integrated analysis of regional systems

edited by P. W. J. Batey, M. Madden · London papers in regional science 15 · a pion publication

integrated analysis of regional systems

p Pion Limited, 207 Brondesbury Park, London NW2 5JN

ISBN 0 85086 116 0

Printed in Great Britain by Page Bros (Norwich) Limited

Contributors

P W J Batey — *Department of Civic Design, University of Liverpool, PO Box 147, Liverpool L69 3BX, England*

S Casini Benvenuti — *IRPET, Via la Farina 27, Florence, Italy*

A Cavalieri — *IRPET, Via la Farina 27, Florence, Italy*

R A Chase — *Department of Agricultural Economics, University of Wisconsin, Madison, WI 53706, USA*

G J D Hewings — *Department of Geography, and Regional Science Program, University of Illinois at Urbana–Champaign, 107-109 Observatory, 901 S. Mathews, Urbana, IL 61801, USA*

J Ledent — *INRS–Urbanisation, Université du Québec, 3465 rue Durocher, Montréal, Québec H2X 2C6, Canada*

F L Leistritz — *Department of Agricultural Economics, North Dakota State University, Fargo, ND 58105, USA*

M Luptáčik — *Institut für Okonometrie und Operations Research, Technische Universität Wien, Argentinierstrasse 8, A-1040 Vienna, Austria*

M Madden — *Department of Civic Design, University of Liverpool, PO Box 147, Liverpool L69 3BX, England*

S H Murdock — *Department of Rural Sociology, Texas A and M University, College Station, TX 77843, USA*

J Oosterhaven — *Faculteit der Economische Wetenschappen, Rijksuniversiteit Groningen, PO Box 800, 9700 AV Groningen, The Netherlands*

T R Plaut — *Bureau of Business Research, University of Texas, Austin, TX 7812, USA*

S H Putman — *Department of City and Regional Planning, University of Pennsylvania, G-3 Fine Arts Building CJ, PA 19104, USA*

J I Round — *Department of Economics, University of Warwick, Coventry CV4 7AL, England*

I Schmoranz — *Institut für Höhere Studien, Stumpergasse 56, A-1060 Vienna, Austria*

B D Solomon — *Federal Energy Regulatory Commission, 825 N. Capital Street NW, Room 507-B, Washington, DC 20426, USA*

J R N Stone

13 *Millington Road, Cambridge CB3 9HW, England*

J van Dijk

Faculteit der Economische Wetenschappen, Rijksuniversiteit Groningen, PO Box 800, 9700 AV Groningen, The Netherlands

M R Weale

Department of Applied Economics, University of Cambridge, Sidgwick Avenue, Cambridge CB3 9DE, England

M Wegener

IRPUD, Universität Dortmund, Postfach 500 500, 4600 Dortmund 50, FRG

Contents

Introduction

P W J BATEY, M MADDEN
University of Liverpool

In the last five years or so, in regional science, economic geography, and demography, a burgeoning interest has been shown in the problems of integration within the field of urban and regional modelling. This interest can be seen largely as a response to the severe limitations of analyses in which a single region or activity is studied in isolation from others. When used in impact analysis or forecasting, a partial approach of this kind may provide results which are misleading, inaccurate, and inconsistent. There is a clear need to specify explicitly the linkages between major activities and to ensure that the analysis of several individual topics or geographical areas proceeds on the basis of a common set of assumptions.

Regional scientists have been aware of these problems for some time. Writing in 1960, Isard drew attention to the importance of drawing together the separate analyses of population, employment, and other activities in a multiregion system. In fact, his classic work, *Methods of Regional Analysis*, contains a whole chapter—"Channels of synthesis"—addressing this issue in conceptual terms. Not until the mid-1970s, however, were there real signs of progress in the development of operational *integrated* urban and regional models. A coherent field, centred around this modelling work, is now emerging and in this volume we bring together a representative selection of some of the most significant research carried out so far.

The volume draws on material presented at the 1984 Annual Conference of the Regional Science Association, British Section held at the University of Kent at Canterbury. Three sessions at the Canterbury meeting were devoted to the theme "Integrated analysis of regional systems" and nine of the papers presented are included in this volume. A further three papers were invited specially for the volume, although not presented at the Canterbury meeting.

As used here, the term 'integration' is interpreted in a broad sense and can be seen to have at least three major facets. First, there is a concern for the integration of various kinds of *regional activity*. Most notably this involves the linking together of demographic and economic activity within regional models, but attention is also given to other activity linkages such as energy and transport and their relationship with population and employment.

Second, the importance of *interregional linkages* is recognised. Several of the models presented enable the transactions (or flows) between a system of two or more regions to be represented explicitly, so that the feedback effects from other parts of the regional system can be taken into account and evaluated.

Last, the question of *conjoining different types of regional model* is addressed. The problems that arise when modelling frameworks are constructed in which, for example, a forecasting model is combined with an optimising model, are examined.

Throughout the volume the emphasis is upon developments in *research* in this field. The effects of this research upon *practice* in urban and regional planning are the subject of a second set of papers—"Integrated forecasting in strategic planning practice"—published in parallel to this volume as a special issue of the *Town Planning Review* (volume 55, part 4, 1984), compiled by the present editors. These papers were presented at the Fourth International Workshop on Strategic Planning, held at the University of Liverpool in April 1984.

The papers assembled in this volume have been organised into four main sections. The first of these is concerned with methodological problems that have a fundamental bearing on the design of regional models. Sections 2 and 3 deal with models from the social accounts/input–output tradition and each of the papers, as well as presenting new technical developments, also includes an empirical example by way of illustration. The final section is devoted to policy applications and the papers demonstrate the value of an integrated approach in the study of particular urban and regional problems. The contents of each of these sections are now considered in more detail.

Section 1 opens with a paper by Wegener in which he provides an extremely useful organising framework for the analysis and comparison of integrated models. Wegener's main concern is with multiactivity models, that is, models that include more than one sector or field of human activity, such as employment, population, housing, and transport. Such models will generally have been developed for forecasting purposes at the regional and subregional level.

Wegener examines how in these models the economic, demographic, and other subsystems are linked and, in particular, which interactions or feedbacks between those subsystems are recognised by the models and by what means. The discussion starts by setting up an 'ideal' comprehensive urban and regional model encompassing as many aspects with potential relevance for regional policymaking as one could possibly conceive. Then a number of typical urban and regional models are reviewed and compared with this comprehensive model in terms of completeness and feedback structure. Two basic approaches to linking the subsystems are distinguished. In 'unified' models *one* algorithm or system of equations is used to model *all* subsystems, whereas in 'composite' models specialised, and hence different, submodels are used for each subsystem. Wegener concludes that unified modelling approaches are superior in terms of coherence and internal consistency, but frequently have to sacrifice essential detail with respect to subsystem specification. Composite approaches, on the other hand, have no restrictions as to how single-activity subsystems are modelled, but present a problem in consistently linking them. Typical examples of both types of model are identified and their advantages and disadvantages discussed.

Wegener's review indicates that the integration of subsystems in multi-activity modelling is a largely unresolved and widely neglected problem. The second paper in this section, by Ledent, pursues this theme further in relation to the consistent modelling of a regional labour market. Ledent's paper draws attention to a severe accuracy problem that affects modelling exercises of this kind. This arises because the aggregate variables of a regional labour market (employment, labour force, and population) and the two variables that are normally derived from them—the unemployment rate and the labour-force participation rate—cannot be derived independently. Two variables among the five must be determined, as residuals, from the other three. Ledent shows that labour force should be one of these two residual variables and suggests that the second should be either employment or the labour-force participation rate. Ledent's paper includes empirical evidence to corroborate these findings. His paper also points to the fact that, in most regional labour-market modelling carried out to date, the consistency problem has not been given the attention it deserves.

Whereas the papers by Wegener and Ledent are concerned largely with activity integration, Hewings's paper, the third in section 1, is an examination of some of the more general problems of integrated modelling. By describing examples of operational models, he illustrates the main issues involved in linking together models of different kinds. He is therefore mainly concerned with 'composite' models (in the sense defined by Wegener). Hewings discusses the practical issues involved in combining an input–output model with a linear programming model in the study of regional energy policy. He also examines the question of whether a linked model provides more or less restrictive assumptions than the use of two models separately: to illustrate this he outlines an attempt to link interregional input–output and commodity-flow models, drawing on the experience of an exercise carried out in South Korea. A further topic discussed by Hewings involves the level of aggregation adopted in integrated modelling, in particular the relative level of aggregation used in representing industries and households in input–output modelling exercises. Hewings is concerned that the household sector should be modelled in greater detail than is normally the case, since household transactions are frequently among the most important within a local economy. Interestingly, several of the more recent input–output studies have begun to put this recommendation into effect, as we shall see when section 3 is examined.

The final paper in this section is also concerned with model-to-model interactions. In this paper, Putman describes a series of experiments carried out using the Integrated Transportation and Land Use Package, ITLUP. His aim is to investigate the effect of progressively increasing the degree of complexity in his suite of models. Starting with a relatively simple combination of two models, one for the location of employment and the other for the location of population, he then refines the model structure by adding trip generation, distribution, and assignment. In a third stage, the representation of the transport system is further improved by the inclusion of modal split. Putman is able to confirm that greater model complexity is accompanied by a closer fit to reality. In its most elaborate form, the ITLUP modelling package is capable of yielding valuable insights about the effects on urban form, particularly on city-centre employment, of abandoning transit systems.

The second section contains two papers which develop the analysis of interregional systems. Both contributions focus on a two-regional system, and apply the concepts of social accounting which were pioneered by Stone, part-author of the first paper. Here Stone and his coauthor Weale present a closed system of two (imaginary) regions incorporating demographic and economic variables. The economic system of each region is represented by an input–output model which is extended into the demographic system in each region by the incorporation of employed and unemployed labour-force variables. The activities of government in each region are restricted to the management of an unemployment fund, and the disbursement of foreign aid.

These economic and government activities are presented in the now familiar production and income accounts, and an accumulation account for each region completes the matrix. The main exogenous variables are the opening stocks of population. The system is solved as a set of simultaneous equations, and a range of experiments to illustrate the properties of the model is carried out. For example, the effect of reducing the foreign aid budget of the 'rich' North region is to increase unemployment in the 'poor' South region by more than the reduction of unemployment in the North, and the achievement of full employment in both regions tends to increase investment by the North in the South.

A particularly welcome feature of this paper is the presentation of the complete data set used by the authors, which should enable readers to carry out their own empirical developments of the model, perhaps following some of the suggestions for future work, such as the introduction of prices or exchange rates, which end the paper.

Round, in his contribution, continues the theme of biregional analysis, using a social accounts matrix (SAM) for Malaysia as an example. He begins by identifying criticisms by Richardson (1978) of regional social accounts, and endeavours to meet these criticisms through presentation of a national SAM for Malaysia, which he develops into a two-regional version for East and West Malaysia. The matrix models input–output relationships via 'make' and 'absorption' matrices. Unlike Stone and Weale's model, however, this system contains no explicit demographic entries—households are represented through wages and consumption, and all entries are measured in money terms. Particular attention is paid to interregional commodity flows, and to problems of import and export pricing where freight costs between regional frontiers exist (as in Malaysia).

Round finishes with some brief descriptions of possible modelling extensions of the SAM base.

The two papers included in section 3 both present interesting extensions of the familiar regional input–output model. In each case, a careful attempt has been made to represent both economic structure and demographic structure within the same unified modelling framework, and special attention has been paid to the modelling of household consumption. Luptáčik and Schmoranz's paper deals with a model designed to assess the effects of changing demographic patterns upon the economy. The model has a closed-loop structure in that household income and consumption are modelled endogenously and, at the same time, changes in demographic structure are allowed to influence certain elements of final demand. The use of the model is demonstrated by reference to a model of the Austrian economy. The economic effects of changing household structure are evaluated and the authors indicate how the model can be used to test alternative social policies, for example, in relation to the payment of child benefits.

The second paper, by van Dijk and Oosterhaven, is principally concerned with the relationship between migration and (un)employment. Their framework is designed to assess the impact—upon production, income, and employment—of the consumption demand of in-migrants. An especially valuable element of the framework is a labour-market submodel which takes into account sectoral wage differentials, payments of social security benefits, and which uses information on the filling of vacancies within the local economy. Van Dijk and Oosterhaven's model has great potential as a policy-testing tool and this is demonstrated by reference to an application in the northern Netherlands, a region characterised by relatively high unemployment rates and net in-migration.

The last section of this volume focuses upon policy applications of integrated regional models. The opening paper in this section, by Leistritz, Chase, and Murdock provides a comprehensive review of socioeconomic impact-assessment models, with the emphasis lying heavily upon examples in the USA. The authors begin by presenting an overview of the general structural features of socioeconomic impact-assessment models, and follow this with a review of the structure and historical development of forty-two models, from Forrester's (1961) Industrial Dynamics Model to the still fairly limited number of models currently under development in the USA. A set of criteria for evaluation of models is outlined, including information requirements, use characteristics, and methodological acceptability, and a selection of seven models is assessed using these criteria. The authors note that economic–demographic interface components of such models are seldom adequately developed, that data availability is, as always, a problem, and that most of the models developed have been designed to deal with conditions of growth.

The next two papers in this section report on empirical applications of integrated econometric models in case studies in the USA. Solomon continues the explicit treatment of socioeconomic impacts with a regional model designed to assess the impacts of synthetic fuels projects. The model integrates economic, demographic, fiscal, and environmental analysis with a spatial component, which enables the author to generate impact assessments at county level in his case study on the Indiana–Kentucky border. Solomon discusses the short history of regional econometric models, before identifying the conceptual structure of his own model, which consists of sets of stochastic and nonstochastic equations representing the responses of employment, wage rates, personal income, population, associated demographic elements (such as migration, labour-force participation, and school membership), and local government revenues and expenditure to a range of exogenous shocks, one of which is the construction of synthetic fuel plants. Three scenarios are presented in the case study, involving the construction of three, one, or no synthetic fuel projects. The implications for energy policy of these scenarios are explored in the concluding section.

In the third paper in this section, Plaut focuses in more detail than Solomon upon the state and local expenditure and revenue implications of exogenous inputs to a system. In this case the study is of Texas, and the exogenous inputs are different oil and gas price and production estimates. Plaut's model is of the same broad type as Solomon's, consisting of a mixture of estimated and deterministic equations that model production, manufacturing, population, and the labour market, but there is no spatial component included. A submodel represents state and local government revenue and expenditure under twenty different heads as these respond to a range of determinants generated elsewhere in the model. The author investigates three scenarios of price and production for oil and gas, and discusses their effects upon state and local government finances in Texas. Not surprisingly, since the Texas economy is energy-production oriented, the low price, low production scenario results in lower state economic and population growth than the other scenarios.

The final paper returns to the issue of biregional input–output modelling which was extensively analysed in section 2 of this volume. Casini Benvenuti and Cavalieri discuss an integrated model, for the Tuscany region of Italy, which sets a group of submodels dealing with exports, private investment, public sector activities, population, labour market, and consumption around an input–output model. This central model is a two-region (Tuscany; rest of Italy) system with endogenised imports and private consumption, which acts as a focal point for the inputs to and outputs from the surrounding submodels.

After a brief section in which the input–output multipliers are split, first, into direct, indirect, and induced effects and, second, by taking advantage of the biregional nature of the table, into internal, spill-over, and feedback effects, a case study is discussed. Here the authors assess the impacts on the Tuscany region and on the rest of Italy of changes in public expenditure, import substitution, exports, and tourist consumption.

In this volume we believe we are able to demonstrate the lively and growing body of research on integrated analysis of regional systems. One of the most heartening aspects of the research is the fact that work is developing both in the theoretical and in the applied fields. For example, the work by Ledent and by Stone and Weale presented in this volume lies very much in the area of theoretical development; this theory is very much complemented by the more practical and applied work of, for example, Solomon, van Dijk and Oosterhaven, or Putman. Here theories are tested in a real-life context, and indications of their policy-relevance identified. Moving still further in the direction of policy-relevance, we have the work by Plaut and by Casini Benvenuti and Cavalieri, which is actually being used by policymakers to establish the impacts of their potential decisions. We can see, then, that the integrated analysis of regional systems is not a theoretically abstract, impractical area of research, nor the mere recycling of already established methods of analysis in different case studies, but a set of developing theories, methods, and policy applications, presenting a challenge to academics, researchers, policy analysts, teachers, and students alike.

Acknowledgement. The editors wish to acknowledge assistance from Economic and Social Research Council in the form of a grant D 00232051.

References
Forrester J W, 1961 *Industrial Dynamics* (MIT Press, Cambridge, MA)
Isard W, 1960 *Methods of Regional Analysis* (MIT Press, Cambridge, MA)
Richardson H W, 1978 *Regional and Urban Economics* (Penguin Books, Harmondsworth, Middx)

Integrated Forecasting Models of Urban and Regional Systems

M WEGENER
University of Dortmund

1 Introduction

The evolution of urban and regional systems is not an autonomous process of nature, but is the result of human decisions—of thousands, millions of decisions, many small and some large, occurring over time as a broad stream of concurrent, unrelated or interrelated, individual or collective, choices.

Planners and public decisionmakers in charge of such systems face a difficult task: to steer a system which, on the one hand, is largely subject to external influences in the form of national policies and long-term economic cycles, and, on the other hand, is largely controlled by private decisions of firms, investors, and other individual or corporate actors. In this situation, it is of vital importance for them to know in advance which of the few and limited policy instruments at their disposal are likely to be most effective and, moreover, will have the most desirable effects.

So urban and regional scientists have tried to develop techniques for forecasting the impacts of public policies on regional development. A prerequisite for this is to understand the forces shaping it, and this means to understand the mechanisms behind the millions of private decisions made every day in the region, which cannot, or can only in an indirect way, be controlled and influenced by the public authority. In their search for understanding the behaviour of private decisionmakers, researchers have tried to identify groups of private actors behaving in similar, regular, and predictable ways, such as travellers, shoppers, workers, households, firms, or organisations. Next, they have tried to separate the decision fields in which these actors pursue their specific activities, such as travel, shopping, finding a job or a residence, establishing a business, investing, producing or shipping commodities. Such decision fields are commonly called markets: the transport market, the labour market, the retail market, the housing market, the construction market, the land market, and other less visible markets like the ones for knowledge and capital. Finally, they have constructed models of these markets: transport, retail, employment, housing, or land-use models.

Characteristically, such models focused on only one, or at most two, of the decision fields or markets at a time and thus comprised only a small section of the activities relevant for regional development. However, the markets interact and these interactions cannot be ignored without missing essential feedback information. This was the motivation for building more comprehensive, multiactivity urban and regional models that explicitly address the interconnectedness of the various urban and regional markets.

Such 'integrated' modelling approaches are the topic of this paper, and, in particular, empirically oriented, spatially disaggregated, multiactivity mathematical models built for the purpose of forecasting the spatiotemporal development of urban and regional systems; where 'multiactivity' indicates that the models include more than one sector or field of human activity, such as employment, population, housing, and transport; and 'urban and regional systems' may be anything from a town to a system of regions in a nation.

The paper is *not* a comprehensive review of all existing models of this kind, but focuses on one aspect of their definition, the multiactivity or *integration* aspect. In particular an analysis is given of how in these models the economic, demographic, etc, subsystems are linked, that is, which interactions or feedbacks between them are recognised in the models and how. The discussion starts from an 'ideal' comprehensive urban–regional model encompassing many conceivable aspects of potential relevance for regional policymaking. Then a few typical urban and regional models will be reviewed and compared with this comprehensive model in terms of completeness and feedback structure. Two basic approaches to linking the subsystems of integrated models are distinguished: in 'unified' models, *one* algorithm or system of equations is used to model *all* subsystems, whereas in 'composite'models specialised, and hence different, submodels are used for each subsystem.

Unified modelling approaches are superior in terms of coherence and internal consistency, but it is frequently necessary to sacrifice essential detail with respect to subsystem specification. Composite approaches, on the other hand, have no restrictions as to how single-activity subsystems are modelled, but face the problem of consistently linking them. In the paper, typical examples of both types of models are identified and their advantages and disadvantages discussed. It is the purpose of the paper to show that the integration of subsystems in multiactivity modelling frameworks is a largely unresolved and widely neglected problem.

2 A model of integrated models

To provide a framework for the subsequent discussion, an 'ideal type' multiactivity urban–regional model is sketched out in this section[1]. Figure 1 is a compact diagrammatic representation of such a model. Each box in the diagram represents a group of variables or rather the set of equations generating them. Adjacency of boxes indicates that their contents are closely interrelated by causal (or definitional) linkages. The directions of links shown are the ones considered to be the most important; in fact, at this level of aggregation most links are bidirectional. The numbers in the boxes are referred to in the following discussion. The letters in circles on the edges of boxes indicate policy instruments.

[1]The idea of using a fictitious model as a frame of reference was borrowed from Bolton (1980a).

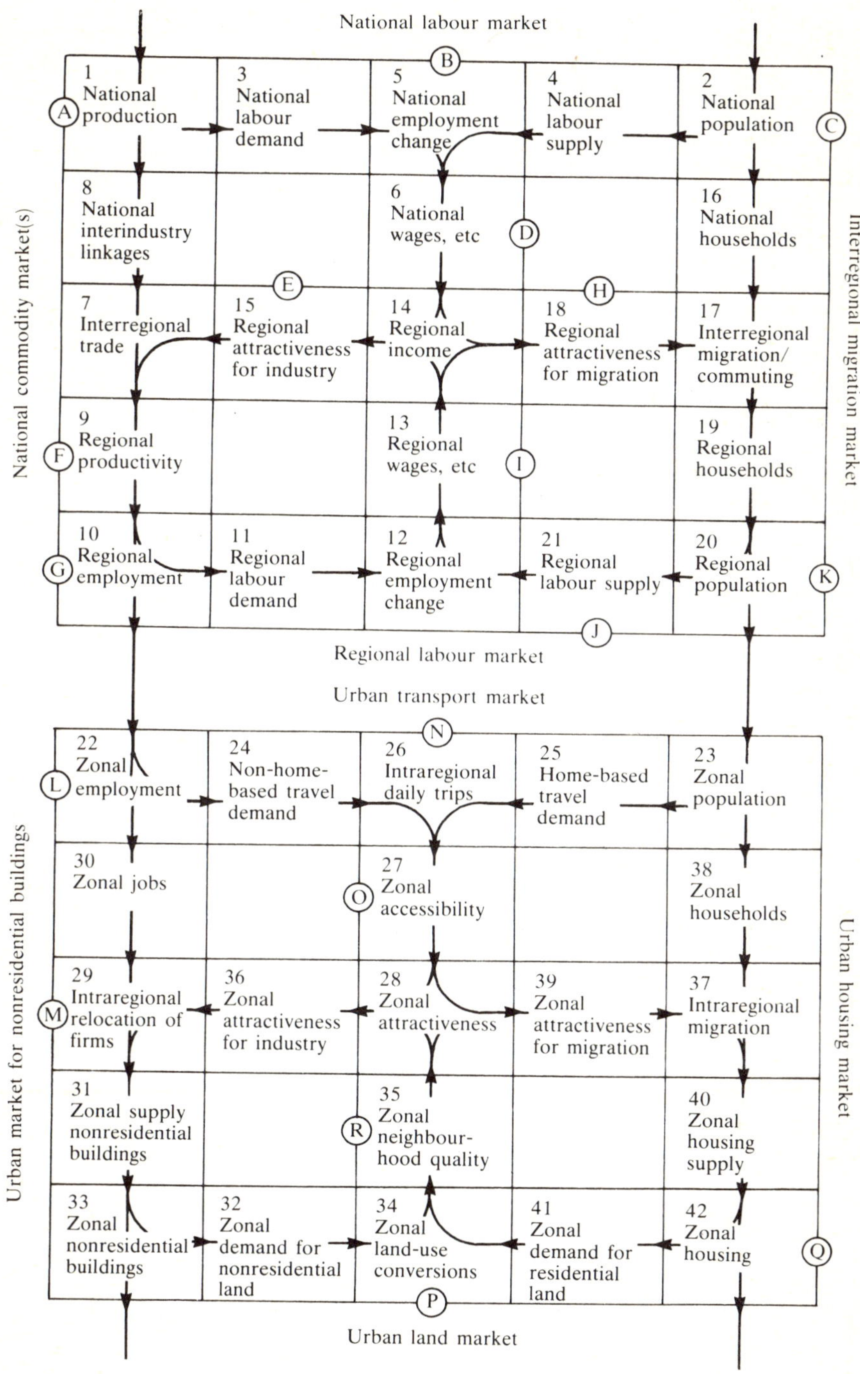

Figure 1. A model of integrated models.

2.1 *Model subsystems*

It is immediately obvious that the model in figure 1 is a two-level system. The top half represents a 'regional' model in a 'national' framework, the lower half an 'urban' model. These designations are only labels indicating the spatial nesting of the two levels; the 'urban' level may equally well comprise a number of communities, and the 'national' framework may also be a state or a province or any larger spatial entity for which aggregate economic and demographic forecasts exist. The 'urban' level is always subdivided into geographical subunits called zones. The 'regional' level is normally multiregional, but may also consist of only one region with the remainder of the 'national' system being the 'rest of the world'. Furthermore, it is possible to conceive of the model as having only one spatial level. In that case, either the 'urban' level is left out entirely, or the 'regional' level is substituted by exogenous trajectories of total employment and population of the urban region.

A second observation that can be made is that the model is organised by markets. Eight markets are distinguished:

the national labour market,
the national commodity market(s),
the national (interregional) migration market[2],
the regional labour market,
the urban transport market,
the urban market for nonresidential buildings,
the urban housing market,
the urban land market.

Each of these markets is placed between two corner boxes of the model diagrams representing major stock variables of the urban–regional system: on the left-hand side, they refer to the production or employment sphere:

national production,
regional employment,
zonal employment,
zonal nonresidential buildings,

whereas on the right-hand side they refer to the population or household sphere:

national population,
regional population,
zonal population,
zonal housing.

---

[2]Interregional migration is not normally understood to be a market, but in fact has all the essential properties of one with potential migrants representing demand and regions representing supply and competing for skilled tax-paying in-migrants.

Each market itself is represented by three boxes: the two outer boxes next to the corner boxes spell out the relevant demand and/or supply variables, and the box in the centre of each market contains the transactions occurring in each of them:

employment change, national
interregional trade flows,
interregional migration,
employment change, regional,
intraregional daily trips,
intraregional relocation of firms,
intraregional migration,
zonal land–use conversions.

Feedbacks between the various markets are represented by the boxes in the centre of each model diagram; they take the form of signals in terms of attractiveness indicators, the most prominent being on the regional–national level regional income, and on the urban level zonal attractiveness including accessibility.

Like any abstraction, the diagram has many weaknesses. An important one is that prices do not appear explicitly, but have to be associated with the demand and supply variables implicitly. Another deficiency is that the transport system is not shown at all at the regional–national level and only implicitly at the urban level. The same applies to land supply, that is, the existing land-use pattern, at the urban level. More serious may be that, at the regional–national level, policy-relevant subsystems, such as the capital market, investment, and credits, are not represented in explicit terms. At the urban level, important policy fields like nontransport infrastructure and environmental policy are not represented directly. Nevertheless, within these limitations, the diagram may serve as a fairly comprehensive representation of an urban–regional system as seen from the point of view of an urban–regional policymaker.

2.2 *Causal links*
Now the most important causal links and feedbacks within this model of a model will be outlined briefly using the numbering system in figure 1.

National production by industrial sector (1) and national population (2) by age and/or sex cohorts (preferably also by nationality, occupational skill, and other classifications) may be endogenously forecast, but more frequently will be taken from national projections prepared by or for the national government; therefore it will not be of concern here how these projections are generated. Given sectoral productivity forecasts (3) and assumptions about the future labour force participation (4), changes in national employment or unemployment rates (5) can be derived, and these together with assumptions about union–industry relations may give rise to forecasts of wages, unemployment benefits, savings, and spending at the national level (6)—but all this, too, may be exogenous to the model.

We next ask, following the top-down convention, how growth or decline of industrial sectors as predicted at the national level will affect individual regions. Here the prediction of interregional trade flows (7) by an inter-regional input–output framework based on nationally derived interindustry linkage coefficients (8) may be one of several possible ways of answering this question, and this will, with appropriate productivity forecasts for the region of interest (9), yield sectoral employment forecasts for the region (10).

Regional employment (10) and the resulting demand for labour (11) will affect the employment–unemployment balance on the regional labour market (12) and hence regional wages, unemployment benefits, savings, and expenditures (13). These make up the most important factor of regional attractiveness—regional income (14)—and, together with other less tangible locational factors, establish the comparative attractiveness of the region for industry (15), in particular for nonbasic industries subsisting on the income generated in the region.

On the population side, a transformation of national population (2) into households (16), the relevant economic agents, seems necessary. House-holds are the decision units for interregional, that is long-distance, migration (17), which is still largely employment-oriented and hence a function of income differences between the regions (18). In-migrant households plus stayer households make up the future households of the region (19), but, in addition, households change in age, income, size, etc, over time, that is, they have to undergo an 'ageing' process. The same applies to regional population (20): it changes through migration as well as through births, ageing, and deaths, and, of course, all changes of house-holds and population need to be consistent in the model. Last, regional population (20) determines the labour supply in the region (21) and thus the employment level (12), income composition (13), total regional income (14), and the attractiveness of the region for industry (15) as well as for further migration (18).

At the urban level of the model, again total employment and total population on the next higher spatial level are the points of departure. Zonal employment (22) and zonal population (23) give rise to non-home-based (24) and home-based (25) travel demand which, subject to the existing transport supply, result in the pattern of daily intraregional freight and person trips (26). This trip pattern reflects the spatial structure of the urban system and gives rise to accessibility indicators (27) which constitute an essential part of the attractiveness of the zones in the region (28).

Future zonal employment by industry (22) is a function of total regional employment by industry (10), but also of intraregional relocation decisions of firms (29). For firms, employment must be converted into jobs (30) for which workplaces of different size and locational requirements must be provided. These represent the demand for offices, factory buildings, shops, or warehouses in the urban market for nonresidential buildings; the supply may consist of new or vacant buildings (31). New industrial and commercial buildings consume land (32) and are added to the existing stock (33), which in addition undergoes processes of degradation, rehabilitation, or displacement. Changes in land use (34) affect the neighbourhood quality of a zone (35), which represents, besides accessibility (27), the other important component of the attractiveness of a zone (28). Zonal attractiveness for industry (36) is an input to relocation decisions of firms (29) and as such may lead to clustering or separation effects between groups of industries.

Future zonal population (23) is the combined outcome of demographic change and migration. Migration can be divided into intraregional migration (37) and in-migration to and out-migration from the region as predicted at the regional–national level in (17). Both kinds of migration again require the transformation of population into households (38). The main determinants of intraregional, that is, short-distance, migration are changes in size and income of households during their life cycle, zonal attractiveness for migration (39), and housing supply (40). Housing supply may be new housing, in which case it has to compete on the land market with other, more profitable, land uses (41), but in large part consists of existing stock vacated by other households (42). As in the case of nonresidential buildings, the housing stock continuously changes in composition through degradation, rehabilitation, or displacement.

2.3 *Policy instruments*

Policy instruments at the national level comprise the traditional instruments of national economic policy, such as taxes, regulations, credits, subsidies, and government consumption (A), unemployment benefits (B), and special transfers, that is, housing allowances, to certain groups of the population (C), but may also include, for instance, interventions into union–industry negotiations through wage or work-time controls (D). Region-specific policies addressing the economy include public infrastructure investments for increasing the attractiveness of the region for industry (E), technology and innovation programmes (F), or direct subsidies to certain industries in the region (G). Other regional policies may address the population of the region either through monetary incentives for in- or out-migration (H), local taxes (I), training programmes for unemployed workers (J), or direct transfer payments given to specific parts of the population in the region (K).

At the urban level, the repertoire of policy instruments to influence the economic development of the urban region is limited. Direct subsidies (L) or relocation assistance (M) given to individual firms may attract some employment or prevent the loss of some, but will not in general fundamentally change the competitive position of the region. More policy options are available to improve the residential quality of the region. Upgraded public transport services (N) or new road construction (O) may increase the accessibility of workplaces and services, land-use controls (P) and neighbour-hood improvement schemes or new public facilities (R) may increase the attractiveness of residential areas, and public housing programmes (Q) may contribute to reducing imbalances in the housing market.

3 Existing integrated models

It would be unreasonable to postulate that any real model should contain all the subsystems, causal links, and policies listed in the preceding section. However, every one of them has been considered important by at least some modellers and might therefore be a candidate for inclusion in an 'integrated' urban–regional model, if the word is to have any meaning at all. Hence it seems worthwhile to take a look at a few existing multiactivity urban and regional models to see which of the subsystems and interrelation-ships are treated in most of them and how. However, no complete review of all existing such models will be attempted here. Such reviews have been undertaken by Bolton and Chinitz (1980) for US multiregional models and by Issaev et al (1982) in the course of an extensive survey on multiregional models at the International Institute for Applied Systems Analysis (IIASA). As far as regional models are concerned, the following passages draw on these sources. The observations on urban models are based in part on an earlier analysis (Wegener, 1982a).

3.1 *Comprehensiveness*

The most striking observation to be made is that to date there exist no urban and regional models that come anywhere near what has been described as an 'integrated' model in the preceding section.

Bolton and Chinitz (1980) looked at six operational multiregional models developed in the United States of America and found that none of them covered even the major components of the economic subsystem. For instance, production and consumption were both endogenised in only four of the six models. Of the forty-nine multiregional 'economic' models studied in the IIASA survey, only ten contained a 'complete' representation of the economic system such that production, employment, investment, and prices or wages were endogenous (Rietveld, 1982), and in eighteen models either production or employment were not represented at all. Population was endogenous in only twenty-five of the forty-nine models, but in only four of these was population broken down into age–sex cohorts, a prerequisite for the application of biometric forecasting techniques. Only seventeen of the models predicted interregional migration flows, and only nine took account of interregional commuting. Not surprisingly, in most models the representation of the labour market was rather crude, with regional unemployment being determined endogenously in only twenty-one of the forty-nine models.

At the urban level, the situation is not much different. It is ironic that there was a, now historical, debate about 'large-scale' urban models

(Lee, 1973), because in fact there never have been, and there are not today, any really comprehensive urban models. This can be demonstrated by looking at a sample of twenty-two multiactivity urban models[3].

Of these twenty-two models, only very few come close to covering all four urban subsystems represented in the lower half of figure 1. Most models remain within the nested employment–population relationship introduced by the Lowry (1964) model, usually with a few extensions into other subsystems. Following the example of the Lowry model, all twenty-two models include a residential location submodel; indeed it is the only subsystem present in all models. The next most frequent activity modelled is retail and/or household-serving employment, which is endogenous in seventeen of the twenty-two models. That is somewhat surprising as these sectors make up only a relatively small fraction of total employment, but may be explained by the fact that well-known model types exist for modelling retail and household-serving employment. Models for locating nonservice employment are contained in only twelve models, which means that in the remaining models the location of basic employment has to be provided exogenously, as virtually all residential location submodels in the sample rely in some way on the work-to-home spatial relationship.

Perhaps the most startling result of the analysis is that only a minority of seven urban models take the ageing of the population and/or the formation of households into account, and only three models explicitly model migration. However, the increase or decrease of population and changes of households in terms of income and size during their life cycle largely determine the volume and composition of the demand for housing in the region. So it is not surprising that only nine models of the sample have an endogenous housing-supply submodel. To have no such submodel means either to assume that housing supply is perfectly elastic to demand changes or to specify the housing supply exogenously. If the number of vacancies in the housing stock is low, specification of the housing supply may eliminate the need for a residential location model altogether. If, however, a housing-supply model is present, a kind of land-use accounting framework seems to be necessary, as scarcity of vacant buildable land is one of the major forces behind the spatial deconcentration of contemporary urban regions. Yet there are three models in the sample which have a housing-supply model, but no land-use submodel. A similar critique may be applicable to the ten models which contain an employment-location

[3] The twenty-two urban models were in chronological order: Lowry (1964; Garin, 1966); EMPIRIC (Hill, 1965); NBER (Kain et al, 1976); Berechman (1976); Boyce (1977); Los (1978); TRANSLOC (Lundqvist, 1978); ARC (Geraldes et al, 1978); ITLUP (Putman, 1980; 1983); TOPAZ (Brotchie et al, 1980); LILT (Mackett, 1980); Toronto (Said and Hutchinson, 1980); Turin (Bertuglia et al, 1980); MRRM (Oguri, 1980); SILUS (Mehta and Dajani, 1981); Brussels (Allen et al, 1981); Choukroun and Harris (1981); Anas (1981; 1982); Beaumont et al (1981); Dortmund (Wegener, 1982b); Merseyside (Madden and Batey, 1983; 1986); Tokyo (Nakamura et al, 1983).

submodel without taking the supply of industrial or commercial land into account. Only four models explicitly model nonresidential buildings, although these may in certain parts of an urban region by far outnumber residential buildings.

If we recall that this category of urban models was originally described as land-use–transportation models, the treatment of the transport subsystem in most of them is disappointing. Seven of the twenty-two models have no endogenous transport submodel at all (some of them use fixed travel times or costs as input); of the remaining fifteen models only eight distinguish more than one mode. However, in ten models, congestion in the transport system is endogenous, which seems to be a misdirection of effort if the rest of the model is rather crude. In only two models is car ownership—one of the most important driving forces of spatial development—endogenously determined as a function of household income.

The last observation points to a common weakness of the majority of urban models: their general lack of economic variables and relationships, namely of prices and elasticities. Housing prices and rents are endogenous in only eight models, land prices in seven models, and rents for industrial or commercial buildings in only one. In line with this obvious lack of interest in the economic side of urban development, in most models, household incomes, if present at all, are exogenous. Only four models contain a representation of the regional labour market, of labour-force participation, and of their combined effect on unemployment and household incomes.

3.2 *Feedback structure*

Even if there exist no really integrated urban and regional models to date, many efforts have been made to link individual subsystems of the urban–regional system, and this has been an area of important theoretical and technical advances. Some of them are summarised below.

One line of development started from the original spatial interaction model as formulated by Wilson (1967) in the framework of entropy maximisation. Used as a transport model, the spatial interaction model predicts transport flows between origins and destinations. Used as a location model, as in the Lowry model, it predicts an equilibrium combination of flows and locations. The latter application has been the starting point for a number of generalisations and extensions aimed at consistently linking two or more subsystems of the urban–regional system by embedding it into a nonlinear constrained optimisation framework. The general idea is to formulate the relationship between two subsystems as constraints of one process on the other and then solve the spatial inter- action model under these constraints. Examples of this kind of integration effort are models linking transport and location (Boyce, 1977; Los, 1978) or models linking two or more urban activities (Brotchie, 1978; Coelho and Williams, 1978; Sharpe and Karlqvist, 1980; Leonardi, 1981).

A second important stream of integration approaches is connected to input–output analysis. Starting from Garin's (1966) matrix formulation of the Lowry model, there have been various efforts to develop Lowry-like allocation models in a linear input–output format (for example, Broadbent, 1973; Macgill, 1977; Batty, 1983). Of the operational models of this kind, the multiactivity spatially disaggregated input–output model by Echenique (Geraldes et al, 1978) and the spatially disaggregated versions of the activity–commodity framework proposed by Madden and Batey (1986) seem to be the most interesting. Other recent approaches in this spirit are the multiregional models of Schinnar (1976) and Gordon and Ledent (1980).

The above approaches have in common that they are 'all of one kind', that is, one type of equation, or one algorithm, is used to represent the whole system modelled. Hence for these and similar models the term 'unified' multiactivity models has become common.

In strong contrast to the modelling philosophy aimed at a unification of formerly heterogeneous modelling approaches, another modelling strategy has been followed by many modellers working in the field of empirical model application. This strategy postulates that each subsystem should be modelled with the most appropriate, that is, most specific, model type available, and, as most subsystems have a different structure, the resulting model types are different. Models constructed along the lines of this modelling strategy will here be called 'composite' models.

A well-known urban model of the 'composite' type is the urban simulation model developed at the National Bureau of Economic Research (Kain et al, 1976). This model contains a considerable number of submodels such as demographic, job-change, household-formation, new construction, housing-market, and rent-formation submodels, and each of them is modelled in an entirely eclectic fashion using whatever available theory or modelling technique appeared to be best suited for its specific purpose. So the model contains, besides various econometric submodels, a probabilistic microsimulation part, a choice part employing logit demand functions, and a programming submodel for determining the spatial allocation of housing demand to housing supply. Further 'composite' urban models are, among others, the ITLUP (Integrated Transportation and Land Use Package) model (Putman, 1980; 1983), the Toronto model (Said and Hutchinson, 1980), the LILT (Leeds Integrated Land-use Transport Model) model (Mackett, 1980), the Dortmund model (Wegener, 1982b), and the Tokyo model (Nakamura et al, 1983). Of the regional models, perhaps the best-known 'composite' model is MIMUS, the Multiuniversity Integrated Multiregional Model of the US (Lakshmanan, 1982), a cooperation between five US universities directed at linking a national economic model with an investment submodel, a labour-market submodel, an industrial complex submodel, a population submodel, and a transportation submodel in a common modelling framework.

Composite modelling approaches have the great advantage of much more flexibility in the choice of variables, relationships, and modelling techniques. However, they have to solve the additional problem of consistently exchanging information between the submodels.

Typically, the submodels contain systems of simultaneous equations, for example, optimisation procedures, within their boundaries, which are designed to be executed only once during a simulation period. However, each of these submodels is connected with at least one other submodel, mostly by a two-way link. This is particularly true for the transport submodel, which is bidirectionally connected with most other submodels. Moreover, several submodels operate on the same model variables at different times during the simulation period. One example is a household-formation model which changes the composition of households in a zone, but so, in a different way, does a residential location or a housing-market submodel. Land use is another example, since all other activities need land and in fact compete for it where it is scarce.

So the decision of the model builder about the sequence in which to process the submodels of a multiactivity model may be crucial. To decide that submodel A is to precede submodel B means that A has priority access to scarce resources, for example, land, but will know what is going on in B only in the next simulation period. Conversely, B may get less from the scarce resources, but can utilise the results of A immediately. By his or her decision on submodel sequence, the model builder in fact decides on the implicit lag structure of the model.

Such problems do not arise in 'unified' modelling approaches which in the way they are defined guarantee consistency in all their parts at all times. However, this advantage has to be paid for by the rigidity and uniformity of the structure which may be suited for many, but not for all, phenomena relevant to urban and regional policymaking. Besides that, some of the most exciting recent theoretical and technical innovations in urban and regional model building, connected, for instance, with dynamics, bifurcation, the simulation of microbehaviour, or the theory of search, have so far occurred outside the unification paradigm, and it still remains to be seen how much of this innovative potential can be amalgamated into the unified methodology. Moreover, unified models are, by definition, monolithic and hence tend to be large, and this is in conflict with the practical requirement of having small transparent modules that have clearly defined interfaces, can be developed and tested independently, and later be assembled to more complex hierarchical model structures.

3.3 *Policy analysis*
Since according to their authors virtually all urban and regional models studied were eventually designed for policy analysis, it is fair to ask what kinds of policies can in fact be investigated using them. Obviously, to forecast the impacts of a policy with a model, the model has to include

that policy among its input variables; however, it may also be sufficient if
the policy can in a plausible way be transformed into a model variable
which is not normally a policy variable (Bolton, 1980b). In contrast,
arbitrary manipulations of input variables not related to realistic policies
merely represent sensitivity tests of the model.

With this distinction one finds that amazingly few policy instruments
currently being applied or discussed by urban or regional policymakers are
actually represented in existing urban and regional models. Admittedly
the analysis is limited because it is based only on the applications named
by the authors of the model; undoubtedly, many modellers would claim
that more policies could be handled by their models. Nevertheless, the
evidence is unequivocal: the majority of existing models are more geared to
forecasting than to policy analysis.

Of the forty-nine regional models included in the IIASA survey, twenty-
two models explicitly contain some representation of national economic
policy in the form of taxes, regulations, credits, subsidies, or levels of
government spending. These policies have in common that they affect the
level and composition of national production and employment and therefore
may be associated with policy type (A) in figure 1. Other kinds of national
policies are included in only a small number of models: four models predict
the impacts of transfers to population (C), three those of wage controls or
work-time legislation (D), and only two look into the effects of unemployment
benefits or social security (B). On the regional level, public infrastructure
investments (E) stand out as the most frequent type of policy, being
represented in fifteen models. Other region-specific policies are very
infrequent in the sample: only three models explicitly treat direct subsidies to
industry in the region (G) or transfers to the regional population (K),
whereas the impacts of technology or innovation programmes (F),
monetary incentives for migration (H), local taxes (I), or labour training
programmes (J) are not represented in any model. For seventeen out of
the forty-nine regional models of the IIASA survey no specific policies are
indicated for evaluation.

In a similar fashion the urban models also are biassed towards a small
subset of the spectrum of potential policies. Of the twenty-two urban
models analysed by the author, eighteen include some sort of zonal land-
use control, either explicitly (where land use is modelled) or in the form of
constraints on activity location (P). Second in frequency are transport
policies: in fifteen models, transport supply can be manipulated in terms of
time, capacity, or cost (O); of course, changes of public transport levels of
service or fares can be investigated only in the eight models where public
transport is present (N). Neighbourhood improvement schemes or new
public facilities (R) can be entered into only three models, and only five
models respond to public housing programmes (Q). Direct subsidies to
new or relocating firms (L, M) are accepted by only one model, whereas
one other model predicts the effects of subsidies or taxes on the regional

level (G, I). Other models show the effects of changes in the national legislation on taxes, social security or other transfers, or on land prices or rent controls (A, B, C), but none of these policies is represented in more than one model.

Many other manipulations of model inputs reported in the literature, such as variations in the regional growth rate or redistributions of certain segments of employment or population in the region, although they may be useful as scenarios, represent sensitivity tests rather than policy alternatives, as these changes are not at the disposal of local, regional, or national policymakers.

4 Conclusions

No straightforward consequences can be drawn out of the observations made in this paper. It has been shown that there exists little agreement between what it might be important to know about an urban or regional system from the point of view of a policymaker and what is actually treated in most existing models. Even models that claim to be integrated models lack either essential submodels or essential causal links between them, or both. It follows that the integration of subsystems in multiactivity urban and regional models is still a largely unresolved and widely neglected problem.

Moreover, it has been shown that there exist in parallel two conflicting modelling philosophies with respect to the building of integrated models, one directed towards unification and the other towards specialisation of model structures. Both strategies have their advantages and disadvantages, and it is impossible to make a judgment at this time as to which of the two will be more successful.

However, the dominant impression derived from the analysis is that the task of building integrated urban–regional models has been too large in the past to be successfully tackled by a single researcher or research group. If integrated models of urban and regional systems are a worthwhile goal, more effective forms of cooperation between specialised research groups working at different places seem to be a necessary condition for further progress.

References

Allen P M, Sanglier M, Boon F, Deneubourg J L, de Palma A, 1981 *Models of Urban Settlement and Structure as Dynamic Self-organizing Systems* Department of Transportation, Washington, DC

Anas A, 1981, "The estimation of multinomial logit models of joint location and mode choice from aggregated data" *Journal of Regional Science* **21** 223–242

Anas A, 1982 *Residential Location Markets and Urban Transportation* (Academic Press, New York)

Batty M, 1983 *Technical Issues in Urban Model Development* Papers in Planning Research 66, University of Wales Institute of Science and Technology, Cardiff

Beaumont J R, Clarke M, Wilson A G, 1981, "The dynamics of urban spatial structure: some exploratory results using difference equations and bifurcation theory" *Environment and Planning A* **13** 1473–1483

Berechman J, 1976, "Interfacing the urban land-use activity system and the transportation system" *Journal of Regional Science* **16** 183–194

Bertuglia C S, Occelli S, Rabino G, Tadei R, 1980, "A model of urban structure and development of Turin: theoretical aspects" *Sistemi Urbani* **1** 59–90

Bolton R, 1980a, "Multiregional models: introduction to a symposium" *Journal of Regional Science* **20** 131–142

Bolton R, 1980b, "The public sector in regional models" paper presented at a National Science Foundation Conference on Assessment of the State of the Art in Regional Modeling, Cambridge, MA; copy obtainable from Professor Bolton, Department of Economics, Williams College, Williamstown, MA

Bolton R, Chinitz B, 1980, "Multiregional modeling" paper presented at the Meetings of the American Economic Association, Denver, CO; copy obtainable from Professor Bolton, Department of Economics, Williams College, Williamstown, MA

Boyce D E, 1977 *Equilibrium Solutions to Combined Urban Residential Location, Modal Choice, and Trip Assignment Models* DP98, Regional Science Research Institute, Philadelphia, PA

Broadbent T A, 1973, "Activity analysis of spatial-allocation models" *Environment and Planning* **5** 673–691

Brotchie J F, 1978, "A model incorporating diversity in urban allocation problems" *Applied Mathematical Modelling* **2** 191–200

Brotchie J F, Dickey J W, Sharpe R, 1980 *TOPAZ—General Planning Technique and Its Applications at the Regional, Urban, and Facility Planning Levels* (Springer, Berlin)

Choukroun J-M, Harris B, 1981, "Modeling complex urban locational systems" in *Essays in Societal Systems Dynamics and Transportation* Ed. D Kahn, Department of Transportation, Washington, DC, pp E12-1-E12-43

Coelho J D, Williams H C W L, 1978, "On the design of land use plans through locational surplus maximisation" *Papers of the Regional Science Association* **40** 71–85

Garin R A, 1966, "A matrix formulation of the Lowry model for intrametropolitan activity location" *Journal of the American Institute of Planners* **32** 361–364

Geraldes P, Echenique M H, Williams I N, 1978, "A spatial economic model for Bilbao" *PTRC Summer Annual Meeting, Warwick*; copy obtainable from Dr Echenique, Marcial Echenique and Partners Ltd, 49–51 High Street, Trumpington, Cambridge CB2 2HZ

Gordon P, Ledent J, 1980, "Modeling the dynamics of a system of metropolitan areas: a demoeconomic approach" *Environment and Planning A* **12** 125–133

Hill D M, 1965, "A growth allocation model for the Boston region" *Journal of the American Institute of Planners* **31** 111–120

Issaev B, Nijkamp P, Rietveld P, Snickars F (Eds), 1982 *Multiregional Economic Modeling: Practice and Prospect* (North-Holland, Amsterdam)

Kain J F, Apgar W C Jr, Ginn J R, 1976 *Simulation of Market Effects of Housing Allowances. Volume I: Description of the NBER Urban Simulation Model* RR77-2, Department of City and Regional Planning, Harvard University, Cambridge, MA

Lakshmanan T R, 1982, "Integrated multiregional economic modeling for the USA" in *Multiregional Economic Modeling: Practice and Prospect* Eds B Issaev, P Nijkamp, P Rietveld, F Snickars (North-Holland, Amsterdam) pp171–188

Lee D B Jr, 1973, "Requiem for large-scale models" *Journal of the American Institute of Planners* **39** 163–178

Leonardi G, 1981, "A general accessibility and congestion-sensitive multiactivity spatial interaction model" *Papers of the Regional Science Association* **47** 3–17

Los M, 1978, "Simultaneous optimization of land use and transportation" *Regional Science and Urban Economics* **8** 21–42

Lowry I S, 1964 *A Model of Metropolis* RM-4035-RC, The Rand Corporation, Santa Monica, CA

Lundqvist L, 1978, "Urban planning of locational structures with due regard to user behaviour" *Environment and Planning A* **10** 1413–1429

Macgill S M, 1977, "The Lowry model as an input–output model and its extension to incorporate full intersectoral relations" *Regional Studies* **12** 337–354

Mackett R L, 1980, "The mathematical representation of a model of the relationships between transport and land use" WP123, Institute for Transport Studies, University of Leeds, Leeds

Madden M, Batey P W J, 1983, "Linked population and economic models: some methodological issues in forecasting, analysis, and policy optimization" *Journal of Regional Science* **23** 141–164

Madden M, Batey P W J, 1986, "A demographic–economic model of a metropolis" in *Developments in Spatial Demography* Eds R Woods, P H Rees (George Allen and Unwin, Hemel Hempstead, Herts) forthcoming

Mehta S, Dajani J S, 1981, "SILUS: the Stanford Infrastructure and Land Use System" report IPM-12, Department of Civil Engineering, Stanford University, Stanford, CA

Nakamura H, Hayashi Y, Miyamoto K, 1983, "A land use–transport model for metropolitan areas" *Papers of the Regional Science Association* **51** 43–63

Oguri Y, 1980, "A metropolitan residential relocation model for the evaluation of housing policies of the Tokyo region" paper presented at the 27th North American Meetings of the Regional Science Association, Milwaukee, 1980; copy obtainable from Dr Oguri, Institute of Socio-Economic Planning, University of Tsukuba, Sakura, Ibaraki, 305

Putman S, 1980, "Integrated policy analysis of metropolitan transportation and location" DOT-P-30-80-32, Department of Transportation, Washington, DC

Putman S, 1983 *Integrated Urban Models: Policy Analysis of Transportation and Land Use* (Pion, London)

Rietveld P, 1982, "A general overview of multiregional economic models" in *Multiregional Economic Modeling: Practice and Prospect* Eds B Issaev, P Nijkamp, P Rietveld, F Snickars (North-Holland, Amsterdam) pp15–33

Said G M, Hutchinson B G, 1980, "An urban systems model for the Toronto region: 1. Model structure" working paper, Department of Civil Engineering, University of Waterloo, Waterloo, Ontario

Schinnar A P, 1976, "A multi-dimensional accounting model for demographic and economic planning" *Environment and Planning A* **8** 455–475

Sharpe R, Karlqvist A, 1980, "Towards a unifying theory for modelling urban systems" *Regional Science and Urban Economics* **10** 241–257

Wegener M, 1982a, "Linking spatial choice models" paper presented at the Workshop on Spatial Choice Models in Housing, Transportation, and Land Use, International Institute for Applied Systems Analysis, Laxenburg, 1982,

Wegener M, 1982b, "Modeling urban decline: a multilevel economic–demographic model of the Dortmund region" *International Regional Science Review* **7** 21–41

Wilson A G, 1967, "A statistical theory of spatial distribution models" *Transportation Research B* **1** 253–269

Consistent Modelling of Employment, Population, Labour Force, and Unemployment in the Statistical Analysis of Regional Growth

J LEDENT
INRS-Urbanisation, Université du Québec, Montréal

1 Introduction

In general, statistical models of regional growth include an endogenous measure of unemployment that reflects the health of the economy at hand. Typically, this measure is derived from a simple submodel that confronts the demand and supply sides of the labour market. In this paper, such a submodel is referred to as a labour-market submodel. According to several researchers who have directed their attention to the connection between migration and urban labour-force dynamics (Miron, 1978; Rogers, 1978), the specification of a labour-market submodel should stress the process whereby firms and households mutually adjust their expectations. Relying on a theory of regional growth with a mixed demand–supply orientation, the submodel should emphasise the endogenous and simultaneous determination of the following five variables:
1 population,
2 labour force,
3 employment,
4 the labour-force participation rate,
5 the unemployment rate.
Such a specification has been used by Chalmers and Greenwood (1978) in the context of an explanatory model and by Ledent and Gordon (1980) in the context of a simulation model.

Unfortunately, existing statistical models of regional growth fail to provide a labour-market submodel with a specification that follows these principles. Thus, in a survey of twenty-three regional models, I found (Ledent, 1981) that
1 all twenty-three models were based on an underlying theory that is exclusively demand-oriented[1], and
2 only seven of the models offered an endogenous and simultaneous determination of the five aforementioned variables.

These observations naturally led me to advocate the development of a more realistic labour-market submodel, for which a minimal formulation—shown here as equations (1)–(11) in table 1—was then proposed. A detailed discussion of this minimal formulation is given elsewhere (see Ledent, 1981).

---

[1] The impact of households on economic activity through their role of labour suppliers, suggested by Borts and Stein (1964), is ignored altogether.

A problem of particular interest arising from such a formulation concerns the coherent treatment of the five main labour-market variables, a problem that originally emerged from the realisation that the derivation of the unemployment-rate variable, following the course suggested by its very definition—expressed as equation (10)—may be troublesome (Ledent, 1978). One way to deal with this problem is to include equation (12) within the minimal formulation of table 1. This formulation then has one more equation than the number of endogenous variables. Hence, one equation must be discarded, but which one?

This paper is devoted to finding the best choice of the equation to discard. First, in section 2, I propose a fundamental exposition of the problem raised by the simultaneous consideration of the five labour-market variables. It eventually leads to the identification of four alternative ways

Table 1. The minimal formulation of a regional labour-market model (source: Ledent, 1981).

(a) Equations[a]

1 Population sector

$$P = \left[\left(1 - \frac{b-d}{2}\right)P_{t-1} + M\right]\bigg/\left(1 + \frac{b-d}{2}\right) \tag{1}$$

$$b = b(w_{t-1}^+, u_{t-1}^-, t) \tag{2}$$

$$d = d(\text{factors to be specified}) \tag{3}$$

$$M = M[\Delta E^+, (u - \bar{u})_{t-1}^-, (w - \bar{w})_{t-1}^+] \tag{4}$$

2 Employment sector

$$E = E' + A \tag{5}$$

$$E' = \sum_{i=1}^{x} E_i \tag{6}$$

$$E_i = \begin{cases} E_i\left[\bar{E}^+, P^+, \rho^+, \left(\dfrac{wP}{E}\right)^-\right] \\ E_i(P^+, w^+, \rho^+) \end{cases} \tag{7b}$$

3 Real per-capita income

$$w = w(\bar{w}^+, w_{t-1}^+, \Delta E^+, \Delta P^-) \tag{8}$$

4 Demoeconomic interface

$$\rho = \frac{L}{P} \tag{9}$$

$$u = 1 - \frac{E}{L} \tag{10}$$

$$\rho = \rho(u^-, w^+, m^+, t^+) \tag{11}$$

$$u = u(\bar{u}^+, u_{t-1}^+, \Delta E^+, \Delta P^-) \tag{12}$$

Table 1 (continued).

(b) Variables
Endogenous variables

P is total population
b is crude birth rate
d is crude death rate
M is net migration flow
E is total employment
E' is wage and salary employment
E_i is employment in sector i
u is unemployment rate

w is real per-capita income
ρ is labour-force participation rate
L is labour force
$\Delta E = E - E_{t-1}$
$\Delta P = P - P_{t-1}$
m is net migration rate, $m = M/\hat{P}$
$\hat{P} = \frac{1}{2}(P_{t-1} + P)$

Exogenous variables
A is other employment
$\bar{E}$ is national civilian employment
$\bar{u}$ is national unemployment rate
$\bar{w}$ is national real per-capita income
t is time trend

Note: This minimal formulation includes a redundant equation. For consistency, one equation among (4), (5), (11), and (12) must be discarded.

[a] An expected positive impact is denoted by a $+$, and an expected negative impact is denoted by a $-$. Use of $t-1$ in subscripts represents a lagged endogenous variable.

[b] The two alternative specifications apply to the goods-producing and service-producing sectors, respectively.

---

of dealing with this problem, that is, four possible choices of the equation to be discarded from the minimal framework in table 1. In section 3, I present a qualitative comparison of these four alternatives followed by a brief illustration.

2 The consistency problem: a fundamental exposition

By definition, unemployment is an accounting concept that results from a direct comparison of the total number of persons in the labour force (L) and the total number of persons actually employed (E). It is generally measured by the ratio (u) of the number of people unemployed to the size of the labour force; that is, u is the unemployment rate:

$$u = \frac{L - E}{L} = 1 - \frac{E}{L}. \tag{10}$$

Because E and L are two variables that take on close values, confidence intervals associated with forecasting an unemployment rate from such a definition are likely to be large. More precisely, they can be expected to cover more than the usual range of variation of such a rate so that the forecast point estimates may well fall outside this range (see Alonso, 1968).

This has clear implications for the construction of a statistical model of regional growth. The endogenous derivation of the unemployment rate from a simple comparison of labour force and employment is likely to affect the credibility of the whole model, especially if the unemployment measure appears as an explanatory variable in several stochastic equations. An economic–demographic model for Arizona (Battelle Columbus Laboratories, 1973) is a good illustration of this point. In this model, the unemployment rate, determined as a residual, is given the central role since most of the important linkages between endogenous variables are carried out through this variable: the unemployment rate affects age-specific fertility and net migration rates as well as sectoral wages. As a result, prediction accuracy for the endogenous variables of the model is low and the 'noise' thus introduced tends to be amplified as the forecasting period is extended. After a while, unemployment rates take on unreasonable values, thus causing the other variables of the model to behave erratically.

Possibly, the best way to overcome the difficulty associated with the derivation of the unemployment rate directly from its definitional equation is to make this variable the dependent variable of a stochastic equation: see equation (12) in table 1—first suggested by Klein and Glickman (1973)— in which the independent variables consist of the national unemployment rate, the one-year lagged value of the dependent variable, and the relative changes in both employment and population.

The substitution of the stochastic equation (12) for the definitional equation (10) in determining the unemployment rate does not affect the validity of the latter, which still holds. Under such circumstances, our minimal formulation now includes one more equation than there are endogenous variables.

This observation raises a problem of coherence between the main labour-market variables, a problem that can be stated simply with the help of figure 1. In practice, the five aggregate variables—population, labour force, employment, the labour-force participation rate, and the unemployment rate—must be predicted. No model can independently forecast all five variables, since they are related by two definitional equations: those defining the labour-force participation rate and the unemployment rate.

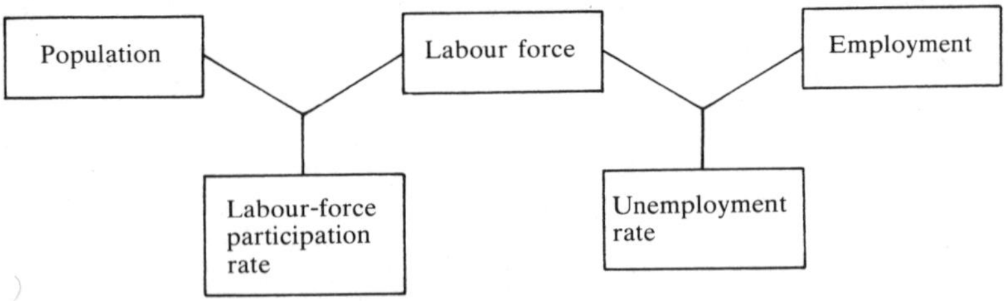

Figure 1. The basic relationships between the main labour-market variables (source: Ledent, 1978, page 547).

Inevitably, this means that two of the five variables have to be calculated as residuals, that is, they have to be obtained from the other three variables—labelled as primary variables—on the basis of the two aforementioned definitional equations. Perhaps the obvious candidates for residuals are the labour-force participation rate and the unemployment rate, since they are not basic numbers. When observed as a residual, however, the unemployment rate may often take on absurd values as was pointed out earlier. Thus, another choice of residual variables appears advisable.

Fundamentally, the *consistency problem* just raised requires one to choose two variables as residuals or, equivalently, three primary variables among the five aforementioned demoeconomic variables. Thus, ten different cases, corresponding to the alternative ways of choosing two (or equivalently three) variables among five, are possible.

From a modelling viewpoint, the labour force and the labour-force participation rate are two variables that are to be handled in a similar way, the second differing from the first only as a result of the control for population size. Simultaneous selection of the two labour-force variables as primary variables can thus be ruled out.

This leaves us with seven cases that involve four rather than five labour-market variables: population, employment, unemployment rate, and a labour-force variable, that is, either labour force or the labour-force participation rate. Among these four variables, three are to be selected as primary variables and the remaining one is to be the main residual variable; the other residual variable being the labour-force variable not retained.

Thus, the seven cases can be classified into four groups according to the main residual variable:
1 group A: population,
2 group B: employment,
3 group C: unemployment rate,
4 group D: labour-force variable.
Each of the first three groups contains two cases that have either labour force [cases A(a), B(a), and C(a)] or the labour-force participation rate [cases A(b), B(b), and C(b)] as a primary variable. By contrast, the last group contains a single case (D) in which neither of the two labour-force variables is a primary variable. All of the seven cases and the corresponding selections of the primary variables are shown in detail in table 2.

Note that existing statistical models of regional growth with a labour-market submodel always treat population and employment as primary variables. In other words, they make use of just three of the seven possible cases identified above, that is, those cases in which the third primary variable is either one of the two labour-force variables [cases C(a) and C(b)] or the unemployment rate (case D). Of the twenty-three models reviewed by me (Ledent, 1981), a vast majority (seventeen) present a formulation that has the unemployment rate as the main residual variable.

The labour-force variable retained as the third primary variable is labour force [case C(a)] in nine instances (for example, see Glickman, 1971) and the labour-force participation rate [case C(b)] in eight instances (for example, see Ghali and Renaud, 1975). Only six of the models reviewed (Klein and Glickman, 1973; Adams et al, 1975; Chang, 1976; Glickman, 1977; Jefferson, 1978; Rubin and Erickson, 1980) have the unemployment rate as the third primary variable (and thus the two labour-force variables as residuals), as is typical of case D.

Last, with regard to the specification of the two labour-force variables, it should be noted that the selection of the labour-force participation rate as a primary variable is more meaningful than, and is thus preferable to, the selection of labour force as a primary variable. Unlike the second, the first allows for an explicit separation of the population-size effect on the level of the labour force. Clearly, labour force is a less important variable and should always be chosen as a nonprimary variable. It would then be determined as a residual using one of the two identities that define the unemployment rate and the labour-force participation rate.

Under such circumstances, the consistency problem can be reformulated. The specification of a regional demoeconomic model involves the joint and simultaneous consideration of four main variables—population (P), employment (E), the labour-force participation rate (ρ), and the unemployment rate (u)—that are linked by an identity,

$$E = (1 - u)\rho P , \tag{13}$$

obtained by combining the identities that define the labour-force participation rate and the unemployment rate. Of necessity, one of these variables must be derived from the others. Since there are four alternative ways of choosing this variable, we are thus left with four alternative cases [A(b), B(b), C(b), and D].

This naturally leads to four variants of our minimal labour-market submodel in table 1, which are obtained by discarding one appropriate

Table 2. The seven alternative cases of the labour-market submodel.

Case	Primary variables[a]	Nonprimary variables[a]	
		main	other
A(a)	E, L, u	P	ρ
A(b)	E, ρ, u	P	L
B(a)	P, L, u	E	ρ
B(b)	P, ρ, u	E	L
C(a)	P, E, L	u	ρ
C(b)	P, E, ρ	u	L
D	P, E, u	L and ρ	

[a] P population, E employment, L labour force, ρ labour-force participation rate, u unemployment rate.

stochastic equation. This equation must have a dependent variable that is, or is directly related to, the variable among the four main labour-market variables chosen as nonprimary:
1 variant A, corresponding to the case A(b) in which population is the main residual variable, follows from taking out the net migration equation (4);
2 variant B, corresponding to the case B(b) in which employment is the main residual variable, is obtained by removing one sectoral employment equation (7);
3 variant C, corresponding to the case C(b) in which the unemployment rate is the main residual variable, results from disregarding equation (12);
4 variant D, corresponding to case D in which the labour-force participation rate is the main residual variable, is obtained by discarding the labour-force participation rate equation (11).

3 Comparison of the four variants
The selection of one variant among variants A–D is not an indifferent matter. Indeed, the choice of the equation to be removed in table 1 has major consequences for our minimal labour-market submodel that are clearly revealed by a comparison of the internal structure that pertains to the four variants: see Ledent (1981, figures 6-1 through 6-4).

Thus, the various linkages that exist between the main labour-market variables may exhibit, from one variant to another, striking differences in their direction. Such differences are the result of the way in which the two identities that define the labour-force participation rate and the unemployment rate are used for the calculation of the two labour-market variables to be estimated as residuals.

As suggested by table 3, these two identities,

$$\rho = \frac{L}{P}, \tag{9}$$

and

$$u = 1 - \frac{E}{L}, \tag{10}$$

are not always used to determine the variables that they define. They may, in some of the variants, be used to determine either of the two labour-market variables appearing on the right-hand side.

It is well known that the addition of two variables yields a more accurate result than their difference. Likewise, their multiplication leads to a more precise result than their quotient (Alonso, 1968). Thus, given the various ways in which the two identities intervene in each variant, we may expect some sizeable differences across variants in the accuracy of the main labour-market variables.

First, the identity (9) that defines the labour-force participation rate is used as such only in variant D. After an adequate transformation, it is used in variant A to derive population and in variants B and C to derive labour force. Noting that the actual use of this identity involves a product of two variables in variants B and C rather than a quotient, as in the alternative variants, we then conclude that identity (9) introduces less inaccuracy in variants B and C than in variants A and D.

Second, the identity (10) that defines the unemployment rate is used as such only in variant C in which, as was seen earlier, it introduces a high inaccuracy resulting from the comparison of two variables (employment and labour force) that take on close values. In other variants, this identity is used to derive employment (variant B) and labour force (variants A and D). Naturally, since the unemployment rate, u, intervenes through $1 - u$, the inaccuracy thus introduced is necessarily much smaller than in variant C, especially in variant B (where $1 - u$ is used in a product rather than in a quotient as in variants A and D).

Combining the above observations we thus conclude that the definitional relationships (9) and (10) introduce into the model an inaccuracy that is, a priori, lowest in variant B, intermediate in variants A and D, and highest in variant C.

Another major difference that can be observed across the four alternative variants arises from the way in which the exogenous information is incorporated. Clearly, the driving force that normally contributes to the determination of the sectoral employment (demand-oriented force) or the net migration flow (supply-oriented force) cannot be incorporated when the employment variable or, alternatively, the population variable is taken as the nonprimary variable. Therefore, in contrast to variants C and D, both of which are demand- and supply-oriented, variants A and B have a more restrictive orientation: a supply orientation in the case of variant B

Table 3. Usage across the four variants of the two identities that define the labour-force participation rate and the unemployment rate.

Variant[a]	Identity that defines	
	labour-force participation rate	unemployment rate
A	$P = \dfrac{L}{\rho}$	$L = \dfrac{E}{1-u}$
B	$L = \rho P$	$E = L(1-u)$
C	$L = \rho P$	$u = 1 - \dfrac{E}{L}$
D	$\rho = \dfrac{L}{P}$	$L = \dfrac{E}{1-u}$

[a]Variant A population as main residual variable, B employment, C unemployment rate, D labour-force participation rate.

and a demand orientation in the case of variant A. Thus, from a theoretical viewpoint, it seems that variants C and D are preferable to variants A and B.

Whereas the driving force that normally contributes to the determination of population change (net migration) is taken out altogether in the case of variant A, the driving force that contributes to the determination of employment change is still at work in variant B; but it only affects the sectoral employment variables determined in an appendage to the submodel that determines the main labour-market variables. This observation naturally suggests that one should perform a slight alteration of variant B so that it takes on a mixed demand–supply orientation, thus making it as acceptable as variants C and D from a theoretical viewpoint. The leading idea here is a reintegration of the determination of the sectoral employments within the principal loop of the model. This can be achieved, for example, by substituting wage and salary employment for total employment in the equations where the latter is used as an explanatory variable (the real per-capita income and unemployment rate equations). Thus, if variant B is amended in this way, only one among the four variants does not allow for a mixed demand–supply approach: variant A which does not incorporate a supply-oriented driving force.

Finally, on combining our conclusions with regard to (1) the handling of the two labour-market identities, and (2) the treatment of exogenous information carried by the driving forces, the following expectations can be put forth. First, variant D (the labour-force participation rate as a nonprimary variable) should be the best performing variant. However, if amended as indicated above, variant B (employment as a nonprimary variable) should be a valid competitor. Second, variants A (population as a nonprimary variable) and C (the unemployment rate as a nonprimary variable) should be much less accurate, mainly because they incorporate less external information (variant A) or are affected by a computing problem (variant C).

Ideally, this qualitative assessment should be substantiated with some pertinent empirical evidence. Unfortunately, given the resources available, the quantitative analysis that is requested for a quantitative comparison of the four variants A – D is here out of reach. A partial empirical assessment restricted to a particular model, however, is provided below as an expedient.

The minimal formulation of table 1 was fitted, using an ordinary least squares (OLS) procedure, to annual data for the rapidly growing metro-politan area of Tucson, AZ, covering the period 1957 – 1977. On the basis of the estimated equations—for which relevant details and comments can be found in Ledent (1981)—an ex post simulation was conducted over the whole observation period.

Table 4 sets out the mean average percentage errors (MAPEs) of the main labour-market variables that were obtained from the simulation of each variant. It indicates that, for all five variables, the lowest MAPE relates to variant D. Clearly, this variant is the best performing; well ahead of variants B (amended as indicated earlier) and A (B has better MAPEs than A for each of the labour-market variables except for labour force). As with variant C—the one in which the unemployment rate is taken as a residual—the accuracy pertaining to four of the five labour-market variables appears to be worse than with D but better than with B and A. The exception is the unemployment rate, for which the MAPE (23.8%) is substantially much worse with C than with the other variants (12.6% to 15.6%), a result that provides a striking confirmation of the earlier speculations about the treatment of the unemployment rate.

Overall, the above illustration appears to give broad support to the qualitative comparison of the four variants that was set forth earlier. The only unexpected result relates to variant C in which the comparatively higher inaccuracy of the unemployment rate does not seem to affect substantially the goodness of fit of the other labour-market variables.

But, as hinted above, the favourable outcome just obtained is not sufficient evidence that these expectations hold universally. Recall that the experiment reported above concerns just an ex post simulation which was performed in relation to a particular model, with a fairly simple equation structure, and a particular region (Tucson Standard Metropolitan Statistical Area) that is often considered atypical. Thus a more systematic analysis that would be

(a) extended to various experiments: ex post and ex ante simulations as well as impact analyses[2];

(b) based on a more detailed equation structure (tailored to the particular theoretical underpinning of each variant); and

Table 4. The Tucson model, ex post forecasts 1957–1977: mean average percentage errors (MAPEs) for the alternative variants.

Variable	Variant[a]			
	A	B	C	D
Population	2.90	2.55	2.55	2.20
Employment	5.08	5.03	4.40	3.42
Labour force	4.60	4.92	4.25	3.37
Labour-force participation rate	2.83	2.81	2.76	2.20
Unemployment rate	15.64	13.42	23.88	12.58

[a]Variant A population as main nonprimary variable, B employment, C unemployment rate, D labour-force participation rate.

[2]According to Carol Taylor (personal communication, 1981), a statistical model of regional growth that ties the local unemployment rate to the national rate—as posited by equation (12)—appears to perform less accurately for impact analysis than a model that defines the local rate residually.

(c) carried out for areas of various socioeconomic and demographic environments,

is needed to ensure that the empirical results do not pertain just to the illustration chosen here and are in fact universal.

4 Summary and conclusion

In this paper the existence has been demonstrated of a severe accuracy problem that affects the consistent modelling of the aggregate variables of a regional labour market (employment, labour force, and population). In brief, these variables and the two that are normally derived from them—the unemployment rate and the labour-force participation rate—cannot be derived independently. Two among them must be determined, as residuals, from the others; these are labour force and one other variable.

It has been shown that the choice of the second residual variable strongly affects the accuracy of the labour-market submodel considered. Qualitative considerations corroborated by partial empirical evidence suggest avoiding the selection of the unemployment rate and that of population. The second residual should be employment or, preferably, the labour-force participation rate. Such a result, however, requires confirmation from a more systematic empirical analysis.

Of course, the modelling problem treated here is not restricted to the particular situation examined in this paper (the regional labour market). It probably has a more general bearing that concerns modelling situations in which several variables are linked by one or several definitional equations. However, it is doubtful that there are many cases in which the accuracy issue can be as acute as in the case dealt with here where one definitional equation involves a comparison (quotient) of two variables that take on close values.

Acknowledgements. The author wishes to thank Carol Taylor, Thomas Plaut, and the editors of this volume for the constructive comments they provided on an earlier draft of this paper.

References

Adams F G, Brooking C G, Glickman N J, 1975, "On the specification and simulation of a regional econometric model: a model of Mississippi" *Review of Economics and Statistics* **57** 286–298

Alonso W, 1968, "Predicting the best with imperfect data" *Journal of the American Institute of Planners* **34** 248–255

Battelle Columbus Laboratories, 1973, "Final report on the Arizona Environmental and Economic Trade-off Model" Arizona Office of Economic Planning and Development, Phoenix, AZ

Borts G H, Stein J, 1964 *Economic Growth in a Free Market* (Columbia University Press, New York)

Chalmers J A, Greenwood M J, 1978, "Labor market adjustment processes: labor force participation, unemployment, and migration" paper prepared for presentation at the Twenty-fifth North American Meetings of the Regional Science Association, Chicago, IL, 10–12 November; copy obtainable from the author at Department of Economics, Arizona State University, Tempe, AZ

Chang H S, 1976, "Tennessee econometric model: phase I" Center for Business and Economic Research, College of Business Administration, University of Tennessee, Knoxville, TN

Ghali N, Renaud B, 1975 *The Structure and Dynamic Properties of a Regional Economy—An Econometric Model for Hawaii* (Lexington Books, Lexington, MA)

Glickman N J, 1971, "An econometric model of the Philadelphia region" *Journal of Regional Science* **11** 15–32

Glickman N J, 1977 *Econometric Analysis of Regional Systems—Explorations in Model Building and Policy Analysis* (Academic Press, New York)

Jefferson C W, 1978, "A regional econometric model of the Northern Ireland economy" *Scottish Journal of Political Economy* **25** 253–272

Klein L A, Glickman N J, 1973, "An econometric model of Pennsylvania" DP295, Department of Economics, University of Pennsylvania, Philadelphia, PA

Ledent J, 1978, "Regional multiplier analysis: a demometric approach" *Environment and Planning A* **10** 537–560

Ledent J, 1981 *Demographic and Economic Interactions in Statistical Models of Regional Growth with an Application to Tucson, Arizona* unpublished PhD dissertation, Centre for Mathematical Studies in Economics and Management Science, Northwestern University, Evanston, IL

Ledent J, Gordon P, 1980, "A demoeconomic model of interregional growth differences" *Geographical Analysis* **12** 55–67

Miron J R, 1978, "Job-search perspectives on migration behavior" *Environment and Planning A* **10** 519–535

Rogers A, 1978, "Demometrics of migration and settlement" in *London Papers in Regional Science 8: Theory and Method in Urban and Regional Analysis* Ed. P W J Batey (Pion, London) pp 1–30

Rubin B M, Erickson R A, 1980, "Specification and performance improvements in regional econometric forecasting models: a model for the Milwaukee Metropolitan Area" *Journal of Regional Science* **20** 11–36

Problems of Integration in the Modelling of Regional Systems

G J D HEWINGS
University of Illinois at Urbana-Champaign

1 Introduction

In the last decade, research in the field of regional and interregional modelling has moved away rather dramatically from the omnipresent concerns with the construction of single-region models to the multifarious issues surrounding the development of integrated models of regional systems. This development, as with many of the earlier growth phases of regional modelling expertise, has continued with very little attention being focused on attempts to standardise procedures and accounting conventions. Hence it has proved to be almost impossible to conduct comparative analyses. In addition, the nature of the linkages that connect models has not been evaluated from the context of possible impacts or distortions which might occur during any forecasting activity. In this paper, I will focus on one major aspect of this problem: the methods and alternative ways in which models can be integrated. Reference will be made to some recent work undertaken on the Korean economy (Kim et al, 1983; Ko and Hewings, 1984), on Greece (Hewings and Romanos, 1981), and to some experimentation with the Ohio River Basin economy (Page et al, 1981).

2 Linking regional and interregional models

Although it may appear surprising that the recent developments in linked models were not a feature of some earlier attempts to model the complete regional system, it is obvious that the sheer frustration occasioned by data collection dampened the enthusiasm for more complex modelling ventures. Isard's "Channels of synthesis" in his *Methods of Regional Analysis* (1960) provides a clear precursor to the more recent developments and anticipates the proposals reported by Isard and Anselin (1982). In the earlier version, very little was documented about the nature of the linkages, in terms of the theoretical foundation or in terms of our ability to implement them empirically. The latter difficulties were highlighted in the work Czamanski (1964) reported for Baltimore, MD, in which he attempted to develop a model to project population and employment simultaneously.

Although one might generally have surmised that the increasing sophistication accompanying the linkage of two or more models would lead to the removal of many problems related to assumptions and the nature of the external to the model economy (that is, the degree to which variables were categorised as endogenous or exogenous), some surprising compromises often have to be made. For example, Czamanski's (1964) elegant theoretical model, with its strong roots in the economic base paradigm, was rather

severely modified in the eventual empirical version. The inclusion of
population equations necessitated a structure in the economic portion of
the model which could not be handled adequately by the traditional
aggregated economic base model. However, the specification of the
disaggregated economic base model, in turn, posed additional problems,
not the least important of which were those imposed by data limitations.

Czamanski's work, and the later extensions by Ledent (1978), reveal
another difficulty attendant upon many attempts to link models: these
concerns surround the issue of combining cross-section and time-series
data in models which contain elements which are both static and dynamic
in nature. Bell and Srinivasan (1983) have recently explored a number of
these issues in the context of economy-wide or computable general
equilibrium (CGE) models. Although the authors correctly claim that
CGE models might be regarded as linear descendants of input–output,
linear programming, and, more generally, activity-analysis models, the
increase in sophistication has not been costless.

A careful reading of Adelman and Robinson's (1978) CGE model for
Korea will reveal a number of instances in which considerable judgment
had to be exercised about the value of a variable for which survey data
were not available. Furthermore, the ability to 'track' linkages and interactions becomes more difficult. However, these compromises may be seen
to be offset by the ability to develop a model providing a more realistic
picture of the totality of potential interactions in a national or regional
economy. In the next sections, some individual issues will be identified
and discussed by reference to some recent empirical work in a variety of
contexts.

3 Linking an input–output and linear programming model for energy analysis

The experience drawn from the Ohio River Basin Energy Demand Study
(ORBES) will be used to illustrate some of the difficulties attendant upon
model-linkage mechanisms (Page et al, 1981). The objective of this modelling
exercise was to provide some way in which an endogenous linear
programming price-substitution energy-demand model could be embedded
within a standard macroaccounting framework. The region chosen (by
political fiat rather than on the basis of socioeconomic integrity) cut across
parts of several states and this presented major data-estimation problems.

Figure 1 illustrates the way in which the standard input–output coefficient
matrix was partitioned into nine submatrices: note, in particular, that flows
are shown in dollars and in some cases in British thermal units (Btu).
One major advantage of this formulation is that it enables the specification
of linkages which are more technologically based and less subject to the
vagaries of the pricing system.

Furthermore, the model enabled the analyst to operate a system in
which signals from the nonenergy sectors could be translated into energy

demands—a fictitious set of nontraded commodities (such as space heating or air conditioning)—which, in turn, could be mapped into a set of energy supplies. The rationale for this arrangement stems from an assumption that consumers of energy products are somewhat indifferent to the nature of the energy supply used for their production. In other words, a consumer is not likely to be aware of the way in which the electricity used to power a home appliance was generated—from traditional power plants using coal, hydro, or oil, from a solar system, or from a nuclear plant.

The utility company, on the other hand, when faced with a set of energy demands for products, may wish to exercise some judgment about the scale of its operations and the nature of the fuel to be used to generate the necessary power. Hence, there is an attempt in the model to relate two market systems—the energy market and the nonenergy or standard interindustry system. Unlike the Hudson–Jorgenson models (Hudson and Jorgenson, 1974), and their derivatives, the endogenous parts of the model are limited to the energy-supply and energy-products submatrices; in the analysis which follows, the coefficients in the rest of the table were assumed to be unchanged during model simulation runs. (When the model was used to simulate the development of a number of scenarios for the economy of the region through to the end of the century, some changes were made in the technological coefficients reflecting 'informed judgment' about the process of structural change.)

Clearly, the strong separability assumptions implicit in this division of the economy create doubts about the 'realism' of any projections. However, one might be able to point to Carter's (1970) work to the effect that structural change may be regarded as analogous to a moving average process and hence justifies the use of constant coefficients in the short run. There is not enough evidence to suggest whether similar structural stability applies also to the division of purchases between regional and interregional—an especially important component of regional systems.

	Energy-supply sectors (Btu)	Energy-product sectors (Btu)	Nonenergy sectors ($)
Energy-supply sectors (Btu)	A_{SS} (Btu/Btu)	A_{SP} (Btu/Btu)	0
Energy-product sectors (Btu)	A_{PS} (Btu/Btu)	0	A_{PI} (Btu/$)
Nonenergy sectors ($)	A_{IS} ($/Btu)	0	A_{II} ($/$)

Figure 1. Partitioned coefficient matrix for the ORBES model.

The model solution procedure, described in figure 2, suggests a very logical framework, given the nature of the assumptions and restrictions highlighted above. The model operates as follows: final demands for the nonenergy sectors are estimated (from scenarios) and are used to solve equation (1):

$$x_I = (I - A_{II})^{-1} y_I. \tag{1}$$

Here I indicates nonenergy sectors; energy-product sectors and energy-supply sectors are indicated by P and S, respectively. Next, the output of the energy-product sectors (x_P) is estimated; this consists of intermediate deliveries to satisfy production in the nonenergy sectors, $A_{PI} x_I$, and final demand in the energy-product sectors, y_P:

$$x_P = A_{PI} x_I + y_P. \tag{2}$$

Thereafter, the supply of energy required (x_S) is estimated in equation (3):

$$x_S = (I - A_{SS})^{-1}(A_{SP} x_P + y_S). \tag{3}$$

The estimates of x_S and x_P are now fed into the linear programming part of the model to provide the optimal allocation of energy supplies to meet the energy-product demands. The linear programming model attempts to produce the needed energy demands (x_P) from the energy supplies (x_S) in

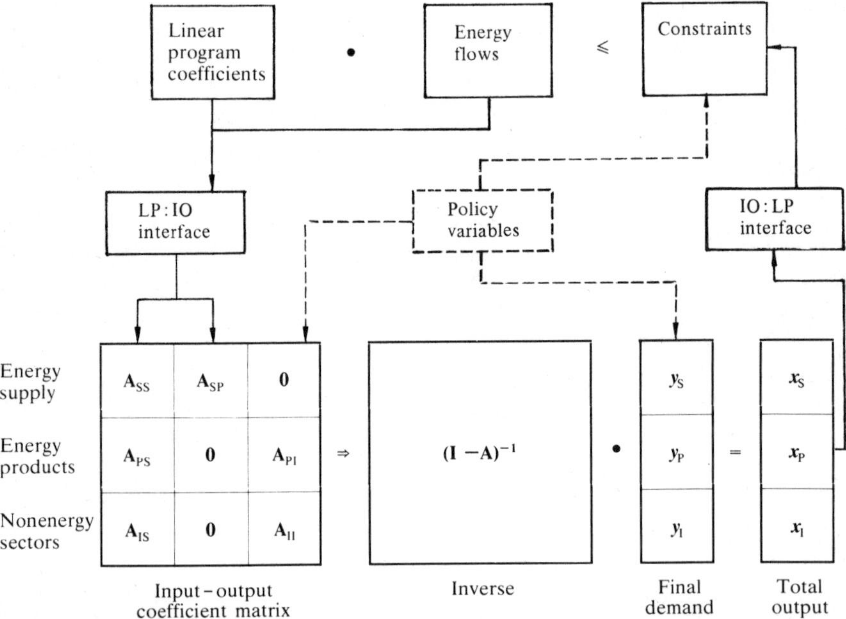

Figure 2. Generalised solution for the combined input–output linear programming (IO–LP) model.

a cost-minimisation framework, subject to the four sets of constraints (the constraint set contains many detailed equations: they are summarised here for ease of exposition):

$$\text{minimise } F = \sum_j c_j z_j , \tag{4}$$

subject to

$$\sum_j \frac{1}{e_{uj}} z_j \leqslant S_u , \tag{5}$$

$$\sum_j d_{vj} z_j = D_v , \tag{6}$$

$$\sum_j n_{wj} z_j \leqslant B_w , \tag{7}$$

$$\sum_j g_{yj} z_j \leqslant G_y , \qquad z_j \geqslant 0. \tag{8}$$

The objective function, (4), provides a simple formulation, namely, that the flow, z_j, from an energy supply to an energy end-use demand classification (for example, natural gas to space heating) multiplied by its associated cost, c_j, of transportation and distribution should be minimised over all energy flows. Equation (5) provides a constraint on the degree to which energy supplies of different kinds (coal, crude petroleum, gas, etc) can be utilised (S_u is the supply of energy type u): the term e_{uj} is a conversion factor relating energy supplies to energy-demand form; for example, it takes approximately 3 Btu of coal to make 2 Btu of gas.

The second constraint set refers to the technological processes involved in converting supplies into products. Here d_{vj} is the unit cost of moving energy-supply type j to demand type v, and D_v is the demand of type v. Constraint set (7) provides limitations imposed by environmental concerns on air and water quality: the term n_{wj} is the amount of pollution of type w generated in the production of energy-demand type j. The right-hand side, B_w, represents the constraint on the total amount of pollution type w allowed in the region. The final set of constraints limits the operating capacities of individual plants producing energy products and provides some data on cost of production (suitably discounted over the expected life of the plant); g_{yj} is the unit cost of providing energy of type j in a production plant of type y, and G_y is the capacity of plant type y.

In the process of deriving a solution for the linear programming part of the model, some of the coefficients in the A_{SS} and A_{SP} matrices (for which base-line estimates are used in both matrices) may be changed and the whole process is repeated until convergence occurs.

However, in running the system, it became apparent that, although the input–output system might conveniently represent the whole of the ORBES economy, this was not true for the linear programming constraints. The set of constraints (7) represents environmental standards—a combination of federal and state mandates. However, the variables represented *region-wide* values which, given the size of the region, were unlikely to be exceeded even if all the plants in the region converted to high-sulphur midwestern coal. In addition, no consideration was given to peak-load problems on the river and railroad systems in the transport of energy supplies to areas of demand. In summary, the linkage mechanism made little sense when both models were developed at the regional level: if the programming constraints were to be truly binding, the model would have to be specified at the subregional level, such as an air-quality maintenance area. Although an attempt was made to link the input–output model with a model to locate energy plants, this link proved to be more elusive. As a result, a priori estimates were made of the feasible number of plants of various size and composition (coal-burning, oil, gas, nuclear; solar was not considered since its potential for significant contributions to energy demand by the end of the century was regarded as negligible).

A more interesting extension would have had the combined input–output and linear programming (IO–LP) model solved in the absence of any locational constraints. Thereafter, the power plants would be sited, taking into account existing plants, available capacity, and potential for conversion to alternative fuel types. With more subregionally specific environmental constraints in operation, the system-wide solution might have been shown to have been infeasible as a result of the violation of environmental constraints or through the inability of certain sites to expand capacity in a timely fashion. These microlevel decisions could then be incorporated into the macrolevel model and the process run again. These iterations would continue until a feasible solution could be found.

The recent attention to the interregional transportation of particulate matter and its contribution to the acid rain problem in the northeastern part of the United States of America—not to mention the flows between subregions within the ORBES area—suggests that the scope of the model would have to be expanded considerably if the greater degree of realism invoked by the use of a semiendogenous input–output model was to be of value. Similar problems of lack of consistency of spatial scale have faced the development of the Merseyside model associated with Madden and Batey (1980): in this case, the issue centred on the specification of labour markets within a regional system.

4 Linking interregional input–output and commodity-flow models

Another issue confronting model-linkage procedures is the concern about the degree to which a linked model may provide more or less restrictive assumptions than the use of the two models separately. The search for some notion of the nature of the modelling 'gestalt' (in terms of assumptions) suggests that most authors have opted for an implied assertion that it would be negative. However, there is also a feeling that the linkage process per se may uncover additional difficulties with the original models—difficulties which were not apparent or not deemed important during the original construction process.

An example of this may be provided from an attempt to combine a commodity-flow model and an input–output model for the South Korean economy (Kim et al, 1983). Wilson's (1970) suggestions along these lines had never been empirically implemented. The first issue that arose in the South Korean study was that the standard industry–industry format of many input–output models was singularly inappropriate when attempts were made to link it to commodity-flow models or to sets of social accounts— unless some careful commodity–industry mapping could be produced. A base-year commodity-flow matrix was used in the process of calibrating the model, which is now described.

An efficient allocation of production to consumption may be found from the following cost-minimisation framework:

$$\text{minimise } C_h = \sum_J \sum_L c_h^{JL} x_h^{JL} , \tag{9}$$

subject to

$$\sum_L x_h^{JL} = X_h^J , \qquad \forall J , \tag{10}$$

$$\sum_J x_h^{JL} = Y_h^L , \qquad \forall L , \tag{11}$$

$$x_h^{JL} \geq 0 , \qquad \forall J, L , \tag{12}$$

$$S_h = - \sum_J \sum_L x_h^{JL} \ln x_h^{JL} , \tag{13}$$

where
c_h^{JL} is the transportation cost from region J to region L for commodity h,
x_h^{JL} is the amount of commodity h shipped from region J to region L,
C_h is the total cost of transporting commodity h in the system,
X_h^J is the production of commodity h in region J,
Y_h^L is the consumption of commodity h in region L,
and S_h can be interpreted as a scalar measure of the level of dispersion or cross-hauling in an observed commodity-flow matrix—in this case, the base-year matrix. This measure accounts for the observed pattern of cross-hauling in most interregional systems and thus avoids the simplifying assumptions of one-way-only flows of any commodity, implicit in most transportation programming models. By addition of constraint (12) to the above transportation problem, the solution is constrained to produce a flow matrix which has the same level of cross-hauling as the observed matrix. The model would now become:

minimise equation (9), subject to equations (10)–(13).

Essentially, the Erlander (1977) reformulation of the Wilson entropy-maximising model has been embellished and cast within an input–output or commodity-flow framework. Total transportation costs are minimised subject to input–output and export–import constraints. Although elegant and suitably sophisticated, the model provides no real improvement in utility for planning and resource-allocation purposes than the use of the two models separately. Why?—because in the transportation system as specified here the question of the source of transportation costs required as one of the inputs of the model is ignored. In its simplest form, the model described in equations (9)–(13) is assumed to describe an economy in which the transportation network has no capacity constraints and, furthermore, one in which transportation costs are assumed to be independent of flow on the network. Some modifications were made—these are shown below.

It is assumed that each link of the network has a cost per unit, c_a, to the user which is an increasing function of the total flow, f_a, on that link:

$$c_a = c_a(f_a). \tag{14}$$

The network equilibrium problem for the version of Wilson's model described earlier is:

$$\text{minimise} \ \sum_a \int_0^{f_a} c_a(t)\,\mathrm{d}t + \sum_h \sum_J (E_h^J + m_h^J)\, d_h^J , \tag{15}$$

subject to

$$x_h^{JL} = \sum_P x_h^{JLP} , \tag{16}$$

$$f_a = \sum_h \sum_J \sum_L \sum_P x_h^{JLP} \delta_{ah}^{JLP} , \tag{17}$$

$$x_h^{JLP} \geqslant 0 , \tag{18}$$

$$S_h = -\sum_J \sum_L x_h^{JL} \ln x_h^{JL} , \qquad \forall h , \tag{19}$$

$$\sum_{J \in \mathscr{P}} E_h^J \leqslant E_h , \qquad \forall h , \tag{20}$$

$$\sum_{J \in \mathscr{P}} m_h^J \leqslant m_h , \qquad \forall h , \tag{21}$$

$$\sum_L x_h^{LJ} + m_h^J + X_h^J = \sum_L x_h^{JL} + \sum_i a_{hi}^J \sum_L x_h^{JL} + Y_h^J + E_h^J , \qquad \forall h, J , \tag{22}$$

where
x_h^{JLP} is the amount of commodity h shipped from region J to region L on path P,
E_h^J is the amount of exports of commodity h from region J,
m_h^J is the amount of imports of commodity h to region J,

d_h^J is the unit cost of exporting or importing commodity h from or to region J,

a_{hi}^J is the technical coefficient for commodity h to commodity i in region J,

$$\delta_{\alpha h}^{JLP} = \begin{cases} 1, & \text{if link } \alpha \text{ is included in path } P \text{ from } J \text{ to } L \text{ for commodity } h, \\ 0, & \text{otherwise,} \end{cases}$$

$$m_h^J \geqslant 0 \,, \quad \forall h, J \,; \qquad X_h^{JL} \geqslant 0 \,, \quad \forall h, J, L \,;$$

$$E_h^J \geqslant 0 \,, \quad \forall h, J \,; \qquad X_h^J \geqslant 0 \,, \quad \forall h, J \,.$$

More recently, some additional distinctions have been introduced to differentiate between shipper behaviour and carrier behaviour (see Friesz et al, 1983), but the major problems of identifying congested networks and translating these results into a suitable form for use in a combined model await further research. In addition, the model described above utilises exogenous estimates of final consumption: the work by Pyatt and Roe (1977), among others, provides eloquent testimony to the inadequacy of that assumption.

5 The issue of aggregation in linked models

Recent work by a number of authors has provided some important insights into the role of aggregation in simple as opposed to linked models. Since it is not unreasonable to assume that the provision of additional resources necessary to complete more sophisticated models is unlikely to be commensurate with needs, some careful attention will have to be focused on the degree to which major components of the linked model will need to be compressed. Regional modellers appear to be moving towards a compromise approach to data collection, especially of survey-based data, which could be characterised as an approach oriented towards the collection of the most important elements of the system rather than towards an exhaustive search for all elements. In principle, given advances in sampling theory, this would appear to pose few problems. However, 'importance' varies in two senses: first, in terms of the uses to which the model is likely to be put and, second, in the degree to which the model will become part of a more sophisticated linked system. An example drawn from the ORBES modelling exercise will illustrate some possible ways in which the issue of aggregation can be handled in a more effective manner. In the next section, the issue of aggregation will be explored in the context of the role of the household sector.

In most cases in input–output model development, some compromise on aggregation has to be made: however, the ultimate choice of the aggregation scheme appears to have been made, in large part, on the basis of financial expediency or the availability of data. Although more-detailed models are usually preferable to more-aggregated versions, this may not always be the case. Concerns with problems of aggregation bias should be placed within the context of the expected uses of the model. As Morimoto (1970) has shown so elegantly, aggregation bias is very dependent upon the nature of changes occurring in the final demand sector and the relationship of these changes within the aggregated sectors of the model. When an input–output model is linked with other models, the issue of aggregation takes on a different dimension.

In the ORBES model, referred to earlier, attention was focused on energy use and its impact on energy supplies and gross regional product. Data available at the regional level precluded the use of the 357 sectors identified at the national level: the question arose as to the 'optimal' aggregation scheme for a model in which energy use was the major concern. The aggregation scheme proceeded in concert with the sensitivity analysis described by Bullard and Sebald (1977). The analysis sought to identify inverse important parameters[1], the perturbation of which would have an important impact upon the solution vector—in this case, the use of energy in the regional economy. However, the linked model (IO–LP) required attention to be focused on total energy demands. It turned out that a number of sectors had some coefficients which were moderately important in an energy sense yet not large enough to be classified as very important. The aggregation of these sectors with other sectors with no coefficients which were either moderately or very important might result in some significant estimation problems in the amount of energy demanded.

Accordingly, the energy sensitivity-analysis was recast from an individual coefficient level to the sector level: columns and rows of the interindustry matrix were perturbed to measure their effect upon total energy demand. The objective was to retain, in nonaggregated form, those sectors which were inverse important: as a result, the 357-sector model was reduced to some fifty-eight sectors in the first instance and eventually to thirty-four sectors. The second reduction was caused by data not being available at the regional level for some sectors (the energy sensitivity-analysis was performed with the national table prior to its adaptation to the regional economy). The procedure may be summarised as follows (more detail is available in Page et al, 1981). Let a_{ij} be an element of the direct coefficient matrix $\mathbf{A}$ and let b_{ij} be a corresponding element of the inverse matrix, $\mathbf{B}$. Let x' and x be the solutions of the perturbed and unperturbed systems of equations and perturb the elements of column j by $(1 + \beta)$ where β is a constant.

Then:

$$x'_i = \frac{x_j}{1 - (b_{ij} - 1)\beta} \, , \tag{23}$$

---

[1]An inverse important parameter is a direct coefficient whose change is likely to have an important impact on the solution vector.

and

$$x'_k - x_k = \frac{\beta b_{kj} x_j}{1 - (b_{jj} - 1)\beta} \simeq \beta b_{kj} x_j \, . \tag{24}$$

A similar sensitivity relation for the ith row of the **A** matrix can be found. It was evident that the energy output was always more sensitive to a column change than to a row change of the same size.

In the analysis just described, the aggregation sensitivity-analysis was performed on the input–output model alone. Bullard (1976) has examined the effects of parametric uncertainty on a combined IO–LP model of the kind used in the ORBES analysis. His conclusions were that, although the error bounds due to parametric uncertainty in the input–output submodel were significant, the errors were much smaller than those caused by uncertainty in the parameters of the linear programming submodel. Clearly, model linking tends to provide results which are not always predictable or consistent. This issue is explored in greater detail in the next section.

6 Aggregation and the role of the household sector

First, regional input–output modellers have conscientiously avoided facing up to the issue that the interindustry linkages may not be the most important parts of the regional system, in terms of the effect of errors in estimation on the results of impact analyses and in terms of the income-generation process and employment creation (see Batey and Madden, 1983). Second, and very closely related to this issue, is the fact that final demand estimation in many models (or at least the personal consumption expenditures) has been estimated as a residual.

A study of the Evros region in Greece (Hewings and Romanos, 1981) shows clearly that such judgment is misplaced: figure 3(a) shows the identification of important coefficients for the interindustry portion of the economy alone and figure 3(b) provides comparable data when the household sector is made endogenous. The concentration of important coefficients in the household sector illustrates this clearly. In a model of the complete economy of Sri Lanka (Hewings, 1983), households provided the major sources of consumption for seven out of twelve sectors and were the major input into nine out of twelve sectors. The case for the development of a more comprehensive set of accounts could not be made more effectively. The type of sensitivity analysis applied to the Evros case was undertaken for the Sri Lankan economy as a whole and for a two-region version developed from these data (see Hewings, 1983, for details). Figures 4(a) and (b) reveal the degree to which the noninterindustry flows dominate the analysis.

Although these findings are revealing, they do beg the question of how one might estimate the important coefficients a priori. One suggestion—to use the national estimates as a guide—proved to be rather inaccurate in the Evros model: only 50% of the coefficients were correctly identified.

This analysis was confined to the interindustry portion of the model; little work has been conducted on the sensitivity of estimation procedures for the household sectors.

In summary, one might stress that in view of the increasingly persuasive arguments propounded in favour of integrated models, the aggregation issue would appear to be better placed in the context of the preceding discussion

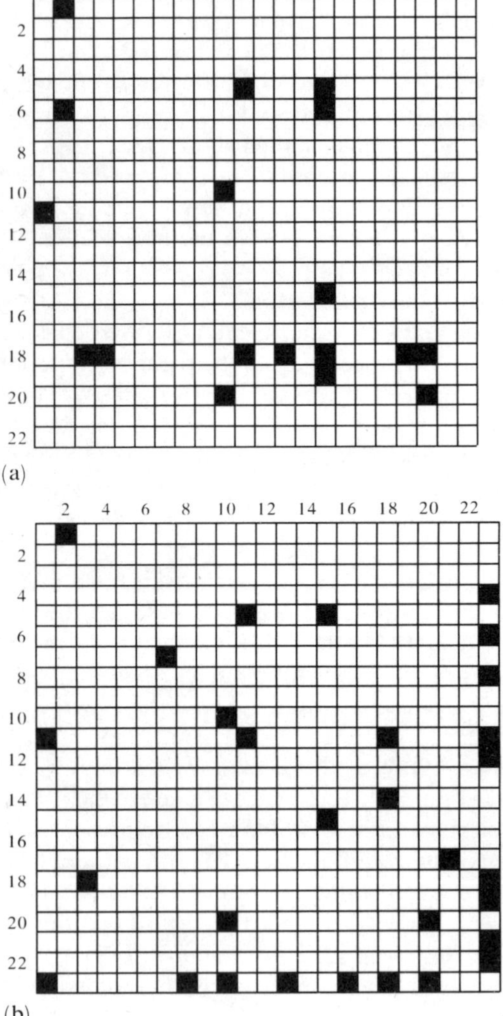

(a)

(b)

Figure 3. Identification of inverse important coefficients (shaded squares) for the Evros region of Greece: (a) for the interindustry portion of the economy alone (22 × 22 matrix); (b) comparable data when the household sector is made endogenous (row and column 23).

rather than in previous contexts in which concerns about aggregation bias were divorced from the uses to which the model might be applied. Furthermore, as the role of nonwage and nonsalary income in proportion to earned income grows, far greater attention must be focused on the disaggregation of household types and income groups and less attention should be devoted to the calculation of minor entries in the interindustry flows matrices. The development of the activity-analysis framework by Batey and Madden (1983) illustrates the importance of accurate representation of the demographic–economic linkages. Rather than dividing the household sector into income groups, households were divided along activity lines— employed, unemployed, and inactive. Batey and Madden were able to show how important the expenditure of social security benefits was to the maintenance of even the existing high levels of unemployment in the region. Without these expenditures, it was estimated that the unemployment rate would have been over 50% higher.

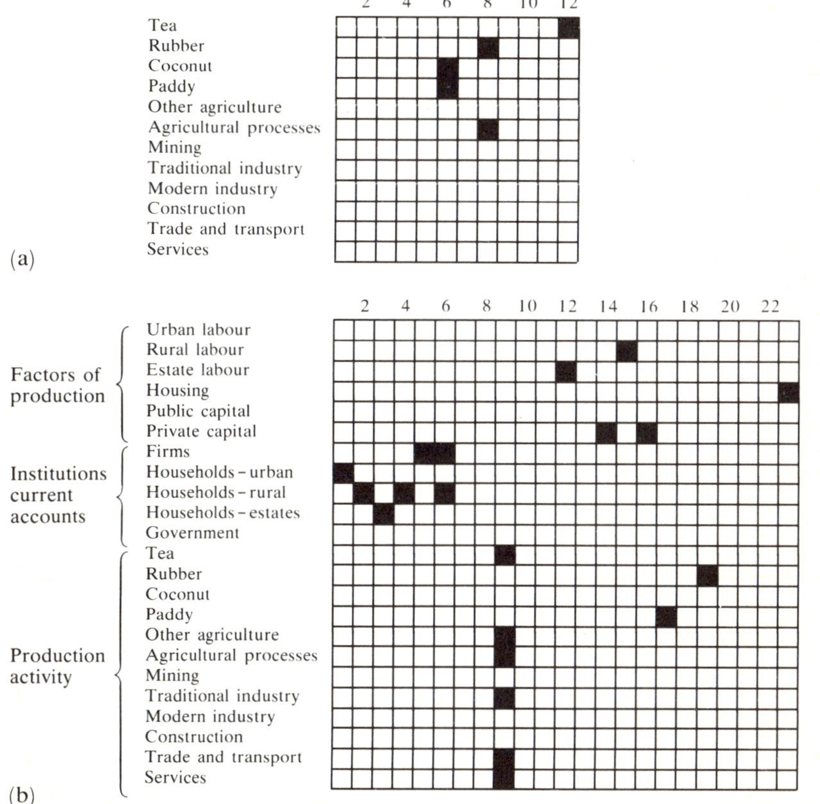

Figure 4. Inverse important parameters (shaded squares) for (a) the interindustry sectors and (b) for the Complete Social Accounting System of the Sri Lankan economy.

These issues go to the very heart of the dilemmas facing regional analytical work. At its crudest level, the choice of modelling paradigm—top-down or bottom-up—places severe constraints on the degree to which regions are assumed to act or not act autonomously. Although Bolton (1980), among others, has viewed this distinction as necessarily a gross oversimplification, it does highlight important aspects of the identification and specification of the driving mechanisms propelling an economy. Closely allied with this issue is the one of consistency: although theoretical issues are often brought to bear on this topic, in actuality, the restrictions imposed by data availability often preclude the implementation of sound theoretical constructs. Taylor and Lysy (1979) provide a very elegant discussion of the problems of closure in CGE models with reference to an aggregated version for the Brazilian economy. When one moves to an n-region economy, the problems would appear to be intensified. Some comments will be made with reference to a regional CGE model in progress for Korea (Ko and Hewings, 1984) and its relation to the role of the household sector.

The earlier work in Greece, the Sri Lankan model, and the excellent application of a social accounting system to the Muda region of Malaysia by Bell et al (1982) point to the critical role of the household sector in the growth path of a regional economy. Tiebout's (1969) model for the State of Washington provided substantiation for the need to distinguish between what he described as extensive and intensive income growth. The first was associated with in-migration, an expansion of the market, and an expectation that new resident households might consume in similar ways to existing residents. These growth processes were derived from additions to the income of the existing residents: since consumer theory suggests that these increments would be unlikely to be spent according to a schedule of average propensities to consume, the effects on the economy would be rather different. At the regional level, the distinction is further compounded by an additional dimension—the division of expenditure between goods produced and sold locally as opposed to those imported. In developing economies, these distinctions are very important ones, given the open nature of the national economy as a whole and the even greater degree of openness at the regional level. Small changes in consumption patterns could lead to large fluctuations in impacts at the regional level. The issue facing the modeller is the degree to which these changes can be incorporated endogenously.

If this were not difficult enough, one is then faced with the issue of treating rural-to-urban migration in general and region-to-region migration in particular. In the simple two-region version of the model, labour was hypothesised to be able to move between sectors, between regions, and to change status (that is, move to or from employment or unemployment). The problems of data estimation here would be enormous: whereas flows between regions may be known, these are rarely broken down by occupation or sector (with both origin and destination labels). Yet the basic underlying assumption of rural-to-urban migration in the developing world according to the Harris–Todaro model (Harris and Todaro, 1970) is that rural individuals move in response to an expectation of a higher income stream in the urban area (suitably modified by the probability of the individual finding employment). In this case, change of location is accompanied also by change in sector of employment. The more general case, of region-to-region migration, presents a problem which probably can only be solved by sample survey data collection.

The need to specify changes in sector of employment reflects the possibilities of significant changes in income and hence in consumption patterns. These in turn will create differing impacts on the structure of production which, in turn, will provide additional job opportunities in some sectors and diminished possibilities in others (again, refer to Batey and Madden, 1983). Even if one were successful in solving this problem, two additional issues have to be addressed. First, the degree to which the migration may be regarded as permanent, seasonal, or of a finite relatively short (one to three years) duration will affect the expenditure patterns of the migrant. These patterns in turn will impinge on the second issue, namely, the amount of earned income repatriated to the original place of residence. In the Korean economy, it is felt that these transfers contribute significantly to the preeminence of Seoul, even though significant numbers of new jobs have been located outside the Seoul region.

This discussion provides some insights into the problem facing modellers in terms of what to make endogenous and what to treat as exogenous. Some recent work by Truchon (1984) provides some opportunities in the spirit of the earlier comments about the use of 'informed estimates' of some key parameters. Truchon shows elegantly how the use of exogenously specified elasticities can be used to induce factor substitution in input–output price models. Defourny and Thorbecke (1984) have provided a link between structural path analysis and social accounting systems—a link which was also alluded to in Hewings (1984). By assuming one can map the social accounting system or even the simple interindustry model onto a network, one can take advantage of some recent developments in network equilibrium modelling. In particular, the notion of a critical path or link (or a set of the same) provides a convenient analogy to the earlier discussion of an important parameter. The placing of bounds on production capacities and individual cells (that is, the degree to which firms within an industry would respond to changes in demand) provides an opportunity to use the input–output model in an analogous fashion to a transportation system in which link costs are dependent on flows (within the bounds established a priori). Without consideration of the price effects, at the regional level, the uncertainties in production may be attributable to the ease with which interregional supply may transplant or be transplanted by regional supply.

There are a number of conceptual problems which remain to be resolved but the development suggests promise and a move towards a more flexible social accounting format.

7 Conclusions
The problem of integration in modelling regional systems promises to be one of the more dynamic in the years to come, as increasing frustration with single models leads to a growing realisation of the advantages of linkage. The challenge to regional science is to provide the necessary theoretical developments to enable less ad hoc linking and more conscientious attention to procedures which could be applied more generally. Regional analysis has not been characterised by its ability to develop consistently defined frameworks which could be used for important comparative analysis and further theoretical development. It is to be hoped that, as linked model developments become more prominent features of regional and interregional analysis, greater care and attention will be devoted to issues of standardisation and accounting conventions.

Acknowledgements. The comments of Jeffery Round and the editors of this volume and the support of National Science Foundation Geography and Regional Science Grant SES 82-0591 are gratefully acknowledged.

References
Adelman I, Robinson S, 1978 *Income Distribution Policy in Developing Countries: A Case Study of Korea* (Stanford University Press, Stanford, CA)
Batey P W J, Madden M, 1983, "The modelling of demographic–economic change within the context of regional decline: analytical procedures and empirical results" *Socio-Economic Planning Sciences* **17** 315–328
Bell C, Hazell P, Slade R, 1982 *Project Selection in Regional Perspective* (Johns Hopkins University Press, Baltimore, MD)
Bell C, Srinivasan T N, 1983, "On the uses and abuses of economy-wide models in development policy analysis" DP DRD 55, World Bank, Washington, DC
Bolton R, 1980, "Multiregional models: an introduction to a symposium" *Journal of Regional Science* **20** 131–142
Bullard C W, 1976, "Error analysis of the combined Illinois–Brookhaven Energy Model" document 218, Center for Advanced Computation, University of Illinois at Urbana-Champaign, Urbana, IL
Bullard C W, Sebald A V, 1977, "Effect of parametric uncertainty and technical change in input–output models" *Review of Economics and Statistics* **59** 75–81
Carter A P, 1970 *Structural Change in the American Economy* (Harvard University Press, Cambridge, MA)
Czamanski S, 1964, "A model of urban growth" *Papers, Regional Science Association* **13** 177–200
Defourny J, Thorbecke E, 1984, "Structural path analysis and multiplier decomposition within a social accounting matrix framework" *Economic Journal* **94** 111–136
Erlander S, 1977, "Accessibility, entropy and the distribution and assignment of traffic" *Transportation Research* **11** 149–153

Friesz T L, Tobin R L, Smith T E, Harker P T, 1983, "A nonlinear complementarity problem and solution procedure for the general derived demand network equilibrium problem" *Journal of Regional Science* **23** 337–359

Harris J, Todaro M P, 1970, "Migration, unemployment and development: a two-sector analysis" *American Economic Review* **60** 126–142

Hewings G J D, 1983, "Regional and interregional accounting systems for development planning under conditions of limited information" in *Urban and Regional Policy Analysis in Developing Countries* Eds L Chatterji, P Nijkamp (Gower, Aldershot, Hants) pp 181–202

Hewings G J D, 1984, "The role of prior information in updating regional input–output models" *Socio-Economic Planning Sciences* **18** 319–336

Hewings G J D, Romanos M C, 1981, "Simulating less developed regional economies under conditions of limited information" *Geographical Analysis* **13** 373–390

Hudson E A, Jorgenson D W, 1974, "US energy policy and economic growth: 1975–2000" *Bell Journal of Economics* **5** 461–514

Isard W, 1960, "Channels of synthesis" in *Methods of Regional Analysis* Ed. W Isard (MIT Press, Cambridge, MA) pp 569–742

Isard W, Anselin L, 1982, "Integration of multiregional models for policy analysis" *Environment and Planning A* **14** 359–376

Kim T J, Boyce D E, Hewings G J D, 1983, "Combined input–output and commodity flow models for interregional development planning: insights from a Korean application" *Geographical Analysis* **15** 330–342

Ko S, Hewings G J D, 1984, "A regional computable general equilibrium model for Korea" *Modeling and Simulation* **15** 451–455

Ledent J, 1978, "Regional multiplier analysis: a demometric approach" *Environment and Planning A* **10** 537–560

Madden M, Batey P W J, 1980, "Achieving consistency in demographic–economic forecasting" *Papers of the Regional Science Association* **44** 91–106

Morimoto Y, 1970, "On aggregation problems in input–output analysis" *Review of Economic Studies* **37** 119–126

Page W P, Gilmore D, Hewings G J D, 1981, "An energy and fuel demand model for the Ohio River Basin energy study region" US Environmental Protection Agency, Washington, DC

Pyatt G, Roe A R, 1977 *Social Accounting for Development Planning* (Cambridge University Press, Cambridge)

Taylor L, Lysy F J, 1979, "Vanishing income distributions" *Journal of Development Economics* **6** 11–29

Tiebout C M, 1969, "An empirical regional input–output projection model: the State of Washington, 1980" *Review of Economics and Statistics* **51** 334–340

Truchon M, 1984, "Using exogenous elasticities to induce factor substitution in input–output price models" *Review of Economics and Statistics* **66** 329–334

Wilson A G, 1970, "Interregional commodity flows: entropy maximizing procedures" *Geographical Analysis* **2** 255–282

Complexity in Urban Systems Modelling:
The Effects of Transit on Urban Form

S H PUTMAN
University of Pennsylvania, Philadelphia

1 Introduction

This paper is a report on a series of tests, to establish the effects of transit on urban form, using the Integrated Transportation and Land Use Package (ITLUP) which has been fully described elsewhere (Putman, 1983). ITLUP has, for more than a decade, provided an organising structure for research, teaching, and practical applications. In its research role it has stimulated investigation into urban spatial model formulation, calibration, integration, and testing. In its teaching role it has provided numerous students with the opportunity for 'hands-on' experience of the advantages and disadvantages of urban modelling. Finally, but certainly not least in importance, ITLUP has assisted a number of metropolitan areas in land-use and transportation planning and policy evaluation. During this entire time, however, this author has maintained a five or more year agenda of unresolved research issues related both to general and to specific modelling questions. This agenda has varied over time as some issues were resolved and new ones appeared to take their places. One persistent item, or rather class of issues, on this agenda has been 'implications of model-to-model interactions'. That class of issues is addressed in this paper.

Some mention of the importance of model-to-model interactions has been made in other accounts of work with ITLUP. Two points are worth repeating here, one regarding regional growth rates and the other regarding changes in sectoral mix. With the exclusion, for the moment, of the operation of constraints, for example, population density limits in particular zones, most spatial interaction models would show a uniform response to a change in regional growth rate. Thus, locator by locator, zone by zone, the effect of 10% regional growth would be double that of 5% regional growth. Note that this does *not* mean that the actual response need be the same in each zone, only that for each zone the response to 10% growth (or decline) will be twice that for 5% growth (or decline). It is the imposition of locational constraints that produces differences in response. This is even more apparent when the location model is linked to a trip-assignment model with link-capacity constraints. Experiments with such models have yielded very interesting and apparently realistic responses to changes in regional growth rates (Putman, 1983).

A second type of important interaction follows from the changes in sectoral mix of regional forecasts. In this case, consider two regional employment forecasts with the same total employment, but with different mixes of, say, manufacturing and service employment. These differences in employment mix result in different household-income distributions. The various house-hold types have different locational behaviour, as do the various employment types. Thus changes in sectoral mix at the regional level will produce a multitude of interrelated spatial location effects at the zonal level both directly, and through the various constraint mechanisms.

The above are model-to-model interactions going from the regional to the intraregional level of detail. They will need more investigation before they can be fully understood. There are further interactions to be examined solely within a level of detail. In a recent paper, attention was called to the potential effects of transport congestion on urban spatial form (Putman, 1984). In that paper it was shown that for two quite different metropolitan areas (San Francisco, CA, and Dortmund, FRG) ITLUP forecast rather high levels of transport congestion in the most densely urbanised zones of the regions. This congestion led, in turn, to long-term decentralisation of population and employment in the regions. These results were obtained using a version of ITLUP that lacked mode-split modelling capability. In two subsequent projects, steps were taken to begin to incorporate a mode-split model into ITLUP and to determine the extent to which different forecasts of long-term spatial patterns would result from this system modification (Keith, 1983; Kim, 1984). Each of the two projects was successful in its own right. The addition of transit allowed some automobile trips to change mode and thus resulted in some attenuation of both congestion and decentralisation. Yet the results were not entirely satisfactory, indicating the need for resolution of several questions on system integration. This paper is about some of the steps taken toward that end.

A set of three groups of computer test runs was completed. There was a twofold purpose to these runs: first, simply to determine the problems involved in adding the mode-split capability to the ITLUP package, and second to examine thoroughly the effects of this addition. The remainder of this paper, after an outline of the three alternative model structures used, is devoted to discussion and analysis of these test results.

2 Definition of test model structures

The three test sequences discussed in this paper were produced by three different model system structures. The first structure was the simplest, with each of the succeeding structures being more complex than its predecessor. The increasing complexity was, in a sense, evolutionary, in that each led to the next along a path of incorporation of additional aspects of reality. The first structure involved the simple linking of two models, one for the location of employment and the other for the location of population. The second structure added to the first: trip generation, distribution, and assignment. The third added mode split to the second.

The first model structure is typical of the way in which 'land-use' models have most often been used in planning. Only two models are involved.

The first is EMPAL, which forecasts the location of four types of employment, at place-of-work, by small area. The second model is DRAM, which forecasts the location of households, usually disaggregated to four income levels, at place-of-residence, also by small area. Both these models have already been described in some detail (Putman, 1983). The sequence of operation of the two models for the first test run (test 1) was simply EMPAL, DRAM. This sequence is shown, along with the data inputs, in figure 1. For the purposes of this test, the sequence was run through three recursions.

Each recursion begins with the execution of EMPAL. To forecast the location of employment of type k in zone j at time $t + 1$, EMPAL uses the following input variables: employment of type k in all zones at time t, population of all types in all zones at time t, total area per zone for all zones, zone-to-zone travel cost (or time) between zone j and all other zones at time $t + 1$, and—as a lagged variable—employment of type k in zone j at time t. The parameters used are derived from data for time t and time $t - 1$. The model requires regional employment forecasts for time $t + 1$.

After the employment location forecasts have been produced by EMPAL, a set of residence location forecasts is produced by DRAM. To forecast the location of residents of type h in zone i at time $t + 1$, DRAM uses the following input variables: residents of all types h in zone i at time t, land used for residential purposes in zone i at time t, the percentage of the developable land in zone i which has already been developed at time t, the vacant developable land in zone i at time t, zone-to-zone travel cost (or time) between zone i and all other zones at time $t + 1$, and employment of all types k in all zones at time $t + 1$. The parameters used are derived from data for time t. The model requires regional population forecasts for time $t + 1$.

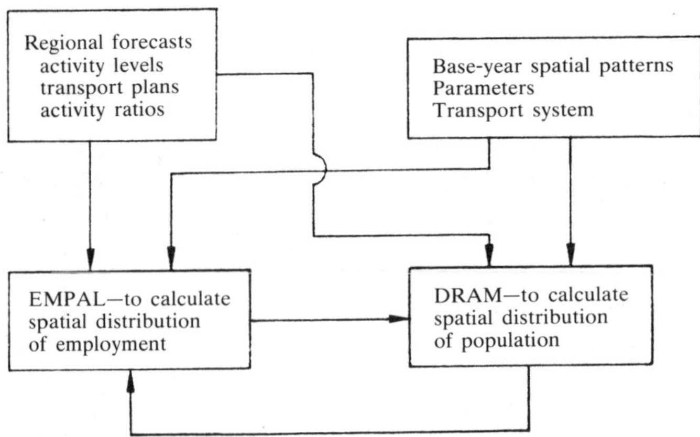

Figure 1. The model system configuration of test 1.

Even though this first model sequence is quite simple, there are still questions left unresolved. One major question is that of sequential versus simultaneous connection of the two models (Putman, 1984). The possibilities range from simple sequential linking of the models, as was done for these experiments, to fully simultaneous linking of the employment and household location models. The question of location-to-transportation feedback, left untouched in this model structure, leads to the discussion of the second structure.

For the second test run (test 2) an additional model was added to the structure and unexercised options from DRAM were switched on. The additional model was NETWRK, a network-assignment model. The overall configuration of this second structure is shown in figure 2. In this configuration, EMPAL does exactly the same task it did in the first structure: employment location forecasting. DRAM, however, now has an augmented role. A matrix of work-to-home trips is generated simultaneously with the calculation of residence location and, subsequently, matrices of home-to-shop and work-to-shop trips are calculated. These three trip matrices are then combined to produce a single matrix of trips from each zone to each other zone. These trips are then taken as input by NETWRK. NETWRK then performs a capacity-constrained assignment of these trips to a representation of the highway network in the region (for time $t + 1$). The resulting congestion of the network yields, after NETWRK does a final tracing of the minimum paths through the congested network, a revised matrix of zone-to-zone travel costs (or times). These become input to the next recursion of the system.

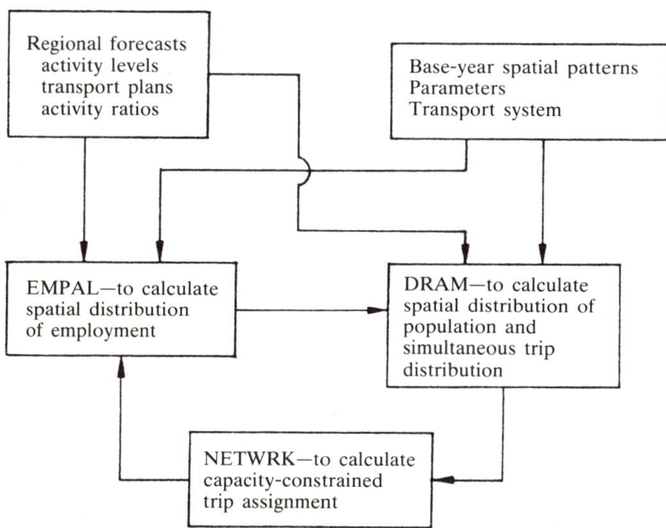

Figure 2. The model system configuration of test 2.

In this modified sequence, too, there are many unresolved questions. These range from problems of conversion of trip probabilities into person trips and then into vehicle trips, to problems of abstract network representation, and selection of a trip-assignment algorithm. There is also the question of modal choice, which leads to the discussion of the third test run.

For the third test run (test 3) only one major model was added: MSPLIT. This addition, however, occasioned the need for several subsidiary procedures. The purpose of this addition was to add a representation of the reality of travellers' mode switching. In addition to the several new models, this third structure also required the augmenting of DRAM to provide for the output of matrices of trips by type. The overall structure of this model system is shown in figure 3. Not shown, but discussed later in this paper, are the supplementary procedures for calculating composite costs and matrices of total trips (after mode split).

In the next three sections of this paper, the tests done with each of these model structures will be presented. In each case the new problems engendered by the increased complexity of the model system will be discussed along with the advantages of the augmented system structure and the differences in the replication of reality in those structures.

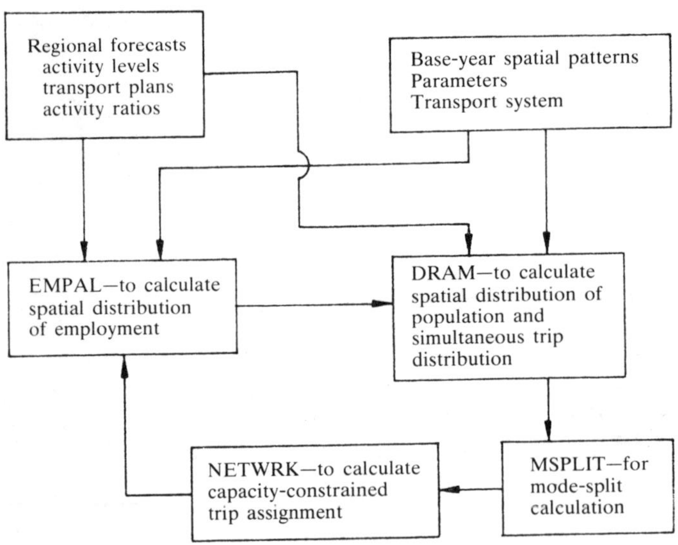

Figure 3. The model system configuration of test 3.

3 Test 1: the simple recursive structure
Test 1, of course, makes use of the simplest of the three model structures described above. The employment model, EMPAL, begins the sequence by producing a forecast of the spatial distribution of employment. This is

followed by the residential model, DRAM, which produces a consequent forecast of the spatial distribution of households. The output of the first model thus becomes the input to the second. The next recursion involves using the output of DRAM as the input to the next run of EMPAL. It should be noted that this is a structure that is indeed sequential. EMPAL makes use of lagged employment data to produce its employment location forecasts. DRAM makes use of lagged household data plus current employment forecasts to produce its residence location forecasts. The fact that both models are disaggregated into several types of locating activity and that each type of location is determined by a multivariate multiparametric function complicates the situation considerably.

Even for this first model structure, questions of model-to-model linkages begin to appear. Quite apart from those questions which might be raised about the internal structure of each model, there are some major issues involving their interconnection. The employment forecasts from EMPAL are disaggregated by type of employment (for example, industrial, service, retail, etc), and by zone, and are at place-of-work. These figures become input to the forecasting of the location of households, by place-of-residence. This household location forecast, in DRAM, begins with the conversion of employees, by employment type, at place-of-work into representative household heads, by household type, but still at place-of-work. These representative households must be transformed into actual numbers of households and then distributed to their place-of-residence.

Many applied models have avoided this problem as they have only one type each of population and employment. In such cases it is only necessary to distribute the employees from their workplaces to their residence locations and then multiply by an employees-per-population ratio. In EMPAL and DRAM the presence of multiple sectors requires a conversion matrix which transforms employees by type to representative heads of households by type. One consequence of this conversion, as mentioned in the introduction, is that as sectoral mix of employment in a region changes so does its sectoral mix (normally income groups) of households. This is, of itself, quite reasonable, but care must be taken, as there is no formal means for updating the conversion matrix during the forecast recursions, that all the households do not wind up in one group. Associated with this are the problems of updating of ratios of persons per household, employees per household, and jobs per employee. In addition, of course, there is the previously noted question of the sequential versus simultaneous linkages of the two models overall.

The existence was noted of these and other questions which are intended to be the subject of future research efforts and the pair of models was run through three iterations (or, more properly, recursions). No time scale is given here, to avoid the further complication, unnecessary for these tests, of justifying the precise values of the regional control totals. It may be

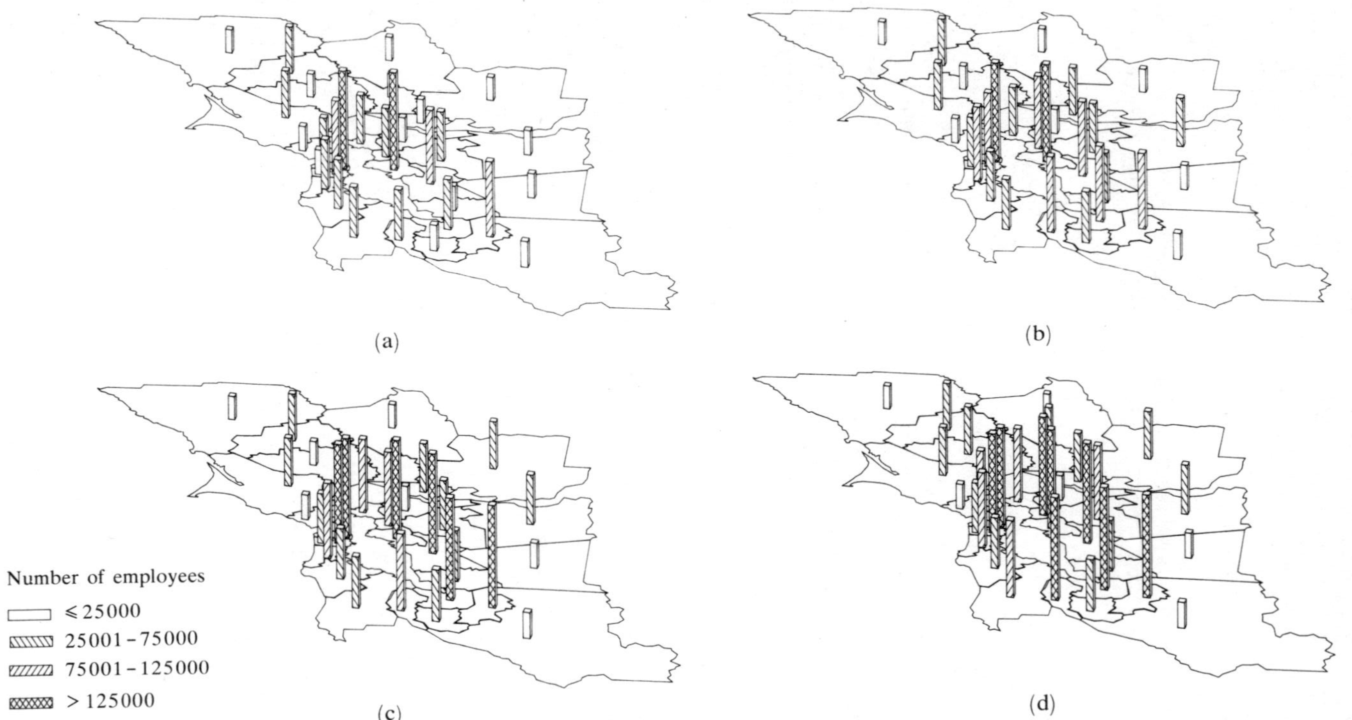

Figure 4. The evolution of the spatial pattern of employment location from test 1 applied to the San Francisco Bay Area (thirty zones): (a) base distribution, (b) first iteration, (c) second iteration, (d) third iteration.

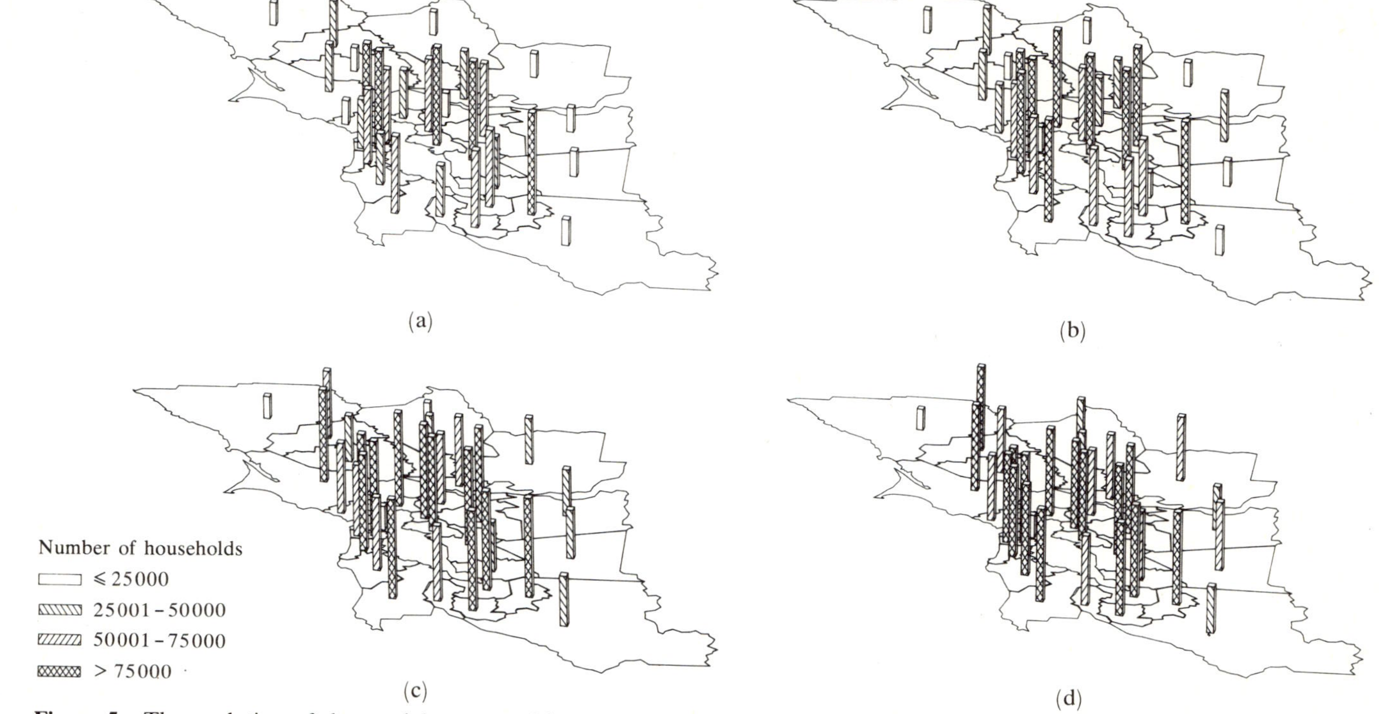

Figure 5. The evolution of the spatial pattern of household location from test 1 applied to the San Francisco Bay Area (thirty zones): (a) base distribution, (b) first iteration, (c) second iteration, (d) third iteration.

assumed that each iteration represents from five to ten years. Thus three iterations may cover a total of twenty to twenty-five years.

Figure 4 shows the evolution of the spatial pattern of employment location in the San Francisco region. The growth and decentralisation of employment in the region is quite clear in the sequence of maps in this figure. It is also quite clear that the changes are not uniform, representing, as is appropriate, changing zonal attractiveness. This attractiveness is partially determined by the subsequent (to each employment forecast) change in household location which, in turn, becomes an input to the next employment forecast. The sequence of household distributions is shown in figure 5 where, again, growth and decentralisation are both clearly visible.

It is worth mentioning here that in these runs no constraints of any sort are imposed. Thus population and/or employment levels and densities are free to vary throughout. Consequently no nonlinear responses result from activity-location constraints, or from transport-congestion constraints (as the transport system characteristics remain unaffected by activity location in this first model structure). Last, it should be noted that calibration of the two models was handled separately, each having been calibrated by the trip-end calibration procedure which has been described elsewhere (Putman, 1983). Clearly, the use of any but the strictly sequential system structure here would also have implications for the calibration method to be used, though it is not clear that many alternatives to sequential calibration exist for models such as these.

The next test series to be described adds a whole new level of difficulties both of calibration and of model linkages.

4 Test 2: integrated model structure 1

The second model structure used in these tests involved utilisation of the trip-distribution capability of DRAM and the linking of a network-assignment program to the end of the EMPAL–DRAM location model pair. Many complications arise from this augmentation of the model set. First, the trip-distribution capability of DRAM yields trip-probability matrices for three trip types; work-to-home, work-to-shop, and home-to-shop. It is necessary to provide the absolute values by which these probability matrices are multiplied to yield actual trips. These should probably be zone-specific and trip-type-specific person-trip generation rates, which should be followed by trip-purpose-specific persons-per-vehicle rates. For the present tests a regional vehicle trip total is used for each trip purpose, and multiplied by the proper probability matrix to yield the matrix of vehicle trips by purpose. There is an obvious need here for further research.

These trip matrices then become input to NETWRK, the network-assignment model. There are a substantial number of unresolved issues connected with this component of the model system as well. The selection of the general approach to be followed, that is, which assignment algorithm, single-path or multipath, iterative incremental, or equilibrium, is always open to discussion. The current series of tests was done using an incremental single-path capacity-constrained assignment algorithm (Putman, 1983). Even without the issue of assignment-algorithm selection there remain other questions. Which volume–delay function is to be used? The traditional functions in common use were derived (several decades ago) from observations of actual on-the-road travel times and trip volumes. Virtually all network modelling involves several (often many) actual roads or highways being represented as one mathematically defined 'link'. The travel time and vehicle capacity of this abstract 'link' are then modified during the trip-assignment process, according to the volume–delay function. First, how well do abstract 'links' represent actual physical facilities, that is, what consistent methods should be used to transform the times and capacities of the actual facilities into abstract link descriptions? Second, are the traditional volume–delay functions too steeply sloping for these aggregated abstract links? Further, what, if anything, is to be done about the issue of generalised cost of travel, which deals with the problems of aggregating several measures of travel difficulty, for example, time or costs, into some single measure for each zone-to-zone pair?

Other issues are associated with the actual model-to-model linkages as well as the procedure to be used in solving the models for numerical answers. A particularly troublesome problem is that of calibration, in a crude sense, of the overall model system. For the test 1 series the zone-to-zone impedances used in calibration were provided by the government agency from whom the initial data set was obtained. They were obtained by using selected nodes from a more complex network then in use by the agency, and by creating a matrix of the travel times between these selected nodes to represent zone-to-zone times for the aggregate zone system used in these tests. These impedances were specified as being representative of afternoon peak-hour travel times and were used in the calibration of EMPAL and DRAM. A similarly prepared future-year impedance matrix was used in the test 1 simulations. The same model parameters prepared for test 1 were used for the test 2 computer runs. Yet, when the DRAM-produced trips were loaded on the aggregated-link highway network, the congested travel times for individual zone-to-zone pairs were four to ten times greater than the original impedances used in test 1. Examination showed the vehicular capacity of the aggregated network to be substantially less than that of a detailed abstracted network for the region, and probably even more substantially less, by comparison, than that of the actual road network. Thus it was necessary to scale the numbers of trips to be loaded, by a process of trial and error, down to the point where the mean minimum-path times on the loaded (congested) abstract network were approximately equal to the zone-to-zone times of the original impedance matrix used in the calibrations and for test 1. This was just the smallest step towards unravelling the enormously complex problem of system calibration for linked models.

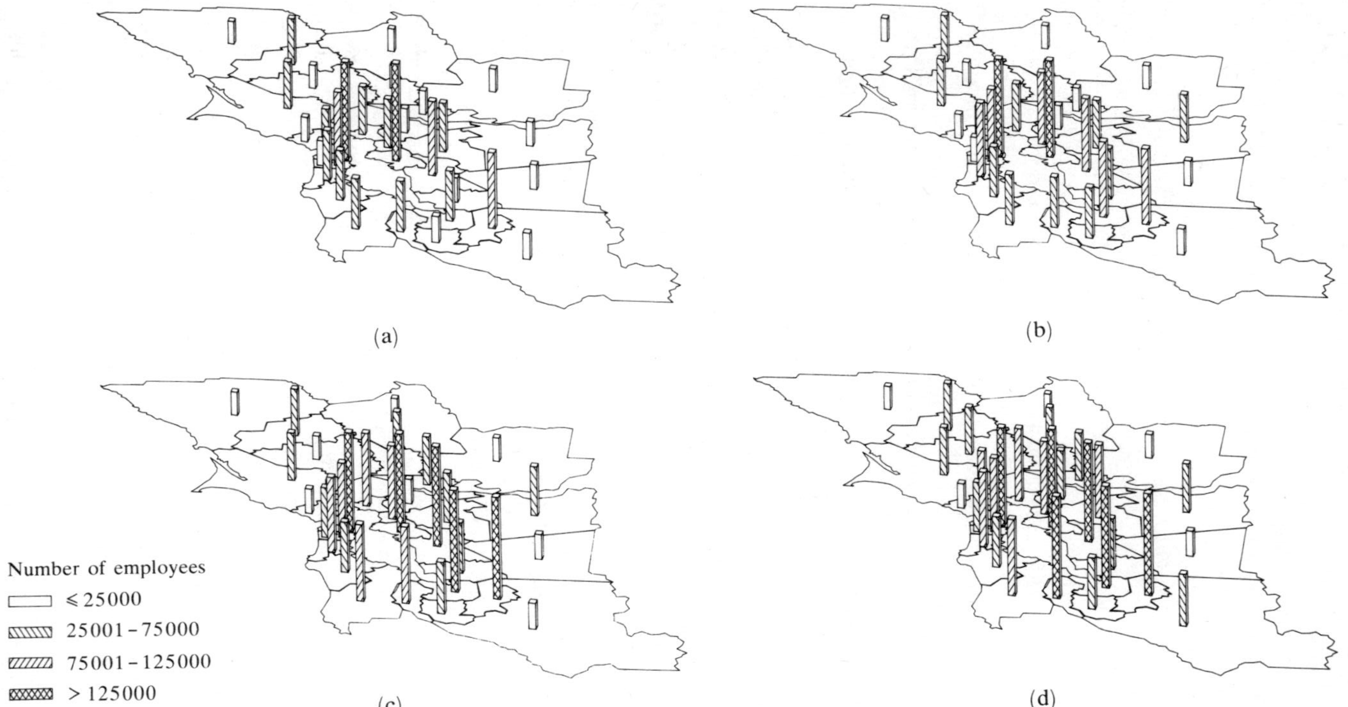

Figure 6. The evolution of the spatial pattern of employment location from test 2 applied to the San Francisco Bay Area (thirty zones): (a) base distribution, (b) first iteration, (c) second iteration, (d) third iteration.

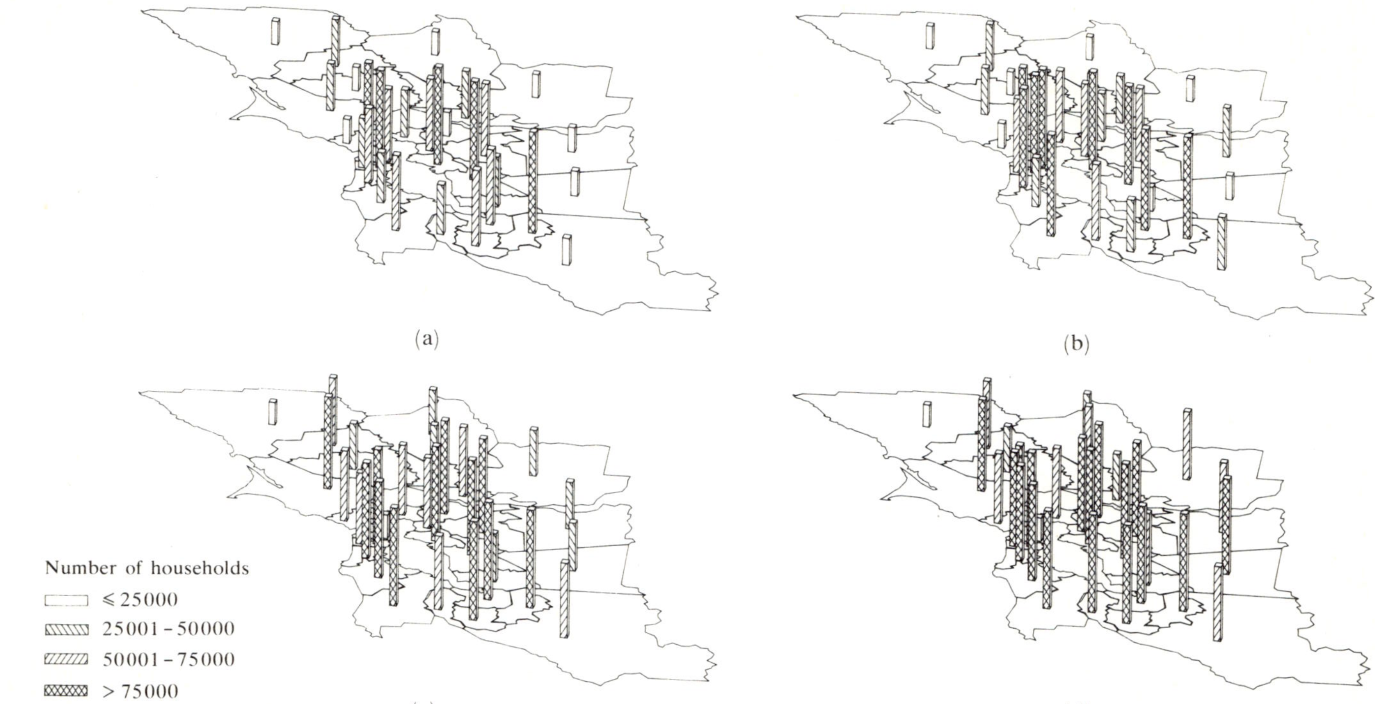

Figure 7. The evolution of the spatial pattern of household location from test 2 applied to the San Francisco Bay Area (thirty zones): (a) base distribution, (b) first iteration, (c) second iteration, (d) third iteration.

All these issues and problems notwithstanding, a series of model runs was made, called test 2, and analogous to test 1. Figure 6 thus shows the evolution of the spatial pattern of employment in the San Francisco region forecast by the system structure of figure 2. Again, the signs of decentralisation are evident. What is rather more interesting is that, even though the model structure and the consequent model outputs of test 2 are different from those of test 1, the resulting *general* spatial patterns are rather similar. This is true for the households too, as can be seen in figure 7 and by comparison of figure 7 with figure 5. Although there clearly are some differences in the results, their overall patterns are rather similar. This says something both about the robustness of urban form, and, perhaps, about the persistence of the 'view' given by the models of the ultimate (steady state) form of the region. It also implies that once a model system is operating more or less properly, a simple look at the outputs will not suffice to verify all the possible questions about reliability of forecasts.

With a view toward increasing this reliability, and also to provide a means for analysing policies pertaining to transit, the model system was further augmented by the addition of a mode-choice procedure to allow travellers to shift between automobile and transit alternatives. These additional model runs, referred to as test 3, are described in the next section of this paper.

5 Test 3: integrated model structure 2

To make any practical use of urban models it is necessary to accept, at face value, a substantial number of assumptions. In the previous discussion of test 1 and test 2 the model structures were shown to rely upon many such assumptions. The addition of modal choice to the system for the test 3 series requires that yet another series of assumptions be made. First, of course, there is consideration of the general structure of the mode-split procedure, for example, predistribution or postdistribution mode split? Then there is the problem of choosing a particular model to use. In the model selected (in this case a multinomial logit formulation) there is the question of variables and, as a subquestion, the matter of selecting a way of calculating generalised costs.

Even when these questions are dealt with, further issues arise. The question of composite cost calculation is a critical and complex one. Here again, the question of system calibration appears. The use of composite costs results in rather different impedance matrices as compared with those used in test 1 and test 2. Should some form of composite cost impedances have been used in the initial calibration (or, a recalibration) of EMPAL and DRAM for test 3? Here the question of zone size also becomes important, as many transit trips are shorter than automobile trips and may take place entirely within a single analysis zone. This implies the need for rather careful consideration of intrazonal trips and intrazonal mode split, as these determine the values of the diagonals of the impedance matrices later input to EMPAL and DRAM, and to which both models are quite sensitive.

Again, despite all these uncertainties, assumptions were made, prototype procedures adopted, and the test 3 simulations were run. The results of these tests are shown in figure 8, for employment, and in figure 9 for households. Again, though there certainly are major differences in the numerical results, the overall spatial patterns are similar to the results from test 1 and test 2. There is perhaps somewhat less congestion-caused dispersion of activities, but it must be admitted that with rather few exceptions (for example, the occasional very different zone employment or population value) none of these test results could be rejected out of hand as being unreasonable.

The question of composite cost calculations will serve, before conclusions are drawn for the paper as a whole, to illustrate the types of problem yet to be resolved. First consider that all spatial interaction models use some c_{ij} or 'difficulty of interaction between zone i and zone j' variable. Depending on the availability of data, the actual values of c_{ij} may be travel time, travel cost, or, in some cases, distance. The question of what, in theory, makes the best measure is not resolved in the current literature. Clearly, the measure must, when possible, take into account the circumstances of the trip-makers, their income, their value-of-time, etc. In practice this is such a complex and poorly defined question that rather simple expedients are taken. In principle, one would like some generalised cost-of-interaction measure which would properly combine all the appropriate factors into a single value. Again, in practice this is often not possible and a simple travel-time or travel-cost measure must be used.

A second aspect of this problem appears with regard to models which represent multimodal transport facilities. Consider, for example, the case of a system which deals with two modes: private automobile, and public transit. To skip over the generalised cost question, assume that for each mode only travel cost is known. How should these two costs, for each $i-j$ zone pair, be used? One alternative is to develop a procedure for combining the modal costs into a composite cost variable prior to their use in the model. The problem then becomes one of determining the precise formulation for such a composite cost calculation. The taking of a simple weighted average was often used in early multimodal analyses. Unfortunately, this formulation has a major drawback. If a new mode is added between zones i and j, and if that new mode is more costly than the prior composite cost (or if there was only one mode to begin with, and if the new mode is more costly than the first mode), then the composite cost increases. This is counterintuitive. Any new mode added to an existing system should result in an improvement in zone-to-zone impedance.

A second alternative follows from an analogy to circuit theory, when several resistances are connected in parallel. In such a case the addition

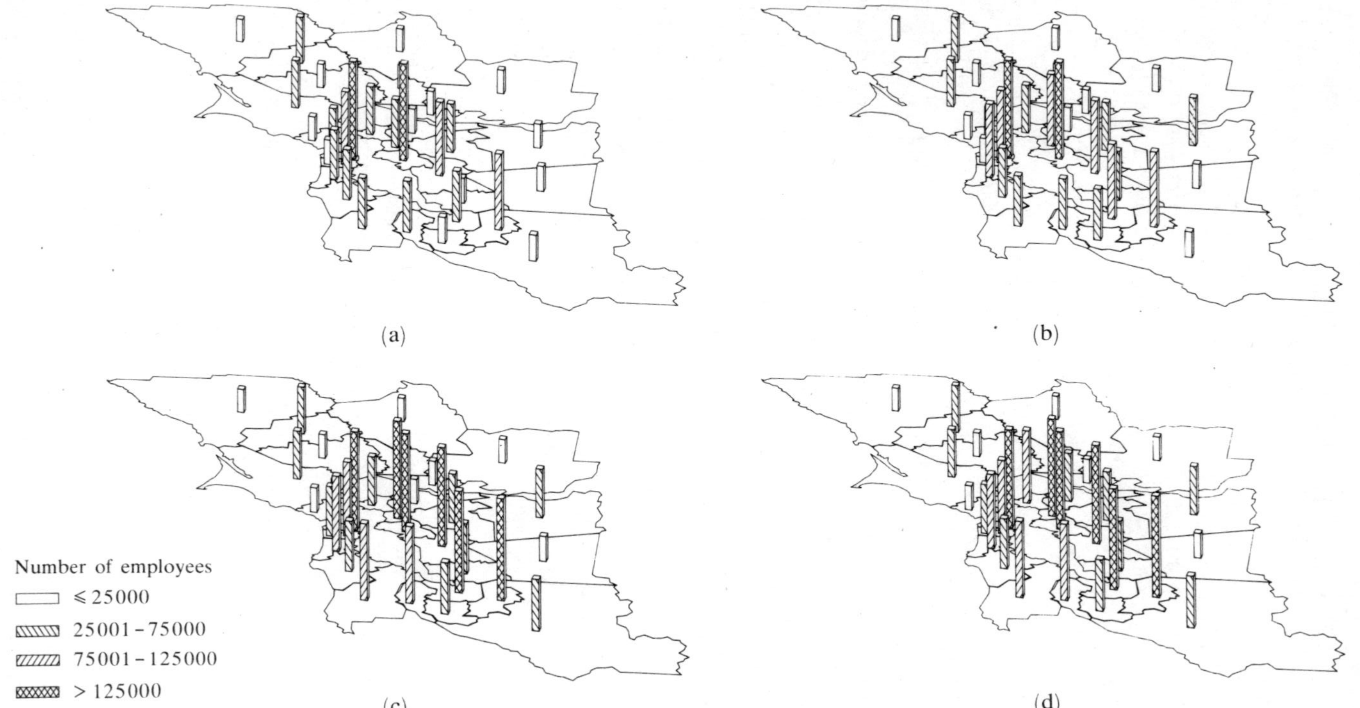

Figure 8. The evolution of the spatial pattern of employment location from test 3 applied to the San Francisco Bay Area (thirty zones): (a) base distribution, (b) first iteration, (c) second iteration, (d) third iteration.

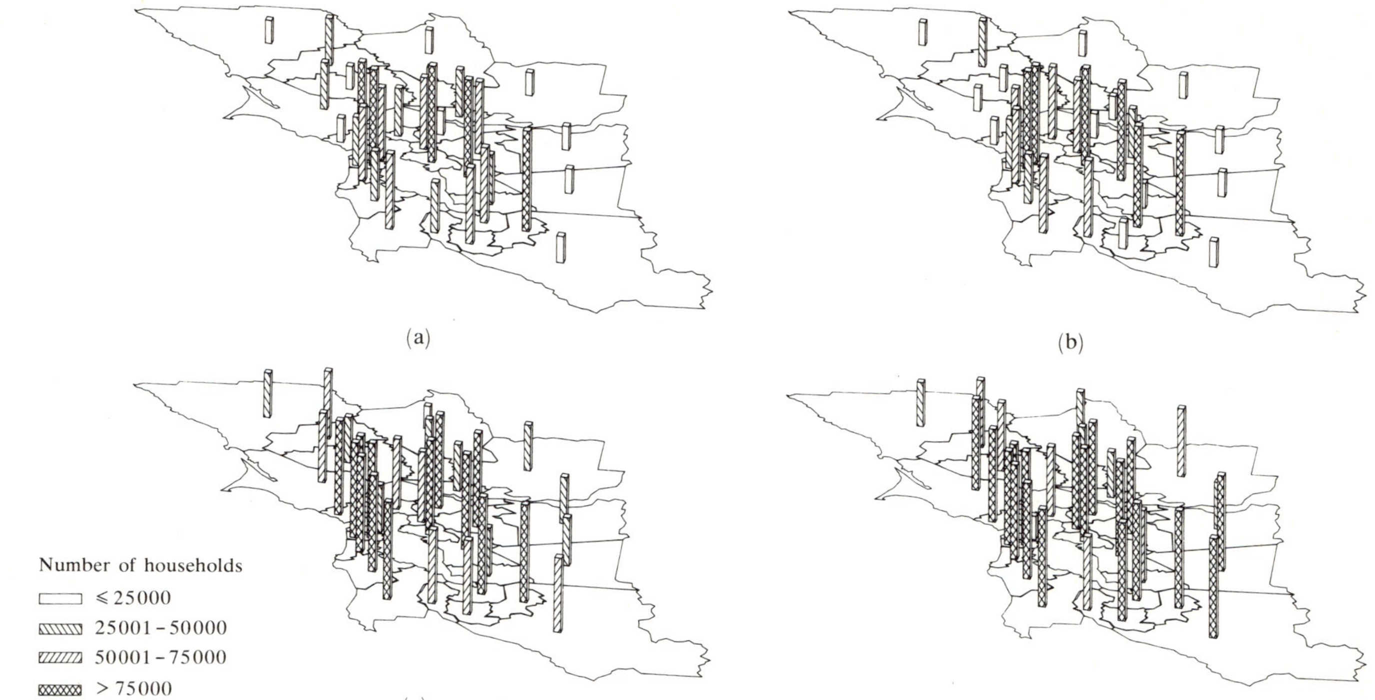

Figure 9. The evolution of the spatial pattern of household location from test 3 applied to the San Francisco Bay Area (thirty zones): (a) base distribution, (b) first iteration, (c) second iteration, (d) third iteration.

of a parallel path, no matter how high its resistance, cannot increase the resulting path resistance. In the case of travel costs, the formula for composite cost, c'_{ij} , would be

$$\frac{1}{c'_{ij}} = \sum_k \frac{1}{c^k_{ij}} \ . \tag{1}$$

Of course, the restriction that c^k_{ij} is nonzero must be imposed to avoid dividing by 0.

Recent work on the ties between random utility theory, probabilistic choice models, and spatial interaction models suggests yet another composite cost function (Wilson et al, 1981). In particular, the following form is suggested.

$$c'_{ij} = -\frac{1}{\lambda} \ln \sum_k \exp\left(-\lambda c^k_{ij}\right), \tag{2}$$

where λ is an empirically derived parameter. The rationale for this formulation is discussed in considerable detail in several papers in the literature (Senior and Williams, 1977; Williams, 1977; Williams and Senior, 1977). The question is, how is the value of λ in the composite cost function to be obtained? The mathematics that produced equation (2) (Williams, 1977) were based on simple one-parameter models of location and mode split. DRAM and MSPLIT are both multiparametric models and thus, in lieu of the analytics, a series of numerical experiments was conducted to gain an understanding of the shape of equation (2), and to learn about its sensitivity to changes in λ and c_{ij} . In reasonable ranges of λ and c^k_{ij} , the function seems to perform adequately, but for use with DRAM and MSPLIT the theoretical inconsistency remains.

The choice of equation (2), for use in ITLUP, required the selection of an arbitrary value of λ. The multinomial logit model used in MSPLIT is multiparametric and does not use travel costs directly, but rather uses differences in travel costs between modes and therefore does not directly yield a value for λ. Thus for these preliminary tests (test 3) an arbitrary value of 0.05 was taken for λ in the composite cost function. This was done to produce some, but not too much, sensitivity of composite cost to addition of modes. This choice clearly implies an additional system-calibration problem as discussed above. Thus the resolution of the composite cost question, itself a secondary question in the model-integration problem, is somewhat elusive. Some structuring of the situation is possible. Elimination of some clearly incorrect alternatives is also possible. But the selection of a 'guaranteed correct' answer does not seem to be possible. As an exemplar of urban systems modelling problems this is an unfortunately too common outcome. In the concluding section of this paper, this situation is discussed in the context of the general issue of complexity in modern science.

6 Conclusion: the issue of complexity in urban systems models

What does all this lead to? If none of these test results is 'obviously' wrong, then is there a way of saying if any of them is 'obviously' right? Which of the many bold assumptions needed to progress from hypothetical model to operational model are critical? How is one to tell? It would be remarkably pretentious to offer here the pretext of a solution to these issues. In lieu of that it is possible to try to place this situation in context. In a recent editorial, Broad (1983) offered some quotes and comments which are particularly relevant here. One such quote, from David Hull, President of the Philosophy of Science Association, is particularly relevant. "In general the simple problems have all been solved, ... the physicists came across some simple problems quite early. But in the social sciences and other areas there may not be any simple problems" (page C1).

It is obvious that in urban systems modelling there are no simple problems. To anyone who has followed developments in this field it is clear that many of the problems are not yet even well defined. The more that is learned, the more is known of the immensity of that which is not yet learned. Progress from the simple robustness of the Lowry model has been considerable. The gradual suffusion of utility theory and choice theory into urban modelling has been salutary. But what of the results of the tests just described? Even though the model structures were different, the results showed substantial similarities. Each succeeding model structure required addition of further assumptions, further compromises between theory and practicality, between the known and the not known.

To some, the admission of uncertainty about the reliability of modelling results provides the grounds for rejection of the entire approach. Yet in any field even the most reliable of forecasts, those concerned with the simplest of phenomena, must have confidence intervals: a band of uncertainty around the forecasts. To ignore the uncertainty which surrounds the traditional 'back-of-the-envelope' or 'seat-of-the-pants' forecast does not mean that it is not there, it *must* be there, and one may be sure that it is large.

For others the response to uncertainty in applied model results has been to abandon almost completely the practical concerns. Here a variety of theoretical considerations supported by extensive mathematical analyses have attempted to unravel some of the knots. Yet all too often the complexity of the subject, as well as the method of approach, has forced these analyses to focus on models which have been greatly reduced by the necessary simplifying assumptions. To a certain degree these analyses trade off substance for precision.

Again, what of the results of the tests described above? The fact is that there is no certain way of knowing which of those results is the most reliable estimate of the evolving spatial patterns of the San Francisco region. It is to be hoped that, as the model structure was modified to reflect additional aspects of reality, it was increasingly able to produce reliable forecasts. Yet each addition to the model system occasioned additional assumptions. Although it is intended that, over time, the sensitivity of the system to each assumption will be examined, the number of experiments implied by this goal is quite staggering. Each assumption, of course, interacts with others and so on through the chain of linked models.

As mentioned above, there is great similarity in, say, the third iteration results of test 2 and test 3 as shown in figures 6-9. Of course, a metropolitan region the size of the San Francisco region is rather stable. Generations of evolving spatial pattern cannot, in reality, be rearranged in a few decades—a model should not forecast such rearrangements. Some zones do show significant differences in total households and some zones show significant differences in employment. In general, particularly if a comparison is made between test 1 and test 3, employment grows in a somewhat more centralised way in test 3 than in test 1. Households, on the other hand, become more decentralised in test 3 than in test 1, but show an evolving decentralisation in both cases.

Taking these tests en bloc there is rather reassuring correspondence to our intuitive understanding of urban spatial dynamics. Test 1 ignores the effects of highway congestion and forecasts regional growth with some decentralisation, but with rather noticeable concentration of both employment and households in zones of base-year concentrations. Test 2 explicitly includes highway congestion by virtue of the integration of the capacity-constrained assignment procedure. The first attempts at test 2 substantially overstated the highway congestion and showed a dramatic decentralisation of the activities in the region. After a crude 'system calibration' to adjust for the aggregation of representative highway links, test 2 was rerun. The final run of test 2 showed decentralisation (perhaps still excessive) both of households and of employment because of highway congestion, particularly congestion in the most urbanised zones. Test 3 augments test 2 by adding mode split to the model structure and a transit system to the data. Some 'system calibration' was required here, too, to adjust the operation of the composite cost calculation. The test 3 results show, compared with test 2, less decentralisation of employment and somewhat more decentralisation of households.

There are some other interesting results from these test runs which become evident on further examination of the actual numerical outputs. First is the aspect of system solution stability. During much of the development of ITLUP there have been recurrent problems of stability of forecasts. In normal use, once the forecast for the final time period has been calculated, the simulations are ended. In ITLUP, because of the congested network feedback loop (see figures 2 and 3) an additional 'equilibrium' run has been required to allow the forecasts to settle down to a stable result. Unfortunately, it has often taken several (sometimes many) such iterations for the system to stabilise. With the addition of the mode-split procedure the solution of the model system has become much more stable.

The regional mode shares, for example, go from 0.688 for automobile and 0.312 for transit for the starting values to 0.758, 0.242; 0.777, 0.223; and 0.778, 0.222, for the three successive iterations. These correspond well to the actual data. The zonal results are equally satisfactory.

Thus, despite the additional assumptions necessary, successive augmentations of the model system configuration yield successive improvements in the correspondence of the model results to perceived reality. Each of the assumptions enumerated above implies a future research task. The substance of the results suggests that the permanent abandonment of transit systems in urban areas may lead to long-term decline in employment in central areas. On a regionwide basis the effect on household location may not be so dramatic, though specific zones will certainly show substantial changes.

All of these results must be understood to have resulted from a blend of both observable fact and assumptions. In urban systems modelling it cannot be otherwise. The task for researchers is to strive to cope with complexity and reduce the uncertainty of results. The task for the users of such research is to adjust to the concept of uncertainty, make intelligent use of what is available, and encourage the researchers in their continued efforts.

References

Broad W J, 1983, "Is science stymied by today's complexity?" *The New York Times* 28 June, pp C1 and C4

Keith R W, 1983, "Incorporation of a mode choice component into the Integrated Transportation and Land Use Package: preliminary empirical results" Urban Simulation Laboratory, Department of City and Regional Planning, University of Pennsylvania, Philadelphia, PA

Kim W J, 1984, "The spatial consequences of incorporating mode split into an Integrated Transportation and Land Use Package (ITLUP): a study of the San Francisco metropolitan area" Urban Simulation Laboratory, Department of City and Regional Planning, University of Pennsylvania, Philadelphia, PA

Putman S H, 1983 *Integrated Urban Models* (Pion, London)

Putman S H, 1984, "Dynamic properties of static-recursive model systems of transportation and location" *Environment and Planning A* **16** 1503–1519

Senior M L, Williams H C W L, 1977, "Model based transport policy assessment 1: the use of alternative forecasting models" *Traffic Engineering and Control* **18** 402–406

Williams H C W L, 1977, "On the formation of travel demand models and economic evaluation measures of user benefit" *Environment and Planning A* **9** 285–344

Williams H C W L, Senior M L, 1977, "Model based transport policy assessment 2: removing fundamental inconsistencies from the models" *Traffic Engineering and Control* **18** 464–469

Wilson A G, Coelho J D, Macgill S M, Williams H C W L, 1981 *Optimization in Locational and Transport Analysis* (John Wiley, Chichester, Sussex)

Two Populations and Their Economies

J R N STONE, M R WEALE
University of Cambridge

1 Introduction

In this paper we describe a model which relates to a closed system of two regions and incorporates both demographic and economic variables. In its present embryonic state it is essentially an input–output model in which the principal exogenous variables are the opening stocks of population. Each of the two regions can be represented by the entries in a set of ten accounts. These accounts can be drawn up in two versions: a demographic–economic version, expressed partly in population numbers and partly in money units; and a purely economic version, expressed throughout in money units.

In the demographic–economic version the first three accounts are production accounts with outputs and intermediate inputs expressed in money and primary inputs expressed in people. The next four accounts relate to the population, divided between a professional and managerial class and other workers, and in each case there may be some unemployed; one side of the accounts shows the numbers of people employed in each branch of production, the numbers unemployed, and the numbers who emigrate, and the other side shows private expenditure expressed in money. The next two accounts are government income and outlay accounts, one relating to an unemployment fund financed by an income tax, the other to the provision and allocation of foreign aid. The tenth and last account is a capital account which receives saving and applies it to the finance of investment at home and abroad. The first seven accounts, being expressed in heterogeneous units, do not balance; the last three, being conventional money accounts, do.

In the purely economic version, people are replaced by their income. Thus in the three production accounts primary inputs are represented by factor incomes which balance final outputs in the usual way. And the four 'population and outlay' accounts become regular income and outlay accounts, with factor incomes and unemployment benefits balancing expenditures and saving. The government and capital accounts remain unchanged. In this version all the accounts balance.

For our examples we have imagined two economies, one rich and one poor; the rich one gives a proportion of its income to the poor one. The populations are all potentially active, though there may be some unemployment; at a later stage it should not be difficult also to introduce the inactive. Migrations are deemed to take place at the beginning of the year and flow directly into employment.

So much for the structure of the system. Now for the data.

2 The data

Eventually we intend to endogenise as many variables as possible but at present the opening stocks of population, the vectors of investment, the coefficients of production and consumption, and the wage, tax, and saving rates are exogenous. These data are set out symbolically in table 1. The layout of this table shows how the two regions, North and South, are related: the top left-hand or northwest quadrant contains the internal transactions of the richer economy and the southeast quadrant those of the poorer; the northeast and the southwest quadrants contain the transactions between the two. Capital letters denote matrices of coefficients and small letters denote vectors of variables. Asterisks indicate entries relating to population numbers. Since the arrangement of the entries for the two regions is symmetrical, the symbols can be defined in pairs, as follows.

In the first and fifth rows:

A_{11}, A_{55} are matrices of domestic interindustry coefficients,

A_{12}, A_{56} are coefficient matrices of consumption goods per unit of gross income,

x_{14}, x_{58} are supply vectors of investment goods for domestic use,

A_{15}, A_{51} are coefficient matrices of exports of intermediate products per unit of the output of the other region,

A_{16}, A_{52} are coefficient matrices of exports of consumption goods per unit of the gross income of the other region,

x_{18}, x_{54} are supply vectors of exports of investment goods to the other region;

in the second and sixth rows:

A_{21}^{*}, A_{65}^{*} are coefficient matrices of domestic manpower per unit of domestic output,

A_{25}^{*}, A_{61}^{*} are coefficient matrices of emigrant manpower per unit of the output of the other region,

x_{2}^{*}, x_{6}^{*} are vectors of the opening stocks of population,

Table 1. The data.

Type of account	No.	1–3	4–7	8, 9	10	11–13	14–17	18,19	20	Pop.[a]	Wages[b]
North											
Production	1–3	A_{11}	A_{12}		x_{14}	A_{15}	A_{16}		x_{18}		
Population/outlay[c]	4–7	A_{21}^{*}				A_{25}^{*}				x_{2}^{*}	
Income/outlay[d]	8, 9		A_{32}								$W_{2}, U_{2} = \frac{1}{2}W_{2}$
Accumulation	10		A_{42}								
South											
Production	11–13	A_{51}	A_{52}		x_{54}	A_{55}	A_{56}		x_{58}		
Population/outlay[c]	14–17	A_{61}^{*}				A_{65}^{*}				x_{6}^{*}	
Income/outlay[d]	18,19						A_{76}				$W_{6}, U_{6} = \frac{1}{2}W_{6}$
Accumulation	20						A_{86}				

[a]Initial population. [b]Wages and benefit rates. [c]Population and private outlay. [d]Public income and outlay.

W_2, W_6 are matrices of wage rates,
U_2, U_6 are matrices of unemployment benefit rates;
in the third and seventh rows:
A_{32}, A_{76} are coefficient matrices containing the proportions, t, of gross income paid in tax and the proportions, g, devoted to foreign aid; here it is assumed that only the North pays foreign aid;
and last, in the fourth and eighth rows:
A_{42}, A_{86} are coefficient matrices of the proportions of gross income saved. With these data the system can be solved.

3 Solving the system

Before we go into the algebra of the system it may be useful to describe the method of solution in a general way. The first step is to calculate the output vectors for the two regions, respectively, y_1 and y_5. These vectors are dependent on terms in y_1, y_5, and the xs. Thus we obtain two simultaneous equations to solve for y_1 and y_5 in terms of the xs and the coefficients. Then, given y_1 and y_5, we can calculate employment and factor incomes; given the initial population and the derived migrant flows we can calculate unemployment and hence, given the rates of unemployment benefits, the income of the unemployed. Finally, given these incomes we can calculate private outlays on domestic products and on imports, taxes, foreign aid, and saving. In the poorer region all the foreign aid received goes to the poorer class, whether employed or unemployed, in proportion to their numbers. The difference between taxes and benefits constitutes the budget surplus (or deficit) and is an addition to (or subtraction from) private saving. Investment abroad where positive is the excess of saving over domestic investment, and where negative appears as the addition to the saving needed in the other region to balance their domestic investment. Imports of intermediate products depend on the outputs into which they enter.

The equations of the model are as follows. For the North

$$
\begin{aligned}
y_1 = {} & A_{11}y_1 + A_{12}[W_2(A_{21}^* + A_{61}^*)y_1 + U_2(x_2^* - A_{21}^*y_1 - A_{25}^*y_5)] + x_{14} \\
& + A_{15}y_5 + A_{16}[W_6(A_{65}^* + A_{25}^*)y_5 + U_6(x_6^* - A_{65}^*y_5 - A_{61}^*y_1) \\
& \qquad\qquad\qquad\qquad\qquad + H\hat{g}_2W_2(A_{21}^* + A_{61}^*)y_1] + x_{18} \\[4pt]
= {} & \{A_{11} + A_{12}[W_2(A_{21}^* + A_{61}^*) - U_2A_{21}^*] \\
& \qquad\qquad\qquad + A_{16}[H\hat{g}_2W_2(A_{21}^* + A_{61}^*) - U_6A_{61}^*]\}y_1 \\
& + \{A_{15} + A_{16}[W_6(A_{65}^* + A_{25}^*) - U_6A_{65}^*] - A_{12}U_2A_{25}^*\}y_5 \\
& + (A_{12}U_2x_2^* + x_{14} + A_{16}U_{16}x_6^* + x_{18}) , \qquad (1)
\end{aligned}
$$

In equation (1), $\hat{g}_2$ denotes a diagonal matrix formed from the vector g_2, which shows the proportions of income each population group in the North pays out in foreign aid; and H is a matrix which channels these payments to the appropriate group in the South. The terms on the right-hand side of the equation are grouped by y_1, and y_5 and the xs. For the South the corresponding equation is

$$
\begin{aligned}
y_5 = {} & \mathbf{A}_{55}y_5 + \mathbf{A}_{56}[\mathbf{W}_6(\mathbf{A}^*_{65} + \mathbf{A}^*_{25})y_5 + \mathbf{U}_6(x^*_6 - \mathbf{A}^*_{65}y_5 - \mathbf{A}^*_{61}y_1) \\
& \qquad\qquad\qquad\qquad\qquad + \mathbf{H}\hat{\mathbf{g}}_2\mathbf{W}_2(\mathbf{A}^*_{61} + \mathbf{A}^*_{21})y_1] + x_{58} \\
& + \mathbf{A}_{51}y_1 + \mathbf{A}_{52}[\mathbf{W}_2(\mathbf{A}^*_{21} + \mathbf{A}^*_{61})y_1 + \mathbf{U}_2(x^*_2 - \mathbf{A}^*_{21}y_1 - \mathbf{A}^*_{25}y_5)] + x_{54} \\
= {} & \{\mathbf{A}_{55} + \mathbf{A}_{56}[\mathbf{W}_6(\mathbf{A}^*_{65} + \mathbf{A}^*_{25}) - \mathbf{U}_6\mathbf{A}^*_{65}] - \mathbf{A}_{52}\mathbf{U}_2\mathbf{A}^*_{25}\}y_5 \\
& + \{\mathbf{A}_{51} + \mathbf{A}_{52}[\mathbf{W}_2(\mathbf{A}^*_{21} + \mathbf{A}^*_{61}) - \mathbf{U}_2\mathbf{A}^*_{21}] + \mathbf{A}_{56}[\mathbf{H}\hat{\mathbf{g}}_2\mathbf{W}_2(\mathbf{A}^*_{61} + \mathbf{A}^*_{21}) \\
& \qquad\qquad\qquad\qquad\qquad\qquad\qquad\qquad\qquad\qquad - \mathbf{U}_6\mathbf{A}^*_{61}]\}y_1 \\
& + (\mathbf{A}_{56}\mathbf{U}_6x^*_6 + x_{58} + \mathbf{A}_{52}\mathbf{U}_2x^*_2 + x_{54}) .
\end{aligned}
\tag{2}
$$

If in equation (1) we denote the matrix of coefficients of y_1 by $\mathbf{B}_1$, the matrix of coefficients of y_5 by $\mathbf{C}_1$, and the term in the xs by $\mathbf{X}_1$, and in equation (2) we denote the matrix of coefficients of y_5 by $\mathbf{B}_5$, the matrix of coefficient of y_1 by $\mathbf{C}_5$, and the term in the xs by $\mathbf{X}_5$, then we can write

$$
y_1 = [\mathbf{I} - (\mathbf{I} - \mathbf{B}_1)^{-1}\mathbf{C}_1(\mathbf{I} - \mathbf{B}_5)^{-1}\mathbf{C}_5]^{-1}(\mathbf{I} - \mathbf{B}_1)^{-1}[\mathbf{X}_1 + \mathbf{C}_1(\mathbf{I} - \mathbf{B}_5)^{-1}\mathbf{X}_5] ,
\tag{3}
$$

and

$$
y_5 = [\mathbf{I} - (\mathbf{I} - \mathbf{B}_5)^{-1}\mathbf{C}_5(\mathbf{I} - \mathbf{B}_1)^{-1}\mathbf{C}_1]^{-1}(\mathbf{I} - \mathbf{B}_5)^{-1}[\mathbf{X}_5 + \mathbf{C}_5(\mathbf{I} - \mathbf{B}_1)^{-1}\mathbf{X}_1] ,
\tag{4}
$$

where $\mathbf{I}$ is the identity matrix.

It is possible to generate full employment by changing the levels of investment. Let us denote employment in the two regions by vectors e_2 and e_6, respectively, where

$$
e_2 = (\mathbf{A}^*_{21} + \mathbf{A}^*_{61})y_1 ,
\tag{5}
$$

and

$$
e_6 = (\mathbf{A}^*_{65} + \mathbf{A}^*_{25})y_5 .
\tag{6}
$$

We can calculate the increases in investment needed to generate full employment by deriving a set of investment–employment multipliers from equations (3)–(6). Since the only terms to change in $\mathbf{X}_1$ and $\mathbf{X}_5$ are x_{14} and x_{58}, respectively, so that $\Delta\mathbf{X}_1 = \Delta x_{14}$, and $\Delta\mathbf{X}_5 = \Delta x_{58}$, it follows that

$$
\begin{aligned}
\begin{bmatrix} \Delta e_2 \\ \Delta e_6 \end{bmatrix} &= \begin{bmatrix} \mathbf{A}^*_{21} + \mathbf{A}^*_{61} & 0 \\ 0 & \mathbf{A}^*_{65} + \mathbf{A}^*_{25} \end{bmatrix} \begin{bmatrix} \mathbf{N}_{11} & \mathbf{N}_{12} \\ \mathbf{N}_{21} & \mathbf{N}_{22} \end{bmatrix} \begin{bmatrix} \Delta x_{14} \\ \Delta x_{58} \end{bmatrix} \\
&= \mathbf{M} \begin{bmatrix} \Delta x_{14} \\ \Delta x_{58} \end{bmatrix} ,
\end{aligned}
\tag{7}
$$

where

$$N_{11} = [I - (I - B_1)^{-1}C_1(I - B_5)^{-1}C_5]^{-1}(I - B_1)^{-1} , \tag{8}$$

$$N_{12} = [I - (I - B_1)^{-1}C_1(I - B_5)^{-1}C_5]^{-1}(I - B_1)^{-1}C_1(I - B_5)^{-1} , \tag{9}$$

$$N_{21} = [I - (I - B_5)^{-1}C_5(I - B_1)^{-1}C_1]^{-1}(I - B_5)^{-1}C_5(I - B_1)^{-1} , \tag{10}$$

$$N_{22} = [I - (I - B_5)^{-1}C_5(I - B_1)^{-1}C_1]^{-1}(I - B_5)^{-1} . \tag{11}$$

In equation (7), the matrix M links changes in four types of employment with changes in six types of investment.

There is a range of possible investment patterns which will lead to a target change in employment. To find a solution we have adopted the expedient of setting the third element of Δx_{14} and Δx_{58} to 0. This means that the third and sixth columns of the matrix M can be removed and, with the new matrix written as $\overline{M}$, equation (7) becomes

$$\begin{bmatrix} \Delta e_2 \\ \Delta e_6 \end{bmatrix} = \overline{M} \begin{bmatrix} \overline{\Delta x}_{14} \\ \overline{\Delta x}_{58} \end{bmatrix} , \tag{12}$$

where the bar indicates the removal of the respective columns and elements. Then the necessary changes in investment are given by inverting the investment–employment multiplier matrix, $\overline{M}$, and we can write

$$\begin{bmatrix} \overline{\Delta x}_{14} \\ \overline{\Delta x}_{58} \end{bmatrix} = \overline{M}^{-1} \begin{bmatrix} \Delta e_2 \\ \Delta e_6 \end{bmatrix} . \tag{13}$$

4 The results

The properties of the model are illustrated by three examples, given in the appendix. In the base run (tables A1 and A2) a given amount of exogenous investment demand takes place in both the North and the South and a transfer is paid by the North to the low-income group of the South. Two variants of this are shown. In one (tables A3 and A4) the transfer is discontinued, whereas in the other (tables A5 and A6) the transfer is maintained and investment is increased so as to generate full employment in both regions.

Considering first the base run (tables A1 and A2) it can be seen that substantial unemployment occurs in both population groups in both regions. But, despite the burden of unemployment in the North, the unemployment benefit fund still manages to make a substantial contribution to saving. Relative to the income of the region the unemployment in the South presents a much larger burden and the Southern fund is dissaving. Despite the transfer, the South is borrowing from the North to finance its investment.

The transfer had the effect of draining spending power from the North and increasing it in the South. Thus its termination (tables A3 and A4) leads to an increase in demand in the North and a reduction in demand in the South. But, principally because production is more labour-intensive than in the North, the increase in unemployment in the South, of 1389 among the second population group, is much larger than the decline in unemployment, of 169, in the North. The increased unemployment adds to the borrowing of the Southern unemployment fund, while the surplus of the Northern fund increases. Obviously the ending of the transfer reduces the current foreign exchange flow to the South and thus foreign investment by the North increases by 597, or 64% of the reduction in the transfer.

Full employment (tables A5 and A6) is achieved by substantial extra investment in both North and South. It is assumed that the extra investment arises from augmented domestic demand for the output of industries 1 and 2 in each region. The increments to investments needed are calculated using the investment–employment multiplier given in equation (7). Full employment removes the need for either unemployment fund to pay out, and thus both funds contribute to saving. It also increases the transfer, which is a constant fraction of gross factor income. But, despite these improvements, the South is unable to finance its extra investment and thus foreign investment by the North is larger, by 855, than in the first sample.

Migration flows depend on industrial gross output. Thus the population flows, although remaining small in absolute terms, are relatively much larger in the full employment case. Particularly visible is the increase in the flow of managers from North to South induced by the enlarged output of industry 2 in the South.

5 The next steps

The form of the model illustrated in these examples is rudimentary and much remains to be done if it is to progress from a toy model to a useful tool for studying the world we live in. It would seem capable of many extensions and generalisations. The following seem to be the topics that should be tackled first:

1 a proper treatment of the composition of the population, in particular the explicit introduction of the economically inactive other than the unemployed;

2 a means of projecting population numbers as depending on birth, survival, and migration rates;

3 the introduction of capital and income from capital, and of the destination of investment;

4 the expansion of the government accounts to include all forms of government activity;

5 the introduction of factor and commodity prices so that their changes influence the composition of production and consumption;

6 a means of introducing different currency units and allowing for the influence of exchange rates.

This list is far from complete. Nevertheless, the inclusion of these changes will entail a considerable amount of work.

APPENDIX
The numerical examples

The three runs described in section 4 are illustrated by six tables showing for each run a demographic–economic matrix and its all-economic counterpart. The data used in the construction of these tables are:

$$\mathbf{A}_{11} = \begin{pmatrix} 0.11940 & 0.05232 & 0.00080 \\ 0.19298 & 0.38921 & 0.05323 \\ 0.12817 & 0.16890 & 0.07177 \end{pmatrix},$$

$$\mathbf{A}_{12} = \begin{pmatrix} 0.00955 & 0.02740 & 0.00955 & 0.02740 \\ 0.10642 & 0.20562 & 0.10642 & 0.20562 \\ 0.31539 & 0.38139 & 0.31539 & 0.38139 \end{pmatrix},$$

$$\mathbf{A}_{15} = \begin{pmatrix} 0 & 0.01818 & 0 \\ 0.02005 & 0.16162 & 0.04179 \\ 0.00996 & 0.04465 & 0.00472 \end{pmatrix},$$

$$\mathbf{A}_{16} = \begin{pmatrix} 0 & 0.03069 & 0 & 0.03069 \\ 0.09627 & 0.17798 & 0.09627 & 0.17798 \\ 0.03210 & 0.01270 & 0.03210 & 0.01270 \end{pmatrix},$$

$$\mathbf{A}_{51} = \begin{pmatrix} 0.02436 & 0.05056 & 0.00020 \\ 0 & 0.00426 & 0.00016 \\ 0 & 0 & 0.00008 \end{pmatrix},$$

$$\mathbf{A}_{52} = \begin{pmatrix} 0.00211 & 0.00611 & 0.00211 & 0.00611 \\ 0.00144 & 0.00339 & 0.00144 & 0.00339 \\ 0.00011 & 0.00013 & 0.00011 & 0.00013 \end{pmatrix},$$

$$\mathbf{A}_{55} = \begin{pmatrix} 0.18852 & 0.13111 & 0.02077 \\ 0.03579 & 0.17980 & 0.05194 \\ 0.03188 & 0.11717 & 0.05430 \end{pmatrix},$$

$$\mathbf{A}_{56} = \begin{pmatrix} 0.10269 & 0.19234 & 0.10269 & 0.19234 \\ 0.12868 & 0.15245 & 0.12868 & 0.15245 \\ 0.12836 & 0.16958 & 0.12836 & 0.16958 \end{pmatrix},$$

$$\mathbf{A}_{32} = \begin{pmatrix} 0.2 & 0.2 & 0.2 & 0.2 \\ 0.05 & 0.05 & 0.02 & 0.02 \end{pmatrix},$$

but
$$\mathbf{A}_{32} = \begin{pmatrix} 0.2 & 0.2 & 0.2 & 0.2 \\ 0 & 0 & 0 & 0 \end{pmatrix} \qquad \text{for tables A3 and A4,}$$

$$\mathbf{A}_{76} = \begin{pmatrix} 0.2 & 0.2 & 0.2 & 0.2 \\ 0 & 0 & 0 & 0 \end{pmatrix} \, ,$$

$$\mathbf{A}_{42} = (0.31500 \quad 0.15596 \quad 0.31500 \quad 0.15596) \, ,$$

$$\mathbf{A}_{86} = (0.31230 \quad 0.02005 \quad 0.31230 \quad 0.02005) \, ,$$

$$\mathbf{A}_{21}^* = \begin{pmatrix} 0.09990 & 0.05575 & 0.14796 \\ 0.22222 & 0.15732 & 0.40385 \end{pmatrix} \, ,$$

$$\mathbf{A}_{61}^* = \begin{pmatrix} 0 & 0 & 0.00004 \\ 0 & 0.00005 & 0.00020 \end{pmatrix} \, ,$$

$$\mathbf{A}_{25}^* = \begin{pmatrix} 0.00013 & 0.00101 & 0.00047 \\ 0 & 0.00020 & 0.00024 \end{pmatrix} \, ,$$

$$\mathbf{A}_{65}^* = \begin{pmatrix} 0.01121 & 0.02828 & 0.12276 \\ 2.42809 & 0.90101 & 1.51086 \end{pmatrix} \, ,$$

$$\mathbf{W}_2 = \begin{pmatrix} 2.93759 & 0 \\ 0 & 1.08656 \end{pmatrix} \, ,$$

$$\mathbf{W}_5 = \begin{pmatrix} 3.28892 & 0 \\ 0 & 0.27867 \end{pmatrix} \, ,$$

$$\mathbf{U}_2 = \tfrac{1}{2}\mathbf{W}_2 \, , \qquad \mathbf{U}_5 = \tfrac{1}{2}\mathbf{W}_5 \, ,$$

$$\hat{\mathbf{g}}_2 = \begin{pmatrix} 0.05 & 0 \\ 0 & 0.02 \end{pmatrix} \, ,$$

but
$$\hat{\mathbf{g}}_2 = \begin{pmatrix} 0 & 0 \\ 0 & 0 \end{pmatrix} \qquad \text{for tables A3 and A4,}$$

$$\mathbf{H} = \begin{pmatrix} 0 & 0 \\ 1 & 1 \end{pmatrix} \, ,$$

$$x_{14} = \begin{pmatrix} 110 \\ 6800 \\ 800 \end{pmatrix}, \qquad x_{48} = \begin{pmatrix} 80 \\ 1040 \\ 61 \end{pmatrix},$$

$$x_{54} = \begin{pmatrix} 0 \\ 0 \\ 0 \end{pmatrix}, \qquad x_{58} = \begin{pmatrix} 114 \\ 320 \\ 0 \end{pmatrix} c$$

but for tables A5 and A6

$$x_{14} = \begin{pmatrix} 403 \\ 12\,640 \\ 800 \end{pmatrix}, \qquad x_{58} = \begin{pmatrix} 52 \\ 4743 \\ 0 \end{pmatrix}.$$

With these parameters the investment–employment multiplier (M of section 3) is given as

$$M = \begin{pmatrix} 0.22874 & 0.21020 & 0.22677 & 0.04682 & 0.08728 & 0.04394 \\ 0.56759 & 0.57716 & 0.61892 & 0.12723 & 0.23733 & 0.11974 \\ 0.00509 & 0.00715 & 0.00325 & 0.04422 & 0.07579 & 0.15383 \\ 0.31908 & 0.48590 & 0.15542 & 3.92525 & 2.50335 & 2.44476 \end{pmatrix},$$

After deleting columns 3 and 6 so as to produce a square matrix and inverting, the matrix, $\bar{M}^{-1}$, which indicates the change in investment needed to produce a unit change in employment is

$$\bar{M}^{-1} = \begin{pmatrix} 45.3507 & -16.5100 & -0.54026 & 0.00036 \\ -45.0588 & 18.2025 & -5.36646 & 0.00784 \\ 1.78948 & -0.83382 & -12.8233 & 0.40490 \\ 0.15965 & -0.12134 & 21.2175 & -0.23698 \end{pmatrix}.$$

Table A1. A demographic – economic matrix for two regions with foreign aid and low investment (population flows are people; other flows in money units).

			North										South											Totals
			1	2	3	4	5	6	7	8	9	10	11	12	13	14	15	16	17	18	19	20	
North																								
Production	primary	1	337	1412	15	127	369	25	70			110	0	48	0	0	158	0	72			80	2821
	secondary	2	544	10501	989	1418	2766	281	524			6800	91	427	87	122	915	58	417			1040	26981
	tertiary	3	362	4557	1333	4203	5130	834	972			800	45	118	10	41	65	19	30			61	18580
Population and outlay — employed	prof./man.	4	282	1504	2749						0		1	3	1								4539
	other	5	627	4245	7504						0		0	1	0								12376
Population and outlay — unempl'd	prof./man.	6								1685	0		0	0	0								1685
	other	7								4579	0		0	0	0								4579
Public income and outlay	unemp. fund	8	0	0	0	2665	2690	496	497														6348
	foreign aid	9	0	0	0	666	269	0	0														935
Accumulation	save/invest.	10	0	0	0	4197	2098	833	398	1384													8910
South																								
Production	primary	11	69	1364	4	28	82	6	16			0	860	346	43	130	988	62	450			114	4563
	secondary	12	0	115	3	19	46	4	9			0	163	475	108	163	783	77	357			320	2642
	tertiary	13	0	0	1	1	2	0	0			0	145	310	113	163	871	77	397			0	2082
Population and outlay — employed	prof./man.	14	0	0	1								51	75	256					0	0		382
	other	15	0	1	4								11079	2381	3145					0	511		16610
Population and outlay — unempl'd	prof./man.	16	0	0	0															369	0		369
	other	17	0	0	0															13757	424		13757
Public income and outlay	unemp. fund	18														254	1028	120	468				1870
	foreign aid	19									935					0	0	0	0				935
Accumulation	save/invest.	20										1200				396	330	187	150	− 648			1615

Key for tables 2 – 7: prof./man. professional and managerial; save/invest. saving and investment. Accounts 4 – 7 and 14 – 17 show population figures. The row totals exclude aid transfers displayed in column 19.

Table A2. The all-economic counterpart of table A1 (all flows in money units; on account of rounding errors row and column totals are not always equal).

			North										South										Totals
			1	2	3	4	5	6	7	8	9	10	11	12	13	14	15	16	17	18	19	20	
North																							
Production	primary	1	337	1412	15	127	369	25	70			110	0	48	0	0	158	0	72			80	2821
	secondary	2	544	10501	989	1418	2766	281	524			6800	91	427	87	122	915	58	417			1040	26981
	tertiary	3	362	4557	1333	4203	5130	834	972			800	45	118	10	41	65	19	30			61	18580
Private income and outlay	employed prof./man.	4	828	4419	8078						0												13325
	employed other	5	681	4614	8157						0												13452
	unempl'd prof./man.	6								2479	0												2479
	unempl'd other	7								2485	0												2485
Public income and outlay	unemp. fund	8				2665	2690	496	497														6348
	foreign aid	9				666	269	0	0												0		935
Accumulation	save/invest.	10				4197	2098	833	398	1384												0	8910
South																							
Production	primary	11	69	1364	4	28	82	6	16			0	860	346	43	130	988	62	450			114	4563
	secondary	12	0	115	3	19	46	4	9			0	163	475	108	163	783	77	357			320	2642
	tertiary	13	0	0	1	1	2	0	0			0	145	310	113	163	871	77	397			0	2082
Private income and outlay	employed prof./man.	14											170	255	844	0	0	0	0		0		1268
	employed other	15											3087	664	877	0	0	0	0		511		5139
	unempl'd prof./man.	16											0	0	0	0	0	0	0	601	0		601
	unempl'd other	17											0	0	0	0	0	0	0	1917	424		2341
Public income and outlay	unemp. fund	18											0	0	0	254	1028	120	468				1870
	foreign aid	19									935		0	0	0	0	0	0	0				935
Accumulation	save/invest.	20										1200	0	0	0	396	330	187	150	−648			1615
Totals			2821	26981	18581	13324	13452	2479	2485	6348	935	8910	4563	2642	2082	1268	5139	601	2341	1870	935	1615	117439

Table A3. A demographic – economic matrix for two regions with no foreign aid and low investment (population flows are people; other flows in money units).

				North										South										Totals
				1	2	3	4	5	6	7	8	9	10	11	12	13	14	15	16	17	18	19	20	
North																								
Production		primary	1	334	1407	15	138	383	24	67			110	0	44	0	0	130	0	65			80	2797
		secondary	2	540	10469	1014	1533	2876	271	505			6800	85	387	76	109	755	65	376			1040	26899
		tertiary	3	358	4543	1367	4543	5334	804	936			800	42	107	9	36	54	22	27			61	19043
Population and outlay	employed	prof./man.	4	279	1500	2818						0		1	2	1								4600
		other	5	622	4232	7690						0		0	0	0								12545
	unempl'd	prof./man.	6								1624	0		0	0	0								1624
		other	7								4410	0		0	0	0								4410
Public income and outlay		unemp. fund	8				2701	2727	478	479														6385
		foreign aid	9				0	0	0	0												0		0
Accumulation		save/invest.	10				4537	2181	803	383	351	0												0	9506
South																								
Production		primary	11	68	1360	4	30	85	5	15			0	799	314	38	116	816	69	406			114	4240
		secondary	12	0	115	3	21	47	4	8			0	152	431	95	145	646	86	322			320	2395
		tertiary	13	0	0	2	1	2	0	0			0	135	281	99	145	719	86	358			0	1829
Population and outlay	employed	prof./man.	14	0	0	1								48	68	224						0		340
		other	15	0	1	4								10296	2158	2763						0		15221
	unempl'd	prof./man.	16	0	0	0															411	0		411
		other	17	0	0	0															15146	0		15146
Public income and outlay		unemp. fund	18														226	848	134	422				1630
		foreign aid	19														0	0	0	0				0
Accumulation		save/invest.	20										1797				352	272	209	136	−1150			1615

Table A4. The all-economic counterpart of table A3 (all flows in money units; on account of rounding errors row and column totals are not always equal).

			North										South										Totals
			1	2	3	4	5	6	7	8	9	10	11	12	13	14	15	16	17	18	19	20	
North																							
Production	primary	1	334	1407	15	138	383	24	67			110	0	44	0	0	130	0	65			80	2797
	secondary	2	540	10469	1014	1533	2876	271	505			6800	85	387	76	109	755	65	376			1040	26899
	tertiary	3	358	4543	1367	4543	5334	804	936			800	42	107	9	36	54	22	27			61	19043
Private income and outlay — employed	prof./man.	4	821	4405	8279						0												13505
	other	5	675	4600	8360						0												13635
— unempl'd	prof./man.	6								2389	0												2389
	other	7								2394	0												2394
Public income and outlay	unemp. fund	8				2701	2727	478	479															6385
	foreign aid	9				0	0	0	0												0			0
Accumulation	save/invest.	10				4537	2181	803	383	1602													0	9506
South																							
Production	primary	11	68	1360	4	30	85	5	15			0	799	314	38	116	816	69	406			114	4240
	secondary	12	0	115	3	21	47	4	8			0	152	431	95	145	646	86	322			320	2395
	tertiary	13	0	0	2	1	2	0	0			0	135	281	99	145	719	86	358			0	1829
Private income and outlay — employed	prof./man.	14											158	231	741	0	0	0	0		0		1130
	other	15											2869	601	770	0	0	0	0		0		4241
— unempl'd	prof./man.	16											0	0	0	0	0	0	0	670	0		670
	other	17											0	0	0	0	0	0	0	2111	0		2111
Public income and outlay	unemp. fund	18											0	0	0	226	848	134	422				1630
	foreign aid	19											0	0	0	0	0	0	0				0
Accumulation	save/invest.	20										1797	0	0	0	352	272	209	136	− 1150			1615
Totals			2796	26900	19043	13505	13635	2389	2394	6385	0	9506	4241	2395	1828	1130	4241	670	2111	1630	0	1615	114166

Table A5. A demographic – economic matrix for two regions with foreign aid and high investment (population flows are people; other flows in money units).

Columns 1–10 = *North*; columns 11–20 = *South*.

Region	Account	Item	No.	1	2	3	4	5	6	7	8	9	10	11	12	13	14	15	16	17	18	19	20	Totals
North																								
Production		primary	1	515	2157	19	174	505	0	0			403	0	161	0	0	299	0	0			80	4313
Production		secondary	2	832	16048	1253	1942	3789	0	0			12640	142	1428	143	241	1734	0	0			1040	41233
Production		tertiary	3	553	6964	1689	5757	7028	0	0			800	71	395	16	80	124	0	0			61	23537
Population and outlay	employed	prof./man.	4	431	2299	3483						0		1	9	2								6224
Population and outlay	employed	other	5	958	6487	9507						0		0	2	1								16955
Population and outlay	unempl'd	prof./man.	6								0	0		0	0	0								0
Population and outlay	unempl'd	other	7								0	0		0	0	0								0
Public income and outlay		unemp. fund	8				3651	3685	0	0														7336
Public income and outlay		foreign aid	9				311	339	0	0												0		1281
Accumulation		save/invest.	10				5749	2874	0	0	7336	0											0	15960
South																								
Production		primary	11	105	2085	5	38	112	0	0			0	1337	1159	71	257	1874	0	0			52	7095
Production		secondary	12	0	176	4	26	62	0	0			0	254	1589	178	322	1485	0	0			4743	8839
Production		tertiary	13	0	0	2	2	2	0	0			0	226	1035	186	321	1652	0	0			0	3427
Population and outlay	employed	prof./man.	14	0	0	1								79	250	420						0		751
Population and outlay	employed	other	15	0	2	5								17223	7962	5175						1281		30367
Population and outlay	unempl'd	prof./man.	16	0	0	0															0	0		0
Population and outlay	unempl'd	other	17	0	0	0															0	0		0
Public income and outlay		unemp. fund	18														501	1948	0	0				2449
Public income and outlay		foreign aid	19									1281					0	0	0	0				1281
Accumulation		save/invest.	20										2117				781	626	0	0	2451			5975

Note: Accounts 4 – 7 and 14 – 17 show population figures. The row totals exclude aid transfers displayed in column 19.

Table A6. The all-economic counterpart of table A5 (all flows in money units; on account of rounding errors row and column totals are not always equal).

			North										South									Totals
			1	2	3	4	5	6	7	8	9	10	11	12	13	14	15	16	17	18	19	20	
North																							
Production	primary	1	515	2157	19	174	505	0	0			403	0	161	0	0	299	0	0			80	4313
	secondary	2	832	16048	1253	1942	3789	0	0			12640	142	1428	143	241	1734	0	0			1040	41233
	tertiary	3	553	6964	1689	5757	7028	0	0			800	71	395	16	80	124	0	0			61	23537
Private income and outlay	employed prof./man.	4	1266	6753	10235						0												18253
	employed other	5	1041	7051	10335						0												18427
	unempl'd prof./man.	6								0	0											0		0
	unempl'd other	7								0	0													0
Public income and outlay	unemp. fund	8				3651	3685	0	0															7336
	foreign aid	9				913	369	0	0													0		1281
Accumulation	save/invest.	10				5749	2874	0	0	7336													0	15960
South																							
Production	primary	11	105	2085	5	38	112	0	0			0	1337	1159	71	257	1874	0	0			52	7095
	secondary	12	0	176	4	26	62	0	0			0	254	1589	178	322	1485	0	0			4743	8839
	tertiary	13	0	0	2	2	2	0	0			0	226	1035	186	321	1652	0	0			0	3427
Private income and outlay	employed prof./man.	14											264	851	1338	0	0	0	0	0			2504
	employed other	15											4800	2219	1442	0	0	0	0		1281		9742
	unempl'd prof./man.	16											0	0	0	0	0	0	0	0	0		0
	unempl'd other	17											0	0	0	0	0	0	0	0	0		0
Public income and outlay	unemp. fund	18											0	0	0	501	1948	0	0				2449
	foreign aid	19									1281		0	0	0	0	0	0	0				1281
Accumulation	save/invest.	20										2117	0	0	0	781	626	0	0	2451			5975
Totals			4312	41233	23542	18253	18428	0	0	7336	1281	15960	7094	8837	3425	2504	9742	0	0	2451	1281	5975	159750

Social Accounting for Regional Economic Systems

J I ROUND
University of Warwick, Coventry

1 Introduction

In the decade of the 1960s considerable interest was shown in the
concepts of social accounting at the regional level. This parallelled an
interest at that time in the formulation of theories of regional economic
growth and early attempts at regional economic model-building. Regions
at the subnational level were considered as though they were spaceless
'mini-nations' and the particular modelling and accounting problems
involved at the regional level focused on the extra degree of openness of
such economies. Important early contributions to the subject were made
by Stone (1961) and by several authors in volumes edited by Hochwald
(1961) and Hirsch (1964; 1966).

By the late 1960s and throughout the 1970s much of regional social
accounting practice tended to be synonymous with input–output analysis,
where quite detailed accounts of transactions between regional production
sectors were constructed, but those transactions and transfers taking place
within the rest of the regional economy were shown in considerably less
detail. Practical examples are legion, but notable studies in this regard are
those by Leven et al (1970), Lee et al (1973), and Polenske (1980).

Following closely the pioneering work of Stone in developing and
extending matrix-accounting concepts, Barnard (1969), Czamanski (1973),
and Sourrouille (1976) all discuss their application at the regional level.
Moreover, as illustrated in Barnard's work for the state of Iowa, to the
extent that a single region is involved, whether it is part of a nation (a
subnational region) or a group of nations (a supranational region), the
conceptual problems are not really very different from those encountered
at the national level. However, the practical accounting problems are
often severe, especially at the subnational level, because there is usually a
higher proportion of activities and institutions which do not have a clearly
defined location. Thus, for example, although multinationals create
accounting problems at the national level, there is an even greater number
of multiplant firms straddling subnational regional boundaries with spatially
diffuse ownership which accentuate these problems at regional levels.

Richardson (1978, pages 31–36) has been very critical of much of the
work on regional social accounts. His arguments were essentially twofold.
First, he pointed to the practical difficulties, particularly those relating to
the measurement of interregional transactions and, second, he raised
questions about the appropriateness of flow accounting at the regional
level. He suggested that information on regional stocks, such as resources

or wealth, would be of more value to regional analysis than income and product accounts, notwithstanding the fact that it is even more difficult to measure regional stocks than interregional flows. Nevertheless, the general tenor of Richardson's criticisms has merit: there was undoubtedly too much emphasis in those early days on replicating national models and techniques at the regional level. This also applied in some measure to social accounting.

In spite of Richardson's remarks, there are several reasons for reexamining some aspects of regional social accounting methodology. First, in view of the interest in examining the relationships between country blocks within the world economy (for example, see Waelbroeck, 1976)[1], it is pertinent to consider the appropriate format to account for flows and transactions between regions defined at the supranational level as well as between small areas. Second, Madden and Batey (1983) and others have been developing linked economic and demographic models. These are very much in the tradition of earlier work by Stone (United Nations, 1975) on social and demographic accounting, and are also related to the BACHUE models constructed by Rogers et al (1978). Such models rely on a matrix-accounting system and due consideration to regional extensions of this system assume some importance. Third, there has been much recent work on using the social accounting matrix (SAM) framework as a basis for policy analysis and planning in developing countries (see Pyatt and Thorbecke, 1976; Pyatt and Round, 1977; and Hayden and Round, 1982). In a study for Malaysia (Pyatt and Round, 1984) a regional dimension was included. In the present paper, I will identify some of the more general results that emerged from this study and will highlight some departures from conventional regional accounting practice.

In the next section the general form of a social accounting matrix will be illustrated using the Malaysian SAM as an example. This provides the necessary background to consider the specific regional issues in section 3. Interregional commodity flows present special problems, and in section 4 a fresh solution is posited to the problem of how to account for freight and transport charges in a consistent manner. Last, in section 5 there is a brief discussion of some implications for modelling regional economic systems, based upon the structure of the SAM framework.

2 An overview of the SAM for Malaysia

The matrix approach to social accounting is far from being a new concept. The immediate intellectual antecedent of the work discussed here is the United Nations System of National Accounts (SNA) (United Nations, 1968). However, Sir Richard Stone, who was the major influence behind the SNA, had earlier demonstrated the SAM approach both to data

---

[1]Equally, there is continuing interest in subnational multiregional models. A useful survey is provided by Issaev et al (1982).

frameworks and to economic modelling in the Cambridge Growth Project (Cambridge, Department of Applied Economics, 1962–1974)[2].

A social accounting matrix (SAM) is simply defined as a single-entry accounting system whereby each macroeconomic account is represented by a column for outgoings and a row for incomings. An entry in the (i, j)th cell represents the transaction which is a receipt by the ith account from account j (or expenditures by account j which are paid to account i). The SAM must therefore be square and its advantages over alternative presentations of data arise from the fact that it is a fully articulated system; that is, each transaction has an identifiable (account) origin and (account) destination. It is this feature which has been exploited to provide a useful understanding of the generation, transmission, distribution, and redistribution of income, and the subsequent expenditure mechanisms within an economy.

A SAM embraces accounts for the whole economic system, which means that for a single national or regional economy it includes accounts for the three basic forms of economic activity—production, consumption, and accumulation—and an account representing transactions with the rest of the world. In the SNA, although it includes a complete SAM, there is a heavy emphasis on the production accounts and input–output, and a consequent reliance on the commodity balances for their compilation. The SAM for Malaysia, in keeping with similar studies for other developing economies, accords the accounts for households and factors of production rather more emphasis than those for production and is consequently more in tune with the aim of monitoring the effects of policy on the living standards of individuals than would an input–output table alone. An incidental feature of a SAM is that Richardson's classification of different types of flow accounts becomes redundant because input–output, income and outlay, and flow of funds accounts are all embraced within a unified and fully articulated system.

Table 1 shows a fairly consolidated version of the SAM for Malaysia in 1970. It shows aggregate transactions between the eleven main accounts of the system, but no detail on the many subaccounts into which several of these main accounts have been subdivided. The cells of the matrix in table 1 contain both schematic and numerical entries. Being an accounting system, row totals equal corresponding column totals, and hence the elements are entirely consistent. Of course, 'consistency' need not imply 'accuracy', but in seeking to eliminate initial inconsistencies between estimates from quite disparate data sources the SAM can sometimes help in identifying which of them should bear most of the burden of adjustment.

The accounts in table 1 are largely self-explanatory and have been ordered to reflect their importance in viewing overall policy objectives.

[2]Of course, even earlier intellectual origins of matrix accounting can be traced through the work of Leontief and as far back as Francois Quesnay in the late 18th century.

Thus 'wants' are a set of accounts for a range of different bundles of goods and services classified according to human needs. In this case they are reflected by thirty-three subaccounts of consumers' expenditures[3]. In column 1, the outlays of the wants accounts show their conversion into receipts by the commodity accounts[4]. With the terminology introduced by Stone and referred to by Czamanski (1973), the matrix in cell (9, 1) is simply a classification convertor. Clearly, in this aggregate SAM, the mapping from household expenditures as wants through a further mapping onto commodities becomes degenerate: both totals simply show the same aggregate of consumers' expenditure.

The next four accounts, 'factors' (account 2) and the institutions' income and outlay accounts for 'households' (account 3), 'companies' (account 4), and 'government' (account 5) are especially noteworthy. The aggregate transactions between these accounts are also reasonably clear from the table. The factor accounts receive value added from domestic production activities [cell (2, 10)] and from abroad [cell (2, 7)] and pay these factor-income receipts to institutions according to their ownership of factors of production. Households receive labour income [cell (3, 2)] in return for the labour services provided; companies (both public and private) receive operating surpluses [cell (4, 2)], before any deduction for depreciation, taxes, etc; and some factor incomes are paid abroad [cell (7, 2)]. However, to understand how the distribution of income arises between different institutions (as well as, at a more disaggregated level, between households), it can be noted from the SAM that factor incomes constitute only part of total income. The other part is transfer income, where households, companies, and government receive and disburse incomes as transfers between themselves. These transfers are shown in the cells intersecting rows 3 to 5 and columns 3 to 5. A principal activity of government is to take part in this transfer (or redistribution) process; indeed, government income is entirely nonfactor income. For example, it receives direct taxes and social security payments from households [cell (5, 3)], direct taxes from private companies [cell (5, 4)], and operating surpluses from government-owned enterprises, as well as current transfers from abroad [cell (5, 7)]. Likewise, part of the outlay of government is in the form of transfers to households [cell (3, 5)] and companies [cell (4, 5)].

Much of the interest in this distributive and redistributive mechanism emerges when the broad groups of accounts depicted in accounts 2, 3, 4, and 5 are disaggregated further. In the Malaysian SAM, fifty-one factor

[3]Pyatt and Thorbecke (1976) envisaged an enlargement of the possible categories to involve nonpecuniary accounts (such as leisure) or, at least, 'wants' which embrace rather more than consumers' expenditure and which would involve certain imputations of benefits (for example, from public expenditure) if the SAM is to be expressed in money terms.

[4]For the most detailed version of the Malaysian SAM there were thirty-three wants accounts and fifty-nine commodity accounts.

Table 1. A social accounting matrix for Malaysia, 1970. Data are in $M million (source: Chander et al, 1980; table based on Pyatt and Round, 1984).

Receipts			Expenditures				
			1	2	3	4	5
	wants	1			Want requirements by households 7528		
	factors	2					
Institutions' current accounts	households	3		Wages and unincorporated business income 8696	Interhousehold transfers 476	Distributed profits 109	Government transfers to households 196
	companies	4		Operating surpluses of companies 1551			Government transfers to companies 134
	government	5			Direct taxes 388	Dirext taxes 992	
Consolidated capital account for domestic institutions		6			Household savings 1101	Company savings 369	Government savings 855
Rest of world	current	7		Factor incomes paid abroad 586	Household transfers abroad 0	Company transfers abroad 230	Government transfers abroad 27
	capital	8					
Production	commodities	9	Conversion of wants into commodities 7528				Government current expenditure 1985
	activities	10					
	indirect taxes	11					
	total	12	Want requirements 7528	Factor payments 10833	Household expenditures 9493	Company expenditures 1700	Government expenditures 3197

Table 1 (continued).

| Expenditures | | | | | | |
6	7	8	9	10	11	12
						Want requirements 7528
	Factor incomes from abroad 232			Value added payments to factors 10601		Factor incomes 10833
	Current transfers from abroad 16					Household incomes 9493
	Current transfers from abroad 15					Company incomes 1700
	Current transfers from abroad 15				Net indirect taxes 1802	Government income 3197
		Capital transfers from abroad − 85				Capital receipts 2240
			Imports 4798			Current payments abroad 5641
Net invest-ment abroad − 124	Balance of payments current deficit 39					Capital payments abroad − 85
Gross fixed capital forma-tion and stock increases 2364	Exports 5324			Intermediate commodity demands 9311		Commodity demands 26512
			Domestic commodity supplies 20403			Gross outputs 20403
			Commodity indirect taxes net of subsidies 1311	Non-commodity indirect taxes 491		Net indirect taxes 1802
Investment 2240	Current receipts from abroad 5641	Capital receipts from abroad − 85	Commodity supplies 26512	Gross inputs 20403	Net indirect taxes 1802	

accounts were distinguished, of which forty-eight were categories of labour according to location (urban or rural) and level of education attained. The household account was disaggregated into thirty-three separate subaccounts according to ethnicity, employment status of the household head, and location. Neither the company nor the government accounts were disaggregated further. Given this detail in terms of the disaggregation of the factoral and institutional accounts, it can be seen that the estimation of submatrices represented by payments of value added to factors, of factor incomes to institutions, and of income transfers between institutions, produces a framework high in information content. Also, by introducing the factor accounts as an intermediate mapping of income from production activities to households and other institutions, there are decided advantages from the point of view of aiding model design. It means that factor accounts can be defined according to the kinds of factor services provided, and this is particularly useful in setting up production functions. Similarly, households can be classified according to household characteristics which may include identifiable target groups in society, such as the urban poor. At the same time, households are composites of individuals each of whom may belong to a different labour market or may be economically inactive. The existence of separate factor and household accounts permits different classifications of factors and households and, even if the classifications were the same, it avoids the necessity of assuming a one-to-one mapping of income between them.

The remaining accounts in table 1 are quite standard and deserve minimal comment. The commodity and activity accounts are shown in rows and columns 9 and 10. This means that the 'make' and 'absorption' matrices are in cells $(10, 9)$ and $(9, 10)$, and these provide the necessary data for input–output.

The structure of accounts for a single-region system are no different from the framework illustrated in table 1 for Malaysia. However, this table and the accompanying motivations behind it provide a basis for considering extensions towards an integrated system of multiregional social accounts which are discussed in the next two sections.

3 A multiregion system of accounts in a SAM framework

A multiregion system poses a different range of problems extending beyond those normally encountered in a single-region system. Apart from the contributions by Stone, Sourrouille, and Czamanski referred to earlier, Hewings (1983) has also attempted to adapt a simplified version of table 1 to fit into a regional context. The solution offered in the present section differs markedly from those of Hewings and other authors, although it develops the kernel of ideas included in Stone's seminal contribution. The particular example referred to concerns the regions of East and West Malaysia, but the conclusions are general and are applicable to other regional systems. Moreover, it should be noted at the outset that the interregional nature of this section is not such a special case as it may at first seem and the results can easily be generalised to the many-region situation.

The choice of regional delineation is especially easy in the Malaysian case, for, although, the Federation contains twelve States, two of these (Sabah and Sarawak) comprise East Malaysia and are separated from Peninsular (West) Malaysia by 500 miles of sea. From a statistical point of view the regional distinction is also an easy one to make since the sources for West Malaysia are independent and are also substantially better than those for East Malaysia both in coverage and quality of data. This created additional compilational difficulties, well known to regional analysis, but these, and the solutions adopted, will not be covered in this paper [details are described in Pyatt and Round (1984, chapter 7)]. An additional feature of general interest encountered in this study, and yet rarely referred to in earlier literature, is exemplified by the position of Singapore as an entrepôt for a variety of commercial and trading activities within Malaysia. Thus, a good deal of merchandise trade between East and West Malaysia is still routed through Singapore, and its position as a financial and commercial centre means that many nonmerchandise transactions and monetary transfers are cleared through Singapore financial intermediaries. In consequence, there are very real difficulties in distinguishing actual East–West flows as opposed to those which involve the intermediation of Singapore, although many of these difficulties have been resolved by the Department of Statistics, Government of Malaysia, prior to the publication of their estimates.

Table 2 shows the two-region analogue of the SAM framework depicted in table 1. It can be viewed as comprising three principal blocks. One block relates to East Malaysia; the second to West Malaysia; and the third to the rest of the world. Each of the blocks for East and West Malaysia contains nine accounts which are the nine domestic accounts in the basic eleven-account SAM of table 1. Transactions between each region and the rest of the world are shown in accounts 7^* and 8^* which are labelled as such in recognition of the fact that they are true international transactions and exclude those which take place between regions.

An important feature of the regional SAM represented by table 2 and which is different from attempts by other authors is the distinction that is drawn between functional flows and geographical flows. A functional flow may be considered to be a transaction or transfer between two agents represented by two of the eleven types of accounts. This is the sense in which all of the SAM elements in table 1 have been viewed. However, when more than one region is involved, and interregional flows have to be considered, the purely geographical transfers (of goods, income, or capital) must be separated from the functional flows which would occur subsequently. Thus, all functional flows are shown in table 2 as if they take place wholly within each region, as indeed most of them do, and geographical (inter-

regional) flows are shown as simply augmenting the receipts in one region
and simultaneously depleting the same account in the other region. This
considerably simplifies the accounting structure and yet, it will be argued,
does not diminish the information content of the resulting multiregion SAM.

One consequence of representing the accounts according to this format is
that interregional transactions and transfers between East and West Malaysia
appear as diagonal entries in the off-diagonal partitions of the table.
Clearly, since gross flows are being represented, it is possible for East to
West transactions to take place at the same time as those from West to East.
Not all of these accounts have interregional transfers associated with them,
and for those that do they may actually be zero flows. Definitional and
actual zeros are distinguished in table 1 by blanks and 0 entries, respectively.
Thus, for instance, the interregional transfers for three accounts are
definitely 0. As noted earlier, the 'wants' accounts (account 1) define a

Table 2. An interregional social accounting matrix for Malaysia, 1970.
Data are in $M million.

Incomes		Expenditures — East Malaysia								
		1	2	3	4	5	6	9	10	11
East Malaysia										
Wants	1			1179.0						
Factors	2								1563.0	
Households	3		1376.0	74.2	10.9	25.0				
Companies	4		149.0			7.8				
Government	5			36.1	32.5					253.0
Cons. cap.	6			196.8	106.6	36.8				
Commodities	9	1179.0				243.0	349.0		1421.9	
Activities	10							3108.7		
Ind. taxes	11							129.2	123.8	
West Malaysia										
Wants	1									
Factors	2		0							
Households	3			0						
Companies	4				0					
Government	5					235.0				
Cons. cap.	6						0			
Commodities	9							218.2		
Activities	10									
Ind. taxes	11									
Rest of world										
Current	7*		50.8		10.0	2.8		1046.7		
Capital	8*						85.0			
Total	12	1179.0	1575.8	1486.1	160.0	550.4	434.0	4502.8	3108.7	253.0

Key: Cons. cap. consolidated capital; Ind. taxes indirect taxes.

mapping between household requirements and the commodities which they implicitly demand: this mapping has no geographical dimension. The appropriate means of representing trade in goods and services are the commodity accounts. Hence, neither 'activities' nor 'indirect taxes' (accounts 10 and 11) can have any interregional transfers: the sole function of activities is to produce commodities, and the indirect tax accounts serve only to collect such taxes and eventually pay them to government. For some other accounts there appear to be zero interregional transfers, such as those for factors and households. It is unlikely that flows were 0 in all these instances but they accord with the estimates provided by the Department of Statistics, Malaysia. Last, it should be noted that not all own-account transfers are interregional flows. Some own-account transfers occur within a region (such as household-to-household transfers in West Malaysia of 401.7) which are still functional flows in the sense defined above.

Table 2 (continued).

Expenditures											
West Malaysia									*Rest of world*		Total
1	2	3	4	5	6	9	10	11	7*	8*	12
											1179.0
	0								12.8		1575.8
		0									1486.1
			0						3.2		160.0
				226.6					2.2		550.4
					93.8						434.0
						98.1			1211.8		4502.8
											3108.7
											253.0
		6349.2									6349.2
							9038.1		219.4		9257.5
	7319.7	401.7	98.0	171.2					16.0		8006.6
	1401.9			125.9					11.9		1539.7
		351.9	959.1					1549.0	12.9		3107.9
		903.8	262.5	818.6						−85.0	1899.9
6349.2				1742.0	2014.9		7891.3		4111.8		22327.4
						17296.1					17296.1
						1182.3	366.7				1549.0
	535.9		220.1	23.6		3750.9					5640.8
					−208.8				38.8		−85.0
6349.2	9257.5	8006.6	1539.7	3107.9	1899.9	22327.4	17296.1	1549.0	5640.8	−85.0	

The accounting framework for multiregion economic systems defined above, although different from those proposed by earlier authors, has much in common with the commodity-accounting framework utilised by Polenske (1980). This is not to say that it implies any particular form of economic model, as will be discussed in section 5. However, it is claimed that this accounting structure is an improvement over more conventional systems from two standpoints. First, the accounts separate out two logically distinct steps in the transmission of interregional flows. The movement of goods, income, or capital between regions does not ordinarily involve a change in their state, apart from their location, but the transactions or transfers between economic agents may subsequently involve a state (or status) change at the new location. Second, it turns out to be more feasible to estimate these interregional flows than it is in conventional systems in which there is an attempt to compound functional and geographical flows in a single step.

Notwithstanding the general attractiveness of this accounting system, problems do exist with regard to recording those interregional transfers which involve transhipment costs. The most obvious and important example where this occurs is in the movements of goods. The accounting implications are dealt with in the next section.

4 Interregional commodity flows in a SAM framework

An historically important debate in the regional input–output literature has concerned the appropriate treatment of interregional commodity flows. Part of the difficulty has arisen through a confusion between the accounting base and the choice of model that is imposed upon it. From an accounting point of view, commodity flows may, in principle, be treated as any other interregional transfer in the manner indicated in the previous section. Thus, in general terms, imports of commodities are portrayed in the SAM framework as augmenting 'domestic' commodity supplies. At a disaggregated level, commodities may be distinguished by qualitative differences or even by price differences if the incidence of commodity taxes, subsidies, or distribution margins leads to a variation in user price. In each case, separate commodity accounts can be distinguished. In this way there is no need to differentiate between complementary and competitive goods, since the first category would be manifested by a commodity supply whose domestic component is 0. A further consequence is that there is no longer a need to value commodities at producer prices or at basic prices. A market-price valuation, whereby prices are those prevailing at the user location, is arguably a more natural valuation. It is also more useful for developing demand systems and production relationships in economy-wide models, as is reflected in the recent spate of computable general equilibrium models (see Dervis et al, 1982) of which input–output models may be considered to be a special case.

The accounting base for a market-price valuation of commodities by users is easily achieved through the distinction drawn between commodity and production-activity accounts. On the supply side of the commodity accounts, the value of the total commodity supplies comprises the following elements. First, there are domestic commodity outputs supplied by production activities which are valued at basic, or ex-factory, prices. These elements heavily dominate the diagonal part of the activity-to-commodity matrix (or 'make' matrix) if there is a close correspondence between the classifications of the accounts for activities and commodities. Second, and also part of the 'make' matrix are the margins supplied by the trade and transport activities. This recognises the special role of these activities in providing the necessary flux to deliver commodities from the point of production to the point of consumption. In the present accounting system, and set out in detail by Pyatt and Round (1984), these margins are considered as part of a whole range of commodity outputs which are supplied by the trade and transport activities, rather than as the supply of a single trade and transport commodity as viewed in more orthodox accounting systems. This is quite simply because they are intrinsic parts of the value of a commodity when considered from the user location; that is, the nature of the commodity has not changed, except for its location. A third component in commodity supply at market prices is the commodity tax element, which can be identified in table 1 in cell (11,9). The final component is imports. In accordance with standard balance-of-payments conventions, imports are valued cif (cost, insurance, freight), that is, they are inclusive of freight charges up to the point of entry but then domestic margins have to be added in moving the goods from there to the user location.

Exports of goods are usually valued fob (free on board) which means they are valued inclusive of all margins (including export duties) at the export frontier. This creates no problem at all with the way in which the SAM has been set up. Indeed, if regional boundaries are adjacent to one another and if there is no cost in moving goods from the export frontier in the exporting region to the import frontier in the importing region, then interregional commodity trade is simply manifested as a diagonal matrix in the region-to-region commodity accounts. However, complications can arise if regional boundaries are not adjacent and there is freight cost between the frontier of the exporting region and the frontier of the importing region, for then fob value will differ from cif value. This is often the case for trade between nations. It is also true as regards trade between East and West Malaysia which, as noted above, are separated by sea and whose trade frequently involves the intermediation of Singapore.

This complication can be fully accommodated in the SAM framework in much the same way as the 'make' matrix dealt with domestic (own-region) freight margins. It can be illustrated as follows. Suppose the commodity-exporting region also supplies the interregional freight services.

These freight services are shown as an export of freight services but, instead of appearing as a diagonal element in the interregional commodity-trade matrix, they are shown as a row of margins in the freight-services row of this matrix. Viewed down the columns, these appear as freight margins which augment the fob value of imports and thereby create import values cif from the point of view of the importing region. Row sums show exports fob from the exporting region. Table 3 illustrates these principles through a highly aggregate version of the matrix for commodity trade from West to East Malaysia. The freight margins in this respect were small, but from a spatial perspective the conceptual arrangement of these accounts is important.

Not all of the freight margins incurred in commodity transhipments are accounted for within the bounds of this example. For instance, freight service may be supplied by the importing region or by the rest of the world, rather than by the exporting region. These also may be accommodated within the SAM framework, although the arrangement is more complex. Details are shown elsewhere (see Pyatt and Round, 1985).

In this section, I have focused on interregional commodity flows, given their obvious importance through trade on the interaction between regional systems. It is equally important to emphasise the special role of trade, transport, and other freight services in a specifically spatial system. Few studies have recognised this within the nexus of input–output and activity analysis, one notable exception being the work of Mennes et al (1969). In principle, the same procedures could apply to the interregional transfers, of factor income, household transfers, and so on. But it is likely that the problem only assumes any significance at all when the interregional transfer involves goods which are costly to transport.

Table 3. Rationalising cif and fob values of interregional commodity flows in the regional Malaysian social accounting matrix. Data are in $M million for 1970 (source: adapted from Pyatt and Round, 1984, tables 8.8 and 8.9).

West Malaysia commodities		East Malaysia commodities				Total (West Malaysia exports fob)
		1	2	3	4	
Agricultural products	1	81.5				81.5
Manufactured products	2		130.8			130.8
Freight services	3	1.4	1.9			3.3
Other services	4				2.6	2.6
Total (East Malaysia imports cif)		82.9	132.7	0	2.6	218.2

5 On regional economic modelling

The demonstration that a SAM framework of the type portrayed in table 1 can be implemented for Malaysia, as well as for several other economies (Pyatt and Round, 1977; Hayden and Round, 1982), with numerous account disaggregations for factors, households and production sectors, has many implications for the modelling of regional economic systems.

First, the broadening of the accounting base to focus attention on factors of production, factor markets, and household behaviour fits in with the modern view that exclusive interest in input–output and production behaviour alone is misplaced, whether at the regional or economy-wide levels. That so much effort has been expended to demonstrate the utility of this framework in developing countries and with considerable success might suggest equivalent payoffs if this were to be used at the regional level. Certainly this could be the case for regions defined at the supra-national level, but for subnational regions a full implementation would necessitate appropriate regional coding in national surveys of households and the labour force, as well as in production surveys. The latter have been shown to be essential prerequisites for implementing SAMs such as the one discussed in this paper.

Second, the most notable feature of the Malaysian SAM is the way in which the mappings of income around the system have been estimated and portrayed in separate and identifiable stages. Two examples can be high-lighted. A conventional approach to the problem of closing a disaggregated production model with respect to household behaviour is to define a mapping of income from production sectors direct to households of different types. However, this sidesteps an important feature of house-holds referred to in section 2, namely, that they may engage in more than one labour market if they are endowed with more than one kind of factor. Without employing a framework which can separate the two stages in mapping factor incomes it would be virtually impossible to accommodate these features within a formal model. This also provides a useful link between economic models and demographic and labour-market models. Another example of this is shown in the general treatment of regional accounts and, specifically, of freight margins. Trade and transport activities play a special role in spatial systems and in most regional input–output studies no distinction whatsoever is drawn between them and other production activities. The regional SAM framework at least allows trade and transport margins to be dealt with in a consistent and logical way: a precursor for formal modelling.

Third, the unconventional treatment of the accounts for interregional commodity flows deserves particular elucidation. It should be noted that they are entirely neutral with regard to one's view of the nature of regional commodities and commodity markets. In an input–output context the framework could be utilised equally well in conjunction with Leontief–Strout models and Isard models. In Leontief–Strout models, consideration would essentially be given to one account for each commodity regardless of the region which produces it. In Isard models separate commodity accounts would be distinguished depending on region of origin and, in consequence, there would be a larger number of commodity accounts to be carried in each of the regions considered. Commodity accounts are chosen according to a variety of distinguishing characteristics and a regional characteristic could be chosen to be one of them.

Fourth, it has been shown elsewhere (Round, 1985) that the framework proposed in tables 1 and 2 provides a useful basis for decomposing the separate effects of different kinds of linkages in an economic system. Although this has been developed in the context of linear models, the nature of linkage is quite general and could be applied to linearised versions of nonlinear models as was discussed in an OECD publication (1979).

6 Conclusions

In this paper, I have set out a modified scheme of accounts, based on a social accounting matrix (SAM), for integrated regional economic systems. The scheme has been demonstrated by means of an SAM for Malaysia and some specifically regional aspects of this system have been considered. Most important of all, it has been argued that the proposed system is high in information content and yet is flexible enough to be implementable in regional systems where a dearth of data tends to be the norm. Some of Richardson's trenchant criticisms are largely overcome by adopting the SAM approach, for it embraces income and outlay, input–output, and flow accounts all within the same framework. At a practical level, this greatly facilitates the estimation of the individual entries, for the accounting balance of one part of the matrix often implies values for entries elsewhere. It does not, as yet, go any way towards meeting Richardson's strongest reservation about present accounting methods, that of providing estimates of regional resources and regional wealth. In principle, these could be included as opening and closing assets and attached to the matrix of flows shown in the regional SAM, but it is well known that such estimates are fraught with difficulties of estimation.

Finally, I have briefly touched on some modelling extensions of the SAM base. This is a wide-ranging topic which, as indicated, is dealt with extensively elsewhere.

Acknowledgement. This paper draws heavily on my joint work with Graham Pyatt, Senior Adviser, Development Research Department, The World Bank. I wish to record my deep gratitude to him although he should not be held jointly responsible for all the ideas expressed herein.

References

Barnard J R, 1969, "A social accounting system for regional development planning" *Journal of Regional Science* **9** 109–115

Cambridge, Department of Applied Economics, 1962–1974 *A Programme for Growth, Volumes 1–14* (Chapman and Hall, Andover, Hants)

Chander R, Gnasegarah S, Pyatt G, Round J I, 1980, "Social accounts and the distribution of income: the Malaysian economy in 1970" *Review of Income and Wealth* **26** 67–85

Czamanski S, 1973 *Regional and Inter-regional Social Accounting* (Lexington Books, Lexington, MA)

Dervis K, de Melo J, Robinson S, 1982 *General Equilibrium Models for Development Policy* (Cambridge University Press, Cambridge)

Hayden C G, Round J I, 1982, "Developments in social accounting methods as applied to the analysis of income distribution and employment issues" *World Development* **10** 451–465

Hewings G J D, 1983, "Design of appropriate accounting systems for regional development in developing countries" *Papers of the Regional Science Association* **51** 179–196

Hirsch W Z (Ed.), 1964 *Elements of Regional Accounts* (The Johns Hopkins University Press, Baltimore, MD)

Hirsch W Z (Ed.), 1966 *Regional Accounts for Policy Decisions* (The Johns Hopkins University Press, Baltimore, MD)

Hochwald W (Ed.), 1961 *Design of Regional Accounts* (The Johns Hopkins University Press, Baltimore, MD)

Issaev B, Nijkamp P, Rietveld P, Snickars F (Eds), 1982 *Studies in Regional Science and Urban Economics 9. Multi-regional Economic Modelling: Practice and Prospect* (North-Holland, Amsterdam)

Lee T H, Moore J R, Lewis D P, 1973 *Regional and Inter-regional Inter-sectoral Flow Analysis* (The University of Tennessee Press, Knoxville, TN)

Leven C L, Legler J B, Shapiro P, 1970 *An Analytical Framework for Regional Development Policy* (MIT Press, Cambridge, MA)

Madden M, Batey P W J, 1983, "Linked population and economic models: some methodological issues in forecasting, analysis, and policy optimisation" *Journal of Regional Science* **23** 141–164

Mennes L B, Tinbergen J, Waardenburg J G, 1969 *The Element of Space in Development Planning* (North-Holland, Amsterdam)

OECD, 1979 *Economic Outlook Occasional Studies, The OECD International Linkage Model* (OECD, Paris)

Polenske K R, 1980 *The US Multi-regional Input–Output Accounts and Model* (Lexington Books, Lexington, MA)

Pyatt G, Round J I, 1977, "Social accounting matrices for development planning" *Review of Income and Wealth* series 23, number 4, pp 339–364

Pyatt G, Round J I, 1984 *Improving the Macroeconomic Data Base: A SAM for Malaysia 1970*, World Bank Staff WP 646, World Bank, Washington DC

Pyatt G, Round J I (Eds), 1985 *Social Accounting Matrices: A Basis for Planning* The World Bank, Washington DC

Pyatt G, Thorbecke E, 1976 *Planning Techniques for a Better Future* (International Labour Office, Geneva)

Richardson H W, 1978 *Regional and Urban Economics* (Penguin Books, Harmondsworth, Middx)

Rogers G, Hopkins M, Wéry R, 1978 *Population, Employment and Inequality: BACHUE–Philippines* (Saxon House, Farnborough, Hants; International Labour Office, Geneva)

Round J I, 1985, "Decomposing multipliers for economic systems involving regional and world trade" *Economic Journal* **95** 383–399

Sourrouille J V, 1976, "Regional accounts: theoretical and practical problems encountered in the recent experience of Argentina" *Review of Income and Wealth* series 22, number 1, pp 13–36

Stone J R N, 1961, "Social accounts at the regional level" in *Regional Economic Planning* Eds W Isard, J Cumberland (OECD, Paris) pp 263–296

United Nations, 1968 *Studies in Methods Series F, Number 2, Revision 3. A System of National Accounts* Statistical Office, United Nations, New York

United Nations, 1975 *Studies in Methods Series F, Number 18. Towards a System of Social and Demographic Statistics* Statistical Office, United Nations, New York

Waelbroeck J (Ed.), 1976 *The Models of Project LINK* (North-Holland, Amsterdam)

Economic Consequences of a Change in Demographic Patterns: An Integrated Approach

M LUPTÁČIK
Technical University, Vienna
I SCHMORANZ
Institute for Advanced Studies, Vienna

1 Introduction

In most empirical studies, changes in consumer demand are defined by changes in income and relative prices. In this context Engel's law is the most powerful instrument of empirical analysis. However, this concentration on the explanation of structural change in income may conceal the influence of demographic factors on the composition and overall development of the consumer demand.

A number of approaches can be found in the literature in which demographic variables are incorporated within demand functions (Barten, 1964; Parks and Barten, 1973; Muellbauer, 1974; Bojer, 1977). In their cross-section study, based on data for the years 1950–1967 for fourteen countries of the Organization for Economic Cooperation and Development, Parks and Barten (1973, page 849) conclude that "the age structure contributes significantly to an explanation of observed differences among countries in the estimated threshold parameters of the linear expenditure demand model".

Change in the level and structure of demand for consumption goods in turn may give rise to changes in production in particular industrial sectors, resulting in changes in the demand for labour as well as changes in primary income distribution, and so forth. The change in the size and structure of the labour force affects the primary income distribution, which determines expenditure patterns and thus the level and structure of private consumption, etc.

Against this background, our objective in this paper is to present a closed model for the quantitative analysis of economic consequences of a change in demographic patterns. For this purpose, a model developed in our previous work (Luptáčik and Schmoranz, 1980) is extended in order to separate the different effects of the above-mentioned dual role of population in the economy. In the next section, we present the mathematical formulation of the model, which is an extension of the input–output model. Section 3 deals with the sensitivity analysis. The data and the empirical results for Austria are discussed in section 4.

2 The mathematical model

A suitable framework for the integrated analysis of the structure of the economy is provided by the open Leontief input–output system.

We start from the basic relation

$$\mathbf{A}x + y = x + m \ ,\tag{1}$$

or

$$x = (\mathbf{I} - \mathbf{A})^{-1}(y - m) \ ,\tag{2}$$

where

$\mathbf{A}$ is an $n \times n$ matrix of technical coefficients, $\mathbf{A} = (a_{ij})$,
$\mathbf{I}$ is an $n \times n$ identity matrix,
x is an n-dimensional gross production vector,
m is an n-dimensional import vector.

For the purpose of our analysis the final demand vector, y, is decomposed into three distinctive components:

$$y = c + y^{\mathrm{D}} + y^{\mathrm{ND}} \ ,\tag{3}$$

where

c denotes private consumption,
y^{D} is that part of public consumption which depends on size and structure of population (schools, hospitals, etc),
y^{ND} is that fraction of final demand which is not directly affected by the demographic structure and is classified as an exogenous variable for the model to be discussed.

Let us start with private consumption, c. Individual consumers are to be found in various types of household, and the household, rather than the individual or family, has been adopted as a consumption unit. A household can be defined as a socioeconomic unit, consisting of individuals who live together, whereas the family comprises only those household members related in kinship, with the exclusion of domestic help, guests, boarders, etc. Households, however, vary considerably in composition and size. For the purpose of an integrated analysis we classify households according to the number of adults, children (persons up to 15 years old), and income receivers. It hardly needs pointing out that the food and clothing needs of a child are different from those of an adult.

It has also been observed that consumer behaviour of large households may be more economical with respect to specific items, as well as all items of consumption taken together, because of the existence of economies of scale. The smaller the household, the higher the per-capita expenditure required to provide a given standard of living.

Therefore, and with respect to the different number of wage earners, the structure of consumption expenditure in the different households varies considerably. It is described by matrix $\mathbf{C}^{\mathrm{H}}$. The coefficients of this matrix, c_{rk}, indicate the proportion of consumption expenditure on commodity group r $(r = 1, ..., m)$ in the total consumption expenditure of the household of type k $(k = 1, ..., h)$. We postulate that these percentage distributions remain stable regardless of a change in the number of households. Substitution of one commodity for another may only take place within the same broad category of each commodity group, and not between one category and another. The number of households of type k is described by a vector d, $d = (d_1, ..., d_h)$, which is given exogenously in our model.

The total expenditure of the household depends on disposable income, in other words, on the number of wage earners. Let

$$q_{kj} = \frac{l_{kj}}{l_j}, \qquad k = 1, ..., h, \quad j = 1, ..., n, \tag{4}$$

be the proportion of employees (wage earners) in sector j who live in household-type k, and let w_{0j} be the wages per unit of production of sector j ($j = 1, ..., n$). Total wage income of the households is denoted by an h-dimensional vector, w:

$$w = Q\hat{W}_0 x \tag{5}$$

where
$\hat{W}_0$ is a diagonal matrix of wage coefficients, w_{0j},
Q is an $h \times n$ matrix of coefficients, q_{kj}, with

$$\sum_{k=1}^{h} q_{kj} = 1 , \qquad j = 1, ..., n. \tag{6}$$

Similarly, it would be possible to include income from profits in our model, merely by modifying matrix $\hat{W}_0$. The elements of the matrix $Q\hat{W}_0$ represent the share of value generated in sector j that is received by household k (see also Grootaert, 1983, matrix V on page 10).

Relation (5) describes the so-called 'primary income distribution', which is the distribution "directly established by flows of income shares from the production system" (Kuznets, 1975, page 790). It results directly from the receipt of wages by households and is closely related to, and affected by, the production structure.

The other source of household income is transfer payments (old age pensions and children's allowances). These are exogenously given for our model and influenced by demographic data. This is a further means by which demographic patterns can affect economic variables.

The total income of the households is then described by an h-dimensional vector, i:

$$i = Q\hat{W}_0 x + t , \tag{7}$$

where t is an h-dimensional vector of transfer payments.
The vector of private consumption, $c^P = (c_1, ..., c_m)$, is now determined by

$$c^P = C^H(I - \hat{S})(Q\hat{W}_0 x + t) \tag{8}$$

where $\hat{\mathbf{S}}$ is an $h \times h$ diagonal matrix of savings ratios and tax rates of the households.

The model distinguishes the primary income distribution [described by equation (5)] from the secondary income distribution which is given after government intervention via taxes and transfers. The secondary income distribution also affects the production structure because it determines the spending patterns of households.

To establish the link between the commodity groups and final demand by industrial sectors we use the transformation (or so-called 'bridge') matrix $\mathbf{T}$. The elements of $\mathbf{T}$, t_{jr} ($j = 1, ..., n$; $r = 1, ..., m$), indicate the proportion of private consumption of commodity group r, produced by sector j. Thus

$$c = \mathbf{T}c^{\mathrm{P}} , \tag{9}$$

where c is the final demand generated by households.
By definition

$$\sum_{j=1}^{n} t_{jr} = 1 , \qquad r = 1, ..., m . \tag{10}$$

Substitution of equation (8) into equation (9) yields

$$c = \mathbf{T}\mathbf{C}^{\mathrm{H}}(\mathbf{I} - \hat{\mathbf{S}})(\mathbf{Q}\hat{\mathbf{W}}_0 x + t) . \tag{11}$$

Setting

$$\mathbf{U} = \mathbf{T}\mathbf{C}^{\mathrm{H}}(\mathbf{I} - \hat{\mathbf{S}})\mathbf{Q}\hat{\mathbf{W}}_0 , \qquad \mathbf{V} = \mathbf{T}\mathbf{C}^{\mathrm{H}}(\mathbf{I} - \hat{\mathbf{S}}) , \tag{12}$$

we get

$$c = \mathbf{U}x + \mathbf{V}t . \tag{13}$$

Thus, $\mathbf{U}$ establishes the link between sectoral gross output and the final demand generated by households. The elements of $\mathbf{U}$ are the labour-input coefficients expressed in terms of goods consumed by the employees (including their children and other members of the household) per unit of sectoral gross output. Thus private consumption is not exogenously given (as in the standard input–output model) but is determined within the model. Matrix $\mathbf{V}$ describes the link between transfer payments and private consumption. Thus, the second term on the right-hand side of equation (13) indicates that part of private consumption that is generated by transfer payments. This formulation allows us to analyse the influence of different instruments of government policy (for example, an increase in children's allowance or a reduction of taxes for households with more children).

Let us now turn to y^{D}, that part of public consumption depending on demographic variables. Largely because of a shortage of data, we postulate that final demand is a linear function of the number of the households.

Let us define the following $h \times h$ matrix,

$$\mathbf{Y}_d^{\mathrm{D}} = \begin{bmatrix} \dfrac{y_{11}^{\mathrm{D}}}{d_1} & \cdots & \dfrac{y_{1k}^{\mathrm{D}}}{d_k} & \cdots & \dfrac{y_{1h}^{\mathrm{D}}}{d_h} \\ \vdots & & \vdots & & \vdots \\ \dfrac{y_{n1}^{\mathrm{D}}}{d_1} & \cdots & \dfrac{y_{nk}^{\mathrm{D}}}{d_k} & \cdots & \dfrac{y_{nh}^{\mathrm{D}}}{d_h} \end{bmatrix} , \tag{14}$$

where

$$\sum_{k=1}^{h} y_{jk}^{\mathrm{D}} = y_j^{\mathrm{D}} , \quad j = 1, ..., n . \tag{15}$$

Then

$$y^{\mathrm{D}} = \mathbf{Y}_d^{\mathrm{D}} d . \tag{16}$$

Substitution of equation (3) into equation (2) leads to

$$x = (\mathbf{I} - \mathbf{A})^{-1}(c + y^{\mathrm{D}} + y^{\mathrm{ND}} - m) = \mathbf{R}c + \mathbf{R}y^{\mathrm{D}} + \mathbf{R}y^{\mathrm{ND}} - \mathbf{R}m , \tag{17}$$

where $\mathbf{R}$ is the Leontief inverse.

At this point it may be helpful to draw together the main elements of our mathematical model by setting the block equation structure of the model within an activity–commodity framework[1]. Such frameworks have been used extensively by Batey (1982; 1985) and Batey and Madden (1981) and have been adopted in the present volume by van Dijk and Oosterhaven (pages 122–147). By expressing the model in this form, we shall be able to see more clearly how the conventional input–output model has been extended and we shall see that the framework provides a convenient means of studying relationships between demographic and economic change.

We consider the model as four main blocks of equations:

$$(\mathbf{I} - \mathbf{A})x - \mathbf{T}c^{\mathrm{P}} - \mathbf{Y}_d^{\mathrm{D}} d = y^{\mathrm{ND}} - m , \tag{18}$$

which corresponds to equation (17),

$$c^{\mathrm{P}} = \mathbf{C}^{\mathrm{H}}(\mathbf{I} - \hat{\mathbf{S}})\mathbf{Q}\hat{\mathbf{W}}_0 x + \mathbf{C}^{\mathrm{H}}(\mathbf{I} - \hat{\mathbf{S}})t \tag{19}$$

which corresponds to equation (8), and

$$\mathbf{I}d = d , \tag{20}$$

$$\mathbf{I}t = t , \tag{21}$$

which both represent exogenous inputs. Assembling these equations as an

---

[1]The presentation of the Luptáčik–Schmoranz model as an activity–commodity framework is due to P W J Batey.

activity–commodity framework, we obtain:

$$\begin{bmatrix} I-A & -T & -Y_d^D & 0 \\ -C^H(I-\hat{S})Q\hat{W}_0 & I & 0 & -C^H(I-\hat{S}) \\ 0 & 0 & I & 0 \\ 0 & 0 & 0 & I \end{bmatrix}\begin{bmatrix} x \\ c^P \\ d \\ t \end{bmatrix} = \begin{bmatrix} y^{ND}-m \\ 0 \\ d \\ t \end{bmatrix}. \quad (22)$$

The framework has three main components: . a matrix of coefficients (partitioned to show how the conventional 'open' input–output model has been extended), a vector of activity levels (unknowns), and a vector of constraints (inputs). Because the matrix of coefficients is square, the equation system can be solved by matrix inversion.

Examining the framework closely, we can see that our model is in effect a closed-loop system and, as Batey (1985) shows, this model has many of the characteristics of a type 2 input–output model. The term $C^H(I-\hat{S})Q\hat{W}_0$ represents the consumption by households per unit of sectoral gross output. The income of households from employment (after savings), by industrial sector (per unit of sectoral gross output) is given by $(I-\hat{S})Q\hat{W}_0$. The bridge matrix T is used to translate the vector of private consumption, by commodity groups, into consumption of industrial commodities. The term Y_d^D is used in conjunction with d to give demographically determined final demand, but since d is exogenous [input via equation (20)], Y_d^D is effectively outside the closed loop of the model.

Inverting the matrix of coefficients and expressing the inverse as four partitions, defined in a similar manner to those in equation (22), we obtain:

$$\begin{bmatrix} x \\ c^P \\ d \\ t \end{bmatrix} = \begin{bmatrix} \Phi & \Lambda \\ & \\ \Pi & \Gamma \end{bmatrix}\begin{bmatrix} y^{ND}-m \\ 0 \\ d \\ t \end{bmatrix}. \quad (23)$$

A standard result in matrix algebra (for example, see Miller, 1966) can be used to express the partitions of the inverse as a function of the partitions in the original matrix of coefficients. In the case of Φ, the upper left-hand quadrant, we obtain

$$\Phi = \left\{(I-A)-[T \ Y_d^D \ 0]\begin{bmatrix} I & 0 & C^H(I-\hat{S}) \\ 0 & I & 0 \\ 0 & 0 & I \end{bmatrix}^{-1}\begin{bmatrix} C^H(I-\hat{S})Q\hat{W}_0 \\ 0 \\ 0 \end{bmatrix}\right\}^{-1} \quad (24)$$

$$= [I-A-TC^H(I-\hat{S})Q\hat{W}_0]^{-1}.$$

But, as we have seen above

$$\mathbf{U} = \mathbf{T}\mathbf{C}^{\mathrm{H}}(\mathbf{I} - \hat{\mathbf{S}})\mathbf{Q}\hat{\mathbf{W}}_0 , \tag{25}$$

so

$$\Phi = (\mathbf{I} - \mathbf{A} - \mathbf{U})^{-1} . \tag{26}$$

Taking this approach a step further, we obtain the following results for Λ, the upper right-hand quadrant of the inverse of the model:

$$\Lambda = \left[\begin{array}{c|c|c} (\mathbf{I} - \mathbf{A} - \mathbf{U})^{-1}\mathbf{T} & (\mathbf{I} - \mathbf{A} - \mathbf{U})^{-1}\mathbf{Y}_d^{\mathrm{D}} & (\mathbf{I} - \mathbf{A} - \mathbf{U})^{-1}\mathbf{T}\mathbf{C}^{\mathrm{H}}(\mathbf{I} - \hat{\mathbf{S}}) \\ (n \times m) & (n \times h) & (n \times h) \end{array} \right] . \tag{27}$$

We note from equation (27) that Λ consists of three main components, all of which contain Φ as a premultiplier. Each of these components represents the effects upon sectoral gross output of a unit change in a given input variable. The first component, $(\mathbf{I} - \mathbf{A} - \mathbf{U})^{-1}\mathbf{T}$, shows the effect of a unit change in household consumption: literally how gross output will fall if consumption occurs outside the study area; the second component, $(\mathbf{I} - \mathbf{A} - \mathbf{U})^{-1}\mathbf{Y}_d^{\mathrm{D}}$, is a demoeconomic multiplier, linking population change with changes in gross output. This multiplier is the subject of further discussion and experimentation in Luptáčik and Schmoranz (1980). Last, the third component, $(\mathbf{I} - \mathbf{A} - \mathbf{U})^{-1}\mathbf{T}\mathbf{C}^{\mathrm{H}}(\mathbf{I} - \hat{\mathbf{S}})$, shows how transfer payments affect sectoral gross output. This term can also be expressed more briefly as $(\mathbf{I} - \mathbf{A} - \mathbf{U})^{-1}\mathbf{V}$, where $\mathbf{V} = \mathbf{T}\mathbf{C}^{\mathrm{H}}(\mathbf{I} - \hat{\mathbf{S}})$.

Combining equations (23), (26), and (27), we obtain a full representation of the constituent elements of sectoral gross output, x:

$$x = (\mathbf{I} - \mathbf{A} - \mathbf{U})^{-1}y^{\mathrm{ND}} - (\mathbf{I} - \mathbf{A} - \mathbf{U})^{-1}m + (\mathbf{I} - \mathbf{A} - \mathbf{U})^{-1}\mathbf{Y}_d^{\mathrm{D}}d$$
$$+ (\mathbf{I} - \mathbf{A} - \mathbf{U})^{-1}\mathbf{V}t . \tag{28}$$

This equation demonstrates clearly that changes in gross output are a function of economic changes (first two terms on right-hand side) and demographic changes (third and fourth terms).

We can see, therefore, that our model represents a closed-loop system in which household consumption is treated as endogenous. In this system, "production leads to income determination, which leads to expenditure patterns, which leads to production requirements needed both to supply the goods and to create the income flows" (Clark, 1975, page 142). Using this model we can now analyse the influence of demographic changes on the economy. This will be done in section 3 by means of sensitivity analysis.

3 Demographic change and economic consequences: sensitivity analysis

In our model the influence of population changes on the economy is reflected in two ways (according to the dual role of demographic variables in the economic development of a country): first, by the vector d (and thereupon y^D, under the assumption of constancy of matrix Y_d^D) and by the vector t; second, through the matrix of labour-input coefficients, U (because of change in matrix Q; all other parts of matrix U remain constant), that is, population as producer. From a mathematical point of view, the following question arises: how does the production vector x change if the vectors y and t, matrix U, and thereupon the inverse matrix $(I - A - U)^{-1}$ change?

Using Noble's theorem about the inversion of matrices (Noble, 1969, chapter 5, page 147) we can write the inverse of the new Leontief matrix in the form

$$R_1 = R_0 + R_0(B^{-1} - R_0)^{-1} R_0 , \tag{29}$$

where

R_0 is the old inverse Leontief matrix, $R_0 = (I - A_0)^{-1}$,
B describes the changes in the matrix of input coefficients A,
     $B = A_1 - A_0$.

Supposing the demographic variables to change, we get a new matrix U_1 and new vectors d_1, y_1, and t_1, other parameters held constant. For brevity, we denote by $\bar{A} = (A + U)$ the matrix of input coefficients including the labour inputs and by $c^t = Vt$ the private consumption generated by transfer payments. Consequently the new vector of production, x_1, corresponding to the new values of demographic variables is given by

$$x_1 = \bar{R}_1 y_1^D + \bar{R}_1 c_1^t + \bar{R}_1 y^{ND} - \bar{R}_1 m , \tag{30}$$

or, since $\bar{R}_1 = (I - \bar{A}_1)^{-1}$, where $\bar{A}_1 = (A + U_1)$,

$$x_1 = (I - \bar{A}_1)^{-1} y_1^D + (I - \bar{A}_1)^{-1} c_1^t + (I - \bar{A}_1)^{-1} y^{ND} - (I - \bar{A}_1)^{-1} m . \tag{31}$$

Substituting equation (29) into equation (30) and rearranging terms yields

$$x_1 = x_0 + Lx_0 + \bar{R}_0 \Delta y^D + L\bar{R}_0 \Delta y^D + \bar{R}_0 \Delta c^t + L\bar{R}_0 \Delta c^t , \tag{32}$$

where

$$x_0 = \bar{R}_0(y_0^D + c_0^t + y^{ND} - m) , \quad \Delta y^D = y_1^D - y_0^D , \quad \Delta c^t = c_1^t - c_0^t , \tag{33}$$

and

$$L = \bar{R}_0(\bar{B}^{-1} - \bar{R}_0)^{-1} , \qquad \text{with} \quad \bar{B} = U_1 - U_0 . \tag{34}$$

Then

$$\Delta x = x_1 - x_0 = Lx_0 + \bar{R}_0 \Delta y^D + L\bar{R}_0 \Delta y^D + \bar{R}_0 \Delta c^t + L\bar{R}_0 \Delta c^t . \tag{35}$$

Noble's theorem about the inversion of matrices allows us to explain variations in gross output caused by demographic changes arising separately

from the population as a producer, on the one hand, and to the population as
a consumer, on the other. The first term on the right-hand side of
equation (35) indicates the change in the sectoral output associated only
with the change in the matrix of primary income distribution. It describes
the influence of population as producer. The second and fourth terms
on the right-hand side of equation (35) represent the influence of a change
of population as consumer. The term $\bar{\mathbf{R}}_0 \, \Delta y^D$ indicates the change in gross
production corresponding to a change of public consumption affected by
the demographic change. Similarly, the term $\bar{\mathbf{R}}_0 \, \Delta c^t$ corresponds to the
change of transfer payments affected by the demographic changes. The
third and fifth terms describe the influence of population as consumers as
well as producers. In this way the change in sectoral gross output can be
partitioned into its various components in additive form.

4 Empirical analysis
4.1 *The database*
Table 1 represents the real private consumption structure of the Austrian
economy. In 1964 more than 50% of private consumption expenditure
was attributed to food, beverages, tobacco, clothing, and footwear. In
1983, only slightly more than 40% was spent on these products. On the
other hand, the share of transportation and communication increased by
more than 60%, and that of entertainment, education, and miscellaneous
goods by nearly 30%. The question now arises as to whether these
structural changes can be attributed to changes in the demographic pattern
or to other influences, mainly income effects.

Table 1. Real private consumption in Austria, 1964–1983 [in billions of Austrian
schillings (that is, 10^9); figures in parentheses are percentages].

Commodity	1964	1969	1974	1979	1983
Food, beverages, tobacco, clothing, and footwear	126834 (51.2)	140815 (47.2)	163194 (42.9)	180284 (40.4)	197909 (40.9)
Heating and lighting	10975 (4.4)	13015 (4.3)	16596 (4.4)	21197 (4.8)	21166 (4.4)
Household operation, rents, furniture	44839 (18.1)	56909 (19.1)	79981 (21.0)	90000 (20.2)	99251 (20.5)
Transport and communication	23911 (9.6)	32585 (10.9)	50909 (13.4)	67387 (15.1)	76211 (15.8)
Medical care and health expenses	16210 (6.5)	19189 (6.4)	22377 (5.9)	23519 (5.3)	26229 (5.4)
Entertainment, education, and miscellaneous	25170 (10.2)	36092 (12.1)	46957 (12.4)	63546 (14.2)	63101 (13.0)
Total private consumption	247939 (100)	298605 (100)	380014 (100)	445933 (100)	483867 (100)

Table 2 shows the demographic pattern of the Austrian population for
1974 and 1983. It can be seen that the total number of households
increased from 2 593 000 to a number of 2 743 000, that is, it increased by
5.7%. In the same period total population increased by only 0.9%, from
7 456 000 to 7 522 000. This means that the average size of households
was 2.87 in 1974 and 2.74 in 1983, a decrease of 4.5%. Changes in the
number of individual types of households are even more pronounced. For
example, the first two types of households increased their numbers by
11% and 27%, respectively. On the other hand, households of types 9
and 10, that is, households with three or more children, each decreased in
number by 39%. These magnitudes together with differences in the

Table 2. Demographic pattern of households in Austria in 1974 and 1983.

Type	Number of			Total number of households (in thousands)		Percentage of total number of wage earners in that type	
	adults	children	wage earners	1974	1983	1974	1983
1	1	0	1	631	700	14.11	15.89
2	1	≥ 1	1	38	48	0.85	1.09
3	2	0	1	275	260	6.16	5.90
4	2	0	2	406	416	18.16	18.89
5	2	1	1	134	120	2.99	2.72
6	2	1	2	103	107	4.63	4.86
7	2	2	1	163	144	3.64	3.27
8	2	2	2	65	70	2.90	3.18
9	2	≥ 3	1	90	55	2.02	1.25
10	2	≥ 3	2	26	16	1.18	0.36
11	3	0	1	35	30	0.79	0.68
12	3	0	2	73	103	3.24	4.68
13	3	0	3	96	125	6.46	8.52
14	3	1	1	17	13	0.39	0.29
15	3	1	2	24	26	1.07	1.18
16	3	1	3	49	51	3.30	3.47
17	3	≥ 2	1	27	12	0.61	0.27
18	3	≥ 2	2	38	24	1.71	1.09
19	3	≥ 2	3	28	15	1.91	1.02
20	4	0	1	9	10	0.21	0.23
21	4	0	2	16	38	0.73	1.73
22	4	0	3	20	38	1.36	2.59
23	4	0	4	27	55	2.45	5.00
24	4	≥ 1	1	12	7	0.28	0.16
25	4	≥ 1	2	33	38	1.45	1.73
26	4	≥ 1	3	34	37	2.27	2.52
27	4	≥ 1	4	26	36	2.34	2.82
28	not specified			98	154	12.79	4.61
Total				2593	2743	100	100

consumption pattern may give a first rough impression of possible sizes of structural changes.

4.2 *The results*

The calculations were made with the help of MUSEM–A82, a multisectoral model for the Austrian economy (see Schmoranz, 1982) with an extension according to our model developed in section 2. The model comprises nineteen production sectors, six consumption and seven nonconsumption final demand categories. The core of the model is the nineteen-sector input–output model, which is based on a provisional input–output table for 1976 (see Richter, 1981). The model is closed, implying that final consumption influences production activity in the different sectors, which in turn creates factor demand and income. Total income is transformed into income per household and finally fed into the demoeconomic multiplier.

The following simulations are of a comparative static character. Taking the demographic patterns of two different points in time, we want to analyse the economic effects of this change in the demographic pattern. For this purpose we assume income per employee, total consumption, and the consumption pattern of 1983 also to hold for 1974.

Table 3 shows the outcomes of three simulations. The figures for simulation 1, 1983A, represent the basic solution, and those for simulation 2, 1974, represent the solution obtained when the demographic pattern of 1974 was fed into the model, all other variables (especially income per employee)

Table 3. Household expenditures resulting from different demographic patterns (source: own calculations).

Commodity	Simulation 1 1983A[a]	Relative differences from simulation 1 (%)	
		simulation 2 1974	simulation 3 1983B
Food, beverages, tobacco, clothing, and footwear	193.866	0.5	1.5
Heating and lighting	20.856	−0.8	1.9
Household operation, rents, furniture	95.037	−0.4	2.1
Transport and communication	74.892	1.5	1.3
Medical care and health expenses	26.260	3.2	0.8
Entertainment, education, and miscellaneous goods	61.620	0.6	1.6
Total private consumption	472.530	0.6	1.5

[a]In billions of Austrian schillings (that is, 10^9).

being held constant. In addition, we wanted to quantify the overall and structural effects of a policy aimed at favouring families with children. In doing so, we increased real disposable income of households with one child by 5%, with two children by 8%, and with three or more children by 10%. The results can be seen under simulation 3, 1983B.

A comparison of simulations 1 and 2 suggests that the overall or aggregate effect deduced from structural change in the demographic pattern between 1974 and 1983 is of a negligible character (table 4). This corresponds to our previous estimates (see Luptáčik and Schmoranz, 1980). If the pattern of 1974 had remained constant up to 1983, real gross national product would be higher by only 0.2%. The effect on private consumption, however, is more pronounced. Total private consumption differs by 0.6%, and the effects on the individual components of this final demand category are even more pronounced. Medical care and health expenses would increase by 3.2%; on the other hand, expenses on heating and lighting would decrease by 0.8%.

The consumption pattern is reflected in the production structure. It is worth noting that the changes shown include only effects derived from demographic factors. Income and price effects, which certainly account for the greater part of the structural change observed, were not considered. The incremental changes shown in table 5 exhibit a wide range of reaction. The strongest increase originates in sectors 08 (crude petroleum) and 03 (manufacture of food, etc), and 16 (transport), reflecting the above average increase in the consumption category 04 (transportation and communication). A slight decrease in production levels results for the sectors 05 (manufacturing of wood) and 12 (electricity, gas, water). This reduction can be explained by economies of scale in household size.

Table 4. Simulation results for selected economic variables (source: own calculations).

Variable	Simulation 1 1983A[a]	Relative differences from simulation 1 (%)	
		simulation 2 1974	simulation 3 1983B
Gross national product, real	843.7	0.2	0.7
Private consumption, real	478.7	0.6	1.3
Investment, real	184.5	0.0	0.0
Imports, real	353.5	0.1	0.2
Disposable income, real	620.9	0.1	0.2
Employment (in thousands)	3160.8	0.1	0.3

[a]In billions of Austrian schillings (that is, 10^9).

The third simulation shows a strong influence on real gross national product. The additional growth of 0.7% can be solely attributed to income effects. Thus, additional income increases the budget deficit by the same order of magnitude. Table 3 shows the effects of simulation 3 on the consumption pattern and table 5 shows the effects on the production structure. The strongest increase is shown for household operation, rents, and furniture, followed by heating and lighting. A below average increase is, unexpectedly, shown for medical care and health expenses.

Table 5. Sectoral (net) production levels resulting from different demographic patterns (source: own calculations).

Production sectors	Simulation 1 1983A[a]	Relative differences from simulation 1 (%)	
		simulation 2 1974	simulation 3 1983B
01 Agriculture, etc	42.5	0.3	0.8
02 Mining, etc	3.5	0.0	0.1
03 Manufacture of food, etc	40.1	0.6	1.6
04 Textiles, etc	19.5	0.3	1.0
05 Manufacture of wood, etc	16.8	− 0.1	0.5
06 Manufacture of paper, etc	16.7	0.2	0.6
07 Manufacture of chemicals	24.2	0.5	1.1
08 Crude petroleum	8.4	0.9	1.8
09 Manufacture of non-metallic mineral products	14.1	0.1	0.4
10 Basic metal industries	18.1	0.2	0.3
11 Manufacture of fabricated metal products	86.5	0.4	0.7
12 Electricity, gas, water	27.0	− 0.2	1.1
13 Construction	58.0	0.1	0.3
14 Trade	121.5	0.4	1.0
15 Restaurants and hotels	21.1	0.1	0.2
16 Transport, etc	51.6	0.6	0.9
17 Financing, etc	101.2	0.1	1.3
18 Social and personal services	32.7	0.4	0.4
19 Public administration and defence	112.0	0.4	0.2
Total gross national product	843.7	0.2	0.7

[a]In billions of Austrian schillings (that is, 10^9).

The empirical analysis of the different effects resulting from the dual role of population in the economy, described by equation (35), is of significant character and leads us to the conclusion that further work on this subject is necessary to understand all influences originating from the demographic structure.

5 Conclusions

The model we have developed is designed to evaluate the economic effects of demographic change, where the different effects due to the dual role of population in the economy can be considered separately.

Two different forms of the model were presented: as a demoeconomic multiplier [equation (18)] which permits—by means of sensitivity analysis— a rapid assessment of the economic effect of changing population size and structure; and within an activity–commodity framework which yields more insight into and detailed results on the nature of demographic–economic interaction. The inverse of the activity–commodity framework contains various—partly novel—multiplier relationships.

The model represents a closed-loop system, which—after some modifications—can be used for analysis of the interactions and interlinkages between (primary) factor demand, income generation, income distribution, and economic activity.

Acknowledgement. We are grateful to P W J Batey for helpful comments on an earlier version of our paper.

References
Barten A P, 1964, "Family composition, prices and expenditure patterns" *Colston Papers* **16** 277–297
Batey P W J, 1982, "Luptáčik's and Schmoranz's demo-economic multiplier: a working note" available from the author, Department of Civic Design, University of Liverpool, Liverpool
Batey P W J, 1985, "Input–output models for regional demographic–economic analysis: some structural comparisons" *Environment and Planning A* **17** 73–99
Batey P W J, Madden M, 1981, "Demographic–economic forecasting within an activity–commodity framework: some theoretical considerations and empirical results" *Environment and Planning A* **13** 1067–1083
Bojer H, 1977, "The effect on consumption of household size and composition" *European Economic Review* **9** 169–193
Clark P, 1975, "Intersectoral consistency and macroeconomic planning" in *Economy-wide Models and Development Planning* Eds C Blitzer, P Clark, L Taylor (Oxford University Press, New York) pp 129–154
Grootaert Ch, 1983 *The Relation Between Final Demand and Income Distribution: With Application to Japan* (Springer, Berlin)
Kuznets S, 1975, "Summary" in *Income Distribution, Employment and Economic Development in Southeast and East Asia* papers and proceedings of the seminar sponsored jointly by the Japan Economic Research Center (JERC) and the Council for Asian Manpower Studies (CAMS), 16–20 December 1974 (JERC, Tokyo; CAMS, Manila) pp 789–799

Luptáčik M, Schmoranz I, 1980, "Demographic changes and economic consequences: demo-economic multiplier for Austria" *Empirical Economics* **5** 55–63

Miller R E, 1966, "Interregional feedback effects in input–output models: some preliminary results" *Papers of the Regional Science Association* **17** 105–125

Muellbauer J, 1974, "Household composition, Engel curves and welfare comparison between households. A duality approach" *European Economic Review* **5** 103–122

Noble B, 1969 *Applied Linear Algebra* (Prentice-Hall, Englewood Cliffs, NJ)

Parks R W, Barten A P, 1973, "A cross country comparison of the effects of prices, income and population composition on consumption patterns" *The Economic Journal* number 331, 834–852

Richter J, 1981 *Strukturen und Interdependenzen der Österreichischen Wirtschaft* Schriftenreihe der Bundeskammer der gewerblichen Wirtschaft 41, Wien

Schmoranz L, 1982, "Allgemeine Wirtschaftsentwicklung" in *Österreich 2000* Ed. C Mandl (R Oldenbourg, Munich) pp 82–101

Regional Impacts of Migrants' Expenditures: An Input–Output/Vacancy-chain Approach

J VAN DIJK, J OOSTERHAVEN
University of Groningen

1 Introduction

Migration of human beings has been an issue of major interest in regional science, economics, and geography. This interest is quite understandable because migration may have substantial effects on the region of origin, the region of destination, and the nation as a whole, as well as on the migrant. Not all aspects of migration, however, have been given equal attention. Sjaastad (1962) noted that migration research dealt mainly with the forces which affect migration and that little has been done to determine the influence of migration as an equilibrating mechanism. This point was confirmed by Greenwood in 1975. In a recent review, Clark (1982) also notes that only scanty attention is paid to the consequences of migration, in particular to its economic effects.

Only the relation between migration and economic growth has been examined to any great extent. This research has concentrated mainly on the question: does migration cause economic growth or does economic growth cause migration? This 'chicken-or-egg' problem is analysed by means of simultaneous equation models. (For details see, among others, Muth, 1971; Greenwood, 1975; 1981; Steinnes, 1978; Dahlberg and Holmlund, 1978; Salvatore, 1984.) In these macroadjustment models, migration is seen as an equilibrating mechanism which optimally allocates the demand and supply of labour and equalises wage rates across regional labour markets. These models rely heavily on aggregate relationships between migration and (un)employment. In reality, however, these are rather complex multidirectional relations with forward and backward linkages that sometimes counteract. Empirical evidence from these kinds of models often shows contradictory or insignificant relations between migration and (un)employment. This is possibly a result of the aggregated nature of macromodels, which are not sufficiently sensitive because of the questionable interaction between the demographic and economic systems (for instance, see Greenwood, 1975; Clark, 1982). Hence, a disaggregated approach seems to be preferable.

A more careful examination of the relation between migration and (un)employment is not only of scientific interest, but is also important from a policy point of view. This may be illustrated by a case study for the northern region of the Netherlands. This region is one of the two regions on which the regional economic policy of the Dutch central government is concentrated (compare Oosterhaven and Folmer, 1983).

The northern region is characterised by a structural shortage of jobs, a situation which has existed almost continuously since World War 2.

Directly after 1945 one of the purposes of regional policy was to move labour from the northern to the western region which had labour shortages. At the end of the 1960s, central government switched to a policy which was intended to spread population and employment more evenly over the country in such a way that congestion in the western regions could be avoided and employment opportunities in the problem regions could be improved. Notwithstanding severe doubts about the effectiveness of this policy of dispersal, the actual migration flows turned around: for the western region from net in-migration to net out-migration and for the northern region from net out-migration to net in-migration. In spite of investment incentives for private firms, relocation of governmental institutions, and migration subsidies, the northern region still shows regional unemployment rates above the national average (for instance, see Oosterhaven and Stol, 1984).

Van Dijk and Bartels (1982) show that, during the period 1973–1979, unemployment in the northern region increased by 7900 persons and the labour force increased by 6400 because of net in-migration of labour. Under the assumptions of homogeneous labour and an ideal matching process, these figures imply that 81% of the rise in unemployment in the north was caused by in-migration. To reach a more realistic conclusion a research project was begun in which the relation between migration and (un)employment was examined at a disaggregated level. A general theoretical framework was developed and applied to the case of the northern region of the Netherlands for 1979. Theoretically, the relation between migration and (un)employment can be disentangled in the following way.

Direct effects Migration of workers directly affects employment and unemployment. The magnitude of the effects depends not only on the number of migrants but also on the type of labour migrant. Three types may be distinguished:
type a: employed migrants who fill jobs for which native unemployed are *also* suited and available. In this case, migration indirectly prevents a decrease in unemployment as migrants preempt the native unemployed;
type b: employed migrants who fill jobs for which *no* native unemployed are suited and available. In this case there is no preemption and without migration, vacancies remain open and employment cannot increase;
type c: unemployed migrants who directly cause an increase in unemployment.

These direct effects were investigated by Van Dijk and Folmer (1985; 1986) who came to the conclusion that in 1979 12% of the migrants who belonged to the labour force were unemployed. Furthermore, they made a comparison between the labour-market characteristics of the age, education, and work experience of the employed migrants and the native unemployed. Individual data were analysed by means of logistic regression.

The results indicate that there are strong differences with respect to these characteristics between the migrants and the unemployed. On the basis of these results it appears that preemption will probably be less than 30% and thus is only of minor importance.

Indirect effects The indirect effects can be split in two parts:
Supply effects The regional labour force increases through labour migration and this affects location decisions of firms. Furthermore, vacancies filled by migrants can be key functions. When such vacancies remain unfilled, other complementary jobs, for which native unemployed are suited, will not become available. The magnitude of these effects is hard to measure, but it seems certain that the indirect supply effects of migration positively influence regional unemployment. This relation is, for example, incorporated in the regional model of the Dutch Central Planning Bureau (CPB, 1981).
Demand effects Because of the expenditure of migrants, regional demand will increase and additional employment will be created in the north.

The measurement of this effect is the problem we focus on in this paper.

When the relation between migration and (un)employment is unravelled in the manner referred to above, it is obvious that the impact of migration on the regional economy is not merely dependent on the magnitude of migration. The effects also depend heavily on the characteristics of the migrants, such as family size and composition, labour-market status, age, education, income, and expenditure pattern. Hence, a disaggregated approach is preferable, in which the above-mentioned effects are investigated at the level of relatively homogeneous subgroups.

The purpose of this paper is to quantify the employment effects of migrants' expenditure. As different groups of migrants exhibit different levels and compositions of consumption expenditure, an input–output approach is required to capture effectively the differences in expenditure impacts. The classical input–output approach, however, has several drawbacks, some of which are especially important in our context.

First, it normally takes no account of the interaction with the labour market. The traditional way of accounting for induced consumption effects is to make an implicit assumption that all new jobs are filled by migrants. In fact, however, some of these jobs are filled by local unemployed who lose their unemployment benefits because of the change in their labour-market status. More generally, it is the way in which vacancies are filled that determines the size and composition of the primary and secondary income changes that cause the changes in endogenous consumption expenditure. In this paper we will remedy this drawback by linking a vacancy-chain model to an input–output model.

Second, besides additional private expenditure, migrants also call for the provision of additional public services. Normally, this effect is not incorporated in the input–output model. Given the size of the public sector this 'demand' effect ought not to be neglected. Hence, our model

will also be extended to account for the population-induced effects on
public consumption.

Finally, the preemption of native unemployed by migrants will influence
the size of the consumption effects. The effect of migrants' expenditure
has to be decreased by the effect that would have occurred if the new jobs
had been filled by local unemployed. Preemption, in fact, prevents this
from happening. Provisionally, however, the rate of preemption is
assumed to be zero, as it is quite small in the study area (see Van Dijk
and Folmer, 1986). In an extended version of our model preemption will
also be included.

The outline of the paper is as follows. In section 2 the size and
composition both of the private and of the public consumption demands of
migrants to the northern region will be estimated. This gives the exogenous
impulses that will be fed into the regional input–output/vacancy-chain
model which is described in section 3. In section 4 the estimated
endogenous effects for different types of in-migrants will be presented. In
section 5 the indirect employment effects due to migrants' expenditure are
compared with the direct effects of labour migration on labour supply.
The paper ends with some conclusions and some policy recommendations.

2 Consumption demand of in-migrants

In this section the estimation of *exogenous* final demand for the products
of twenty-seven northern industries and for government services located in
the north is described. From the introduction it is clear that the effects of
migration have to be studied for more or less homogeneous subgroups.
Therefore, final demand is estimated for eleven subgroups, which are
chosen on the basis of characteristics which appeared to be the most
important determinants of the level and composition of consumption
demand (CBS, 1984; Van Weeren and Van Praag, 1984).

The level of total consumption demand for these eleven types of
migrant families is estimated by means of three types of data which are all
provided by the Dutch Central Bureau of Statistics (CBS). First, the total
number of migrants is extracted from the Labour Force Survey 1979
(CBS, 1983a; 1983b), which contains individual data. Expenditure
patterns, however, are only available for families. Hence, the individual
migrants have to be translated into migrant families. Fortunately, it is
possible to distinguish between family heads (including singles), on the one
hand, and remaining family members, on the other hand. Furthermore,
for each individual, information about family size, employment status, and
education is available. Therefore, in this section the number and
characteristics of family heads are used to identify the number and type of
consumption units (that is, families) for the calculation of total demand.
In contrast, the labour-market model in the next section is based on
individuals as measurement units.

Second, the average level of private consumption expenditure per type of family is derived from the Budget Survey 1978–1981 (CBS, 1984) which, as pointed out above, contains only data on the spending of whole families and not that of individual consumers. In using these data, we do, of course, make the (plausible) assumption that migrant families consume as much as the average families having the same characteristics.

Third, we need data on the amount of consumption by migrants of public goods and quasipublic goods for which the employment effects cannot be related to individual expenditure. The figures from the Budget Survey show only the consumption of government products as far as direct full payments are concerned. For our purpose we are especially interested in the level of public services that is directly related to the size of the regional population and in the number of civil servants needed to produce these services.

This part of total government employment was estimated by means of the so-called 'minimum requirements technique', which is traditionally used to estimate the size of the nonbasic sector in economic base models (compare Richardson, 1978, page 90). For the years 1977 to 1979 for each of the eleven Dutch provinces, the number of civil servants per thousand inhabitants was calculated. No outlying low rates were found. Hence, the lowest rate of thirty-seven civil servants per thousand inhabitants (which occurred twice) was accepted as the minimum population-induced amount of public-sector employment. Because of the linear nature of the minimum requirements technique this implies that the average effect equals the marginal effect. To make this number of thirty-seven civil servants comparable with the private consumption demand figures, it is multiplied by the average production per civil servant in 1979. This leads to a consumption of northern government services of Dfl.3182 per inhabitant per year.

Differences in this figure between various types of families, however, need to be considered. Families without children, for instance, hardly use educational services unless they are students. In the latter case they will consume a relatively high amount of educational services. The use of facilities such as police and local government administration, however, will differ only with the size of the family. Studies by the Social–Cultural Planning Bureau (SCPB) indicate that some 60% of all government production consists of public goods which cannot be related to specific individuals or households (SCPB, 1981; 1983). The use of the other 40% is directly attributable and depends on the characteristics of households and individuals. From the SCPB studies we derive that students consume 2.14 times the average consumption of government services per capita, whereas the low-income group, which accounts for approximately 63% of the inactive and for all of the employed and unemployed singles group, consumes only 0.49 times the average. The remaining family types consume 1.06 times the average of Dfl.3182 multiplied by family size.

Table 1 contains the main results of the above estimation procedure. The number of migrant families with inactive heads is quite small. Therefore, this group will be aggregated throughout the paper. The column for consumption per family clearly shows the significance of disaggregation according to family type, as large differences in total consumption demand are shown.

Next, the way in which total consumption is spent by each type of family is of importance, because it determines which regional industries will be affected by the migrants' consumption shown in table 1. Unfortunately, the only available budget data show consumption expenditures over groups of goods (CBS, 1984). They contain no data on the industrial and regional origin of the goods concerned. Furthermore, no distinction is made between the factory price (fob—free on board), the retail margin, and the value added tax (VAT).

Figure 1 shows the three major steps that are needed to transfer the budget data into patterns of consumption demand that fit into the input – output framework. The lower right-hand corner represents the data on exogenous final demand of migrant families—these data are actually needed as model input in the next section.

Table 1. Number of migrant families and total private and public (northern government services) consumption demand per type of family in 1979 in the north of the Netherlands [sources: own calculations from data which are described in CBS (1983a; 1983b; 1984) and SCPB (1981; 1983)].

Type of family	Migrant families		Consumption per family (Dfl.)
	number	average size	
Head in the labour force			
1 single	779	1.0	24 284
2 family of two persons	1137	2.0	38 776
3 family of three or more, head with low education	724	4.1	48 181
4 family of three or more, head with medium education	918	4.2	54 375
5 family of three or more, head with high education	729	4.0	62 807
Total	4287	3.0	45 155
Heads, who are students	1466	1.0	17 533
Heads, who are inactive[a]	889	2.4	34 668
Total	6642	2.5	37 624

[a]These figures are aggregated from detailed data for five types of migrants of which the head is inactive: (1) retired singles, (2) families of two or more with retired head, (3) singles who are not in the labour force, (4) families of two or more of which the head is not in the labour force, (5) miscellaneous.

First, the available consumption data for a hundred groups of goods have to be rearranged in consumption patterns over twenty-seven industries. Expenditure on a specific group of goods has to be assigned to the industry in which most of these goods are produced. The construction of such a 'wiring diagram' is a subjective activity. With such a scheme it is possible to show which part of the migrants' consumption is spent on the products of a specific industry.

Second, VAT, foreign imports, and the retail margin are subtracted with the aid of National Account data for 1979 (CBS, 1981). This leads to an estimation of the proportion of total consumption demand going to the twenty-seven domestic industries and to domestic retail margin.

Last, regional import shares for the northern household sector are derived from the regional input–output tables for the northern region for 1975 (CBS, 1982; FNEI, 1983). When these shares are applied to the shares of domestic industries in total consumption demand, the corresponding northern shares result.

The results of the above procedure are presented in table 2 for the three main types of migrant families. The results for five subgroups of the employed plus unemployed group are shown in the appendix. The consumption of northern government services is divided into a small part for which the northern consumers actually pay and a large part which is financed through the national tax system. The paid part is derived from the budget data, where it is seen as a part of total private consumption.

The public part is calculated as the difference between the estimated minimally required government services and those government services for which an actual payment is made. The public part is also expressed as a ‰ of total private consumption expenditures, which equals 1000‰. These figures show that the neglect of public consumption leads to a significant underestimation of total consumption in the north. Public

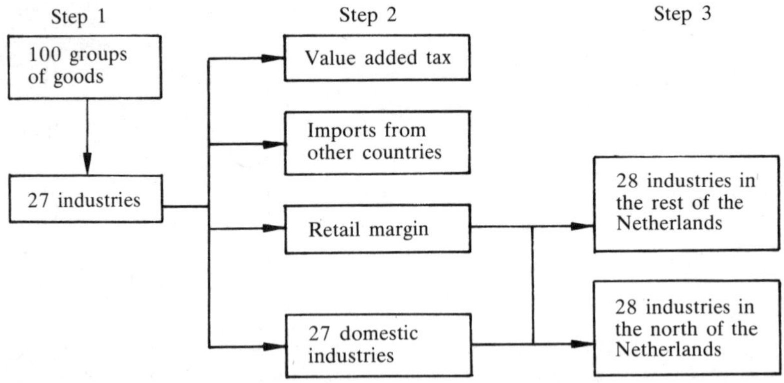

Figure 1. Construction procedure for migrant consumption patterns over regional industries.

Table 2. Consumption expenditure by three types of migrant families for twenty-eight industries in 1979 [in ‰ of total private spending; source: own computations from raw data of 1979 survey of family expenditure patterns; for information about the data see CBS (1984)].

SIC[a]	Industry	Type of migrant family		
		employed plus unemployed[b]	students	inactive[c]
0	Agriculture	9.7	9.6	10.6
19	Mining, quarrying	0.1	0.2	0.1
20.1–20.2	Food (animal products)	18.2	8.4	22.6
20.3–21.3	Other food products	12.7	12.3	15.2
21.4–21.7	Beverages, tobacco	2.2	2.3	2.2
22	Textiles	0.0	0.0	0.0
23–24	Clothing, leather	1.5	1.1	1.5
25	Wood, furniture	2.0	0.9	1.9
26	Paper	0.0	0.0	0.0
27	Printing, publishing	4.4	7.2	4.2
12, 28	Oil, gas, refineries	0.0	0.0	0.0
29–31	Chemical, rubber	0.5	0.3	0.6
32	Building materials	0.8	0.9	0.7
33	Basic metals	0.0	0.0	0.0
34–35	Metal processing, machinery	0.1	0.1	0.1
36	Electrical equipment	0.4	0.6	0.4
37	Transport equipment	0.5	0.2	0.4
38–39	Other manufacturing	0.1	0.0	0.1
40	Electricity, gas, water	34.1	20.5	41.5
51–52	Construction, installation	14.5	11.8	14.3
6	Trade, hotels, repair	139.7	157.4	143.5
7	Transport, communication	41.4	59.4	38.8
81–82	Banks, insurance	1.1	0.8	1.1
83–85	Real estate, business	126.5	165.0	139.6
93	Medical, other health	70.2	45.6	64.6
95–96	Culture, recreational services	62.7	77.1	55.3
9	Other services	38.0	46.0	32.1
	Paid government services	20.3	10.0	18.1
Subtotal northern industries[d]		606	638	609
Value added tax		78.1	66.7	76.4
Import from other countries		120.2	86.8	119.0
Import from rest of The Netherlands		198.7	207.9	195.7
Total private consumption expenditure[d]		1000	1000	1000
Northern public government services for which no direct payments are required		230.2	345.3	217.9
Total[d,e]		1230	1345	1218

[a]SIC Standard Industrial Classification.
[b]These are average figures for all families with a head who is in the labour force (employed or unemployed) which are based on detailed data for five types of migrant families (see appendix).
[c]These average figures for all families with an inactive head are also based on five types of migrant families (see note table 1). These are available upon request from the authors.
[d]Discrepancies in the totals are caused by a cumulation of weighting and rounding errors.
[e]These totals correspond to the figures for total consumption in guilders reported in table 1.

consumption by students equals 54% of their private spending on northern products and for the other two groups (employed and unemployed, and inactive) it is 38%.

Next, we will discuss how the exogenous final demand of migrants and the expenditure coefficients are used to estimate employment and income effects.

3 A regional input–output labour-market model
In the above section it should have become clear that different types of migrants not only have different levels of income but also have different ways in which they spend their income and different needs for government services. Furthermore, consumption goods and services are provided locally in different proportions. Last, the industries (including government services) that produce these items have different input patterns, with different proportions of each input being purchased locally. To take account of these differences when we estimate the impacts of the consumption demand of migrants, we need to use a regional input–output model.

Besides intermediate inputs, industries also need primary (factor) inputs. Of these, labour is the most important, not only because it is the yardstick against which we wish to measure the significance of the consumption demand effects, but also because workers need inputs (consumption) too, and this causes further indirect effects. The traditional way to deal with these consumption-induced effects is to add an extra row and column for households to the input–output model (compare Richardson, 1972).

Elsewhere, we have indicated that this way of treating households as an industry ignores the functioning of the regional labour market and this leads to incorrect estimates of income and employment. The presumed additional income and consumption, for instance, has to be corrected for the decrease in income because less social security benefits are paid, because there exists a (negative) institutional relation between labour incomes and those social security benefits that depend on a person's labour-market status (Oosterhaven, 1981, chapter 6).

In this paper we wish to remedy this neglect of the labour market more fundamentally than has been done in other interindustry models that are used for impact and projection analysis (see Batey, 1985, for a review of a series of demographic–economic impact models). To this end, we will make a systematic distinction between the number of vacancies to be filled in the period under consideration and the number of new jobs. This is because very often a vacancy is filled by someone who was employed and the filling of the first vacancy will cause a second vacancy and so on. At the end of this Markovian process the last vacancy in a chain will be filled by an unemployed worker, or a new participant will enter the labour force, or the vacancy will remain open. It should be clear that job-to-job changes as well as the entry of unemployed or new participants will cause various types of income changes.

Below we will describe this process by means of an 'integrated input–output/vacancy-chain model'. We will discuss the model equation by equation, indicating the empirical sources used and presenting the main results.

3.1 *The input–output equation*

We start with the definition equation of input–output analysis, which in our case explains the change in the total production per regional industry (Δx_i; $i = 1, ..., N$) from the changes in five components of total demand, namely

$$\Delta x = A\Delta x + q^w\Delta c^w + q^u\Delta c^u + q^n\Delta c^n + \Delta f_{ex} , \tag{1}$$

where

Δx is an N-dimensional vector of changes in sectoral production levels,

A is an $N \times N$ matrix of regional intermediate input coefficients per industry,

q^w is an N-dimensional vector of regional consumption expenditure coefficients that relate to people with (relatively high) labour incomes,

Δc^w is the change in total consumption from labour incomes,

q^u is an N-dimensional vector of expenditure coefficients that relate to people with (medium–high) unemployment benefits,

Δc^u is the change in total consumption from unemployment benefits (that is, in our case the Dutch WW, WWV, and WAO schemes that are tied to previous labour incomes),

q^n is an N-dimensional vector with expenditure coefficients that relate to people with (subsistence-level) nonactive benefits,

Δc^n is the change in total consumption from nonactive benefits (that is, in our case the Dutch RWW and ABW schemes that are *not* tied to any labour income),

Δf_{ex} is an N-dimensional vector of changes in exogenous final demand (that is, in our case the consumption demand of in-migrants).

A description of the Dutch social security schemes has been given by Grais (1983).

Matrix A stems from the most recent input–output table for the northern Netherlands, which was constructed for 1975 by the Federation of Northern Economic Institutes [FNEI (1983); see Oosterhaven (1984) for a review of the construction procedures and reliability of Dutch regional and interregional input–output tables]. This table, and hence our model, contains twenty-eight sectors (including government services).

We assume that the q vectors for employed and unemployed individuals are the same and are equal to the q vectors for employed and unemployed families. The vectors q^w and q^u are calculated in the same way as the q vectors in table 2 (see figure 1), but are based on the consumption pattern of average employed and unemployed families, instead of migrant families.

The consumption pattern for the inactive with subsistence benefits is assumed to be equal to the pattern for students in table 2, because this group of inactive people consists mainly of school-leavers, who have more or less the same consumption patterns as students.

Traditionally, a distinction is made between types of income growth: *intensive* growth for workers with increases in labour income; *extensive* growth for migrants and people with no previous labour incomes; and *redistributive* growth for unemployed losing their benefits because of obtaining work (see Oosterhaven, 1981; Batey, 1985). This distinction is made because average consumption coefficients need to be used in the case of extensive growth, whereas marginal coefficients are required in the two other cases.

It should be noted that this distinction is *not* necessary when the household sector is disaggregated in the same manner as in equation (1). When a person's labour-market status changes, the effect of this change on his or her consumption behaviour is estimated as the difference between the corresponding two terms of equation (1). Hence, in fact, marginal expenditure coefficients are used, as in the case with redistributive and intensive growth. In the case of a migrant or of people who lose no benefits, only one term of equation (1) applies, at least if we assume that no preemption takes place. So, the average q vectors are used as in the case with extensive growth.

3.2 *The vacancy-chain model*

Next, the number of new jobs or job closures per regional sector (Δe_i) is determined as a function of the change in production level and the increase in labour productivity, that is,

$$\Delta e = \hat{L}\Delta x - \hat{P}^w e_{t-1} , \tag{2}$$

where

Δe is an N-dimensional vector of changes in employment in each industry,

$\hat{L}$ is an N-dimensional diagonal matrix of marginal employment coefficients,

$\hat{P}^w$ is an N-dimensional diagonal matrix of increases in labour productivity,

e_{t-1} is an N-dimensional vector of base-year employment levels in each industry.

Equation (2) is necessary to determine the total number of vacancies in each industry (v_i) that may be filled during the period under consideration. This total equals

$$v = Tv + \Delta e + \Delta v_{ex} , \tag{3}$$

where

v is an N-dimensional vector of the total number of vacancies that may be filled during the period under consideration,

$\mathbf{T}$ is an $N \times N$ matrix of transition probabilities (t_{ij}) of people leaving industry i to take up jobs in industry j,

Δv_{ex} is an N-dimensional vector of exogenous changes in v.

Exogenous changes in the number of vacancies are influenced by two basically different causes. First, vacancies may be created because people leave their jobs for jobs in other regions (that is, emigrants), because of (early) retirements, and because of industrial disability. Such vacancies might be explained by means of the equation

$$\Delta v_{\mathrm{ex}} = \hat{\mathbf{R}} e_{t-1} , \tag{4}$$

where $\hat{\mathbf{R}}$ is an N-dimensional diagonal matrix with departure rates per regional sector.

Second, the number of vacancies caused by frictions in the matching process on the labour market might change.

Rogerson and MacKinnon (1982), for example, show with a simulation model that migration lowers the number of frictional vacancies. For ease of exposition, however, we will assume the number of frictional vacancies to be constant. This implies that we assume that all endogenously created vacancies will be filled during the period under consideration and that all existing vacancies remain unfilled.

Next, we turn to the way in which these vacancies are taken up. First, workers from the same or from other regional industries take up some of the vacancies [that is, $\mathbf{T}v$, compare equation (3)]. The other vacancies are filled up as follows:

$$m = \hat{\mathbf{T}}^{m} v , \tag{5}$$

$$\Delta u = -\hat{\mathbf{T}}^{u} v , \tag{6}$$

$$\Delta n = -(t^{n})^{\mathrm{T}} v , \tag{7}$$

$$\Delta r = -(t^{r})^{\mathrm{T}} v , \tag{8}$$

where

$\hat{\mathbf{T}}^{m}, \hat{\mathbf{T}}^{u}$ are N-dimensional diagonal matrices of transition probabilities for regional industry, corresponding to:

m a vector of in-migrants obtaining jobs, and

Δu a vector of unemployed who received unemployment benefits; the in-migrants and unemployed are specified for each regional sector where they take up vacancies because their incomes differ by sector (see section 3.3);

$(t^{n})^{\mathrm{T}}, (t^{r})^{\mathrm{T}}$ are N-dimensional vectors of transition probabilities for regional industry, corresponding to:

the number of economically inactive persons who received (subsistence) inactive person benefits;

Δr is the number of economically inactive persons who had no benefits at all.

In the last two cases only the total number of people is needed.

As we assume that all endogenous vacancies are taken up by the above-mentioned five categories of people, the following condition must hold

$$i^{\mathrm{T}}\mathbf{T} + (t^{\mathrm{m}})^{\mathrm{T}} + (t^{\mathrm{u}})^{\mathrm{T}} + (t^{\mathrm{n}})^{\mathrm{T}} + (t^{\mathrm{r}})^{\mathrm{T}} = i^{\mathrm{T}} , \qquad (9)$$

that is, the column sums of all transition probabilities equal 1.

When all endogenous vacancies are filled, the change in the number of people working in each industry (Δl_i) will have to equal the change in the number of jobs (Δe_i). This is easily proven as the first number equals the difference between the numbers of vacancies taken up and the vacancies created by people leaving for jobs in (other) regional industries:

$$\Delta l = v - \mathbf{T}v . \qquad (10)$$

From equation (3) it may be derived that:

$$v = (\mathbf{I} - \mathbf{T})^{-1}(\Delta e + \Delta v_{\mathrm{ex}}) , \qquad (11)$$

(where $\mathbf{I}$ is the identity matrix). If the exogenous change in vacancies (Δv_{ex}) is equal to 0, substitution of equation (11) into equation (10) gives

$$\Delta l = \Delta e . \qquad (12)$$

From equation (11) it also follows that the vacancy-chain model is a submodel that can be solved independently of the rest of the model, because equation (11) can be substituted into equations (5)–(8), which gives

$$m = \hat{\mathbf{T}}^{\mathrm{m}}(\mathbf{I} - \mathbf{T})^{-1}(\Delta e + \Delta v_{\mathrm{ex}}) , \qquad (13)$$

$$\Delta u = -\hat{\mathbf{T}}^{\mathrm{u}}(\mathbf{I} - \mathbf{T})^{-1}(\Delta e + \Delta v_{\mathrm{ex}}) , \qquad (14)$$

$$\Delta n = -(t^{\mathrm{n}})^{\mathrm{T}}(\mathbf{I} - \mathbf{T})^{-1}(\Delta e + \Delta v_{\mathrm{ex}}) , \qquad (15)$$

$$\Delta r = -(t^{\mathrm{r}})^{\mathrm{T}}(\mathbf{I} - \mathbf{T})^{-1}(\Delta e + \Delta v_{\mathrm{ex}}) . \qquad (16)$$

Table 3 gives the values of the transition probabilities for the north for 1979 for nine aggregated sectors and the above five groups. It is clear that the industrial sector is the most important sectoral source from which all sectors draw new workers. Furthermore, it is clear that intrasectoral moves provide a lot of new workers (from approximately 25% to approximately 65%). Of all categories of formerly nonemployed in the north, those with subsistence benefits (mainly school-leavers) are the most important new suppliers of labour. Migrants take up 5–17% of the vacancies filled.

Table 3. Origin of workers who got a job in 1979 by sector in the north of the Netherlands in percentages [source: these figures are our own computations from the raw data of the Labour Force Survey 1979 from the Dutch Central Bureau of Statistics (for details about these data see CBS, 1983a)].

Origin of workers: sector[a]	Sector of employment in 1979[a]								
	1	2	3	4	5	6	7	8	9
1	13	0	1	8	3	1	0	1	0
2	0	9	0	0	0	0	0	0	0
3	1	9	24	13	13	8	13	8	4
4	0	0	0	9	0	0	0	0	0
5	5	0	5	28	39	1	6	3	1
6	3	0	10	0	4	26	17	3	3
7	1	0	1	0	1	1	22	3	0
8	1	9	2	8	1	2	0	15	3
9	0	19	3	0	2	6	7	3	22
Subtotal[b]	24	46	46	65	62	44	65	36	33
In-migrants	7	18	7	17	4	5	10	13	14
Unemployed	11	10	6	0	6	7	5	5	6
Economically inactive with benefits	42	20	37	18	26	34	17	41	38
Economically inactive without benefits	15	6	3	0	1	9	3	5	9
Subtotal[b]	74	54	54	35	38	56	35	64	67
Total[b]	100	100	100	100	100	100	100	100	100

Note. The percentages are based on man-years. Therefore, part-time workers are reduced to full-time equivalents. This is done by multiplying the number of workers in each category by the ratio of number of workers to number of full-time jobs at the sector of destination. This can be justified because for these groups the characteristics of the sector determine the number of part-time jobs. An exception is made for the inactive persons without benefits. Now the man-years are calculated by using the ratio of number of workers to number of full-time jobs for this specific group. For this group, which consists mainly of spouses, we assume that the number of part-timers is determined by characteristics of this specific group and not by the sectoral characteristics.
[a] Sectors are 1 agriculture, 2 mining and quarrying, 3 industry, 4 electricity, gas, and water, 5 construction, 6 trade, hotels, and repair, 7 transport and communication, 8 commercial services, 9 other services.
[b] Discrepancies in the totals are caused by a cumulation of weighting and rounding errors.

3.3 *The income–consumption model*

The last part of our integrated model ties the above vacancy-chain model to the input–output equation. First, we determine the change in total consumption of employed people, viz,

$$\Delta c^{w} = (c^{q})^{T}\hat{\mathbf{W}}\Delta e + \Delta c^{w}_{ex} , \tag{17}$$

where

Δc^{w} is the change in total consumption expenditures of employed people;

c^{q} is an N-dimensional vector of average consumption quotes per industry (FNEI, 1983). The quotes depend on the average wage level per industry and account for taxes, social security premiums, and private savings.

$\hat{\mathbf{W}}$ is an N-dimensional diagonal matrix of average gross labour incomes per industry;

Δc^{w}_{ex} is the consumption change originating from changes in exogenous incomes of workers.

In our impact study we have to reckon with the fact that the extra consumption expenditure of migrants is already treated exogenously (compare section 2). Hence, that part of the change in labour incomes that accrues to migrants has to be deducted from equation (17) to avoid double counting the expenditure of migrants, because migrants who take up endogenous vacancies have already been included within exogenous final demand. So, for the purpose of our impact study equation (17) has to be replaced by

$$\Delta c^{w} = (c^{q})^{T}\hat{\mathbf{W}}(\Delta e - m) \ . \tag{18}$$

Second, we determine the decrease in total consumption expenditure of those who received unemployment benefits before they filled an endogenously created vacancy. For this category it appears that their unemployment benefits equal about 80% of the average wage of all sectors (SCPB, 1981, page 59). In line with this figure we assume that their unemployment benefits are equal to approximately 80% of the average sectoral labour income in the sector in which they become employed,

$$\Delta c^{u} = 0.80(c^{qu})^{T}\hat{\mathbf{W}}\Delta u + \Delta c^{u}_{ex} \ , \tag{19}$$

where

c^{qu} is an N-dimensional vector with consumption quotes for unemployed; these depend on the level of the former unemployment benefits $(0.80\hat{\mathbf{W}})$—hence, they are larger than the corresponding c^{q} in equation (17);

Δc^{u}_{ex} is the consumption change originating from exogenous changes in numbers of unemployed or exogenous income changes of unemployed.

Last, we have to determine the decrease in consumption expenditure of economically inactive persons with benefits. For this category an equal (subsistence) social benefit of Dfl.12 227 at 1979 prices (computed from CBS, 1980) is assumed to apply to all economically inactive persons who get a job. Because people with a subsistence benefit are assumed to be unable to save any money, the average consumption propensity that corresponds to this income will be equal to 1.

$$\Delta c^{n} = 12\,227\,\Delta n + \Delta c^{n}_{ex} ,\tag{20}$$

where Δc^{n}_{ex} is the consumption change originating from exogenous changes in the incomes of economically inactive persons and in their number.

Furthermore, we assume that, apart from their new labour incomes, migrants and economically inactive persons without benefits experience no other endogenous changes in income.

This completes our model. The structural equations of the model are equations (1)–(3), (6)–(8), and (17)–(20). Insight into the workings of the model as well as the ease of solving its structural form are improved by reducing its size.

3.4 *The solution of the integrated model*
The first step towards a solution of the model may best be taken by substituting the employment equation (2) into equations (3) and (17), respectively; and substituting equations (6) and (7) into equations (19) and (20), respectively. This leads to the following partially reduced form

$$\Delta x = A\Delta x + q^{w}\Delta c^{w} + q^{u}\Delta c^{u} + q^{n}\Delta c^{n} + \Delta f_{ex} ,\tag{1}$$

$$v = Tv + \hat{L}\Delta x - \hat{P}^{w}e_{t-1} + \Delta v_{ex} ,\tag{21}$$

$$\Delta c^{w} = (c^{q})^{T}\hat{W}(\hat{L}\Delta x - \hat{P}^{w}e_{t-1}) + \Delta c^{w}_{ex} ,\tag{22}$$

$$\Delta c^{u} = -0.80(c^{qu})^{T}\hat{W}\hat{T}^{u}v + \Delta c^{u}_{ex} ,\tag{23}$$

$$\Delta c^{n} = -12\,227(t^{n})^{T}v + \Delta c^{n}_{ex} .\tag{24}$$

Equations (1) and (21)–(24) may be written in one large matrix:

$$
\begin{array}{c}
\begin{array}{c} (1) \\ (21) \\ (22) \\ (23) \\ (24) \end{array}
\left[
\begin{array}{cc|ccc}
(I-A) & 0 & -q^{w} & -q^{u} & -q^{n} \\
-\hat{L} & (I-T) & 0 & 0 & 0 \\ \hline
-(c^{q})^{T}\hat{W}\hat{L} & 0^{T} & 1 & 0 & 0 \\
0^{T} & 0.80(c^{qu})^{T}\hat{W}\hat{T}^{u} & 0 & 1 & 0 \\
0^{T} & 12\,227(t^{n})^{T} & 0 & 0 & 1
\end{array}
\right]
\left[
\begin{array}{c}
\Delta x \\ v \\ \Delta c^{w} \\ \Delta c^{u} \\ \Delta c^{n}
\end{array}
\right]
\end{array}
$$

$$
= \left[
\begin{array}{c}
\Delta f_{ex} \\
\Delta v_{ex} - \hat{P}^{w}e_{t-1} \\
\Delta c^{w}_{ex} - (c^{q})^{T}\hat{W}\hat{P}^{w}e_{t-1} \\
\Delta c^{u}_{ex} \\
\Delta c^{n}_{ex}
\end{array}
\right]\tag{25}
$$

where the numbers on the left-hand side are the equation numbers, the numbers along the top are the dimensions of the symbols, the entries in the second column on the left-hand side are endogenous variables, and the entries in the right-hand column are exogenous and lagged endogenous variables.

The upper left-hand quadrant of the first matrix shows the direct interindustry relations. Sectors purchase each other's products ($\mathbf{A}$) and hire each other's workers ($\mathbf{T}$). The upper left-hand quadrant has, however, a block-triangular structure. Production changes influence the vacancy chains, but there does not exist a direct reverse influence. The influence of the vacancy-chain process runs via the lower left-hand quadrant, where production changes and the filling of vacancies codetermine the size and nature of regional income changes. Via the upper right-hand quadrant, the resulting changes in consumption expenditure again influence regional production levels.

The final solution of our model runs along the same lines. First, the vacancy equation (21) is substituted into equations (23) and (24). Next, equations (22)–(24) are substituted into equation (1), which gives

$$\Delta x = \mathbf{A}\Delta x + q^{\mathrm{w}}(c^{\mathrm{q}})^{\mathrm{T}}\hat{\mathbf{W}}\hat{\mathbf{L}}\Delta x - q^{\mathrm{u}}0.80(c^{\mathrm{qu}})^{\mathrm{T}}\hat{\mathbf{W}}\hat{\mathbf{T}}^{\mathrm{u}}(\mathbf{I}-\mathbf{T})^{-1}\hat{\mathbf{L}}\Delta x$$

$$- q^{\mathrm{n}}12\,227(t^{\mathrm{n}})^{\mathrm{T}}(\mathbf{I}-\mathbf{T})^{-1}\hat{\mathbf{L}}\Delta x + \Delta f_{\mathrm{ex}} + r_{\mathrm{ex}} \,, \tag{26}$$

where r_{ex} represents the exogenous and the lagged endogenous variables, that is,

$$r_{\mathrm{ex}} = q^{\mathrm{w}}[\Delta c_{\mathrm{ex}}^{\mathrm{w}} - (c^{\mathrm{q}})^{\mathrm{T}}\hat{\mathbf{W}}\hat{\mathbf{P}}^{\mathrm{w}}e_{t-1}] + q^{\mathrm{u}}[\Delta c_{\mathrm{ex}}^{\mathrm{u}}$$

$$+ 0.80(c^{\mathrm{qu}})^{\mathrm{T}}\hat{\mathbf{W}}\hat{\mathbf{T}}^{\mathrm{u}}(\mathbf{I}-\mathbf{T})^{-1}(\hat{\mathbf{P}}^{\mathrm{w}}e_{t-1} - \Delta v_{\mathrm{ex}})]$$

$$+ q^{\mathrm{n}}[\Delta c_{\mathrm{ex}}^{\mathrm{n}} + 12\,227(t^{\mathrm{n}})^{\mathrm{T}}(\mathbf{I}-\mathbf{T})^{-1}(\hat{\mathbf{P}}^{\mathrm{w}}e_{t-1} - \Delta v_{\mathrm{ex}})] \,. \tag{27}$$

Equation (26) is easily solved:

$$\Delta x = [\mathbf{I}-\mathbf{A} - q^{\mathrm{w}}(c^{\mathrm{q}})^{\mathrm{T}}\hat{\mathbf{W}}\hat{\mathbf{L}} + q^{\mathrm{u}}0.80(c^{\mathrm{qu}})^{\mathrm{T}}\hat{\mathbf{W}}\hat{\mathbf{T}}^{\mathrm{u}}(\mathbf{I}-\mathbf{T})^{-1}\hat{\mathbf{L}}$$

$$+ q^{\mathrm{n}}12\,227(t^{\mathrm{n}})^{\mathrm{T}}(\mathbf{I}-\mathbf{T})^{-1}\hat{\mathbf{L}}]^{-1}(\Delta f_{\mathrm{ex}} + r_{\mathrm{ex}})$$

$$\equiv (\mathbf{I}-\mathbf{A} - \mathbf{Q}^{\mathrm{w}} + \mathbf{Q}^{\mathrm{u}} + \mathbf{Q}^{\mathrm{n}})^{-1}(\Delta f_{\mathrm{ex}} + r_{\mathrm{ex}}) \,, \tag{28}$$

where $\mathbf{Q}^{\mathrm{w}}$, $\mathbf{Q}^{\mathrm{u}}$, and $\mathbf{Q}^{\mathrm{n}}$ are defined implicitly in equation (28).

With equation (28) all other model equations may be solved by subsequent substitution. The solutions for employment and endogenous in-migration of workers, for instance [compare equations (2) and (5)] have the following forms:

$$\Delta e = \hat{\mathbf{L}}(\mathbf{I}-\mathbf{A} - \mathbf{Q}^{\mathrm{w}} + \mathbf{Q}^{\mathrm{u}} + \mathbf{Q}^{\mathrm{n}})^{-1}(\Delta f_{\mathrm{ex}} + r_{\mathrm{ex}}) - \hat{\mathbf{P}}^{\mathrm{w}}e_{t-1} \,, \tag{29}$$

$$m = \hat{\mathbf{T}}^{\mathrm{m}}(\mathbf{I}-\mathbf{T})^{-1}\hat{\mathbf{L}}(\mathbf{I}-\mathbf{A} - \mathbf{Q}^{\mathrm{w}} + \mathbf{Q}^{\mathrm{u}} + \mathbf{Q}^{\mathrm{n}})^{-1}(\Delta f_{\mathrm{ex}} + r_{\mathrm{ex}})$$

$$+ \hat{\mathbf{T}}^{\mathrm{m}}(\mathbf{I}-\mathbf{T})^{-1}(\Delta v_{\mathrm{ex}} - \hat{\mathbf{P}}^{\mathrm{w}}e_{t-1}) \,. \tag{30}$$

Finally, we will evaluate the empirical significance of our more elaborate treatment of the way in which regional income increases are influenced by the functioning of the labour market and the social security system. This will be done by comparing the normalised employment multipliers.

Table 4. Normalised regional employment multipliers for twenty-eight sectors for the northern Netherlands.

SIC[a]	Classical models		type 2	Our models	excluding migration
	type 1			general	
	1975	1979			
0	1.35	1.28	1.65	1.44	1.40
19	1.22	1.65	2.69	2.22	1.93
20.1 – 20.2	4.84	5.37	6.83	6.00	5.83
20.3 – 21.3	1.97	1.92	2.44	2.16	2.09
21.4 – 21.7	1.29	1.40	1.89	1.61	1.55
22	1.10	1.07	1.24	1.14	1.11
23 – 24	1.06	1.07	1.42	1.17	1.13
25	1.18	1.18	1.48	1.30	1.26
26	1.45	1.52	1.98	1.72	1.66
27	1.30	1.28	1.59	1.41	1.37
12,28	1.58	1.47	1.88	1.68	1.61
29 – 31	1.22	1.28	1.73	1.49	1.42
32	1.18	1.15	1.43	1.28	1.24
33	1.55	1.43	1.92	1.70	1.60
34 – 35	1.15	1.15	1.44	1.27	1.23
36	1.29	1.28	1.63	1.45	1.40
37	1.27	1.26	1.55	1.38	1.34
38 – 39	1.07	1.11	1.50	1.25	1.20
40	1.10	1.14	1.61	1.45	1.25
51 – 52	1.27	1.28	1.64	1.42	1.38
6	1.13	1.13	1.47	1.27	1.23
7	1.13	1.13	1.46	1.30	1.22
81 – 82	1.28	1.26	1.58	1.43	1.36
83 – 85	1.30	1.30	1.73	1.50	1.42
93	1.09	1.08	1.35	1.21	1.16
95 – 96	1.09	1.10	1.49	1.29	1.21
9	1.01	1.01	1.28	1.11	1.05
PGS	1.20	1.15	1.47	1.33	1.27

[a]SIC Standard Industrial Classification; see table 1 for definition of industries; PGS paid government services.

Note: The employment coefficients for 1975 ($\hat{\mathbf{L}}$) are directly derived from FNEI (1983). The available coefficients for 1979 only relate to wage-earner employment (CBS, 1983b). They have been augmented by the national ratio of number of self-employed and wage earners to number of wage earners. In the case of agriculture and trade the northern 1975 ratios are slightly decreased in accordance with the national decrease for those industries. The other regional ratios are held constant because the national change is negligible. Normalised regional employment multipliers reflect the total change in regional employment divided by the direct change in employment corresponding to a change in exogenous final demand.

Type 1 multiplier $= \hat{\mathbf{I}}^{\mathrm{T}}(\mathbf{I} - \mathbf{A})^{-1}\hat{\mathbf{L}}^{-1}$; type 2 multiplier $= \hat{\mathbf{I}}^{\mathrm{T}}(\mathbf{I} - \mathbf{A} - \mathbf{Q}^{\mathrm{w}})^{-1}\hat{\mathbf{L}}^{-1}$.

Our general model multiplier $= \hat{\mathbf{I}}^{\mathrm{T}}(\mathbf{I} - \mathbf{A} - \mathbf{Q}^{\mathrm{w}} + \mathbf{Q}^{\mathrm{u}} + \mathbf{Q}^{\mathrm{n}})^{-1}\hat{\mathbf{L}}^{-1}$.

Our migration impact model multiplier $= \hat{\mathbf{I}}^{\mathrm{T}}(\mathbf{I} - \mathbf{A} - \mathbf{Q}^{\mathrm{w}} + \mathbf{Q}^{\mathrm{u}} + \mathbf{Q}^{\mathrm{n}} + \mathbf{Q}^{\mathrm{m}})^{-1}\hat{\mathbf{L}}^{-1}$.

Before we do so, the importance of a correct estimation of the employment coefficients ($\hat{L}$) needs to be emphasised. The first two columns of table 4 show the so-called type 1 multipliers as calculated with employment coefficients for 1975 (the year from which the input–output table stems) and 1979 (the year of our case study), respectively. It is clear that the differential growth of prices and of labour productivity between various industries is of great empirical significance and should not therefore be neglected.

Next, the traditional so-called type 1 and type 2 multipliers may be compared (compare Richardson, 1972). Table 4 shows that the indirect and induced effects (type 2) are one to five times as high as the indirect effects (type 1) only. This is not surprising, as the type 2 multiplier incorrectly assumes that all new jobs are being filled up by migrants (see Oosterhaven, 1981, chapter 6).

Now, we turn to the multipliers from our general model [equation (29)]. Our multipliers lie roughly halfway between the type 1 and type 2 multipliers. The empirical reasons for this result may be found in table 3 and equations (19) and (20). Directly or indirectly [that is, $(\hat{T}^m + \hat{T}^r)(I - T)^{-1}$] only a small fraction of the new jobs are taken up by migrants and people without benefits. A larger proportion are directly or indirectly taken up by unemployed and by formerly economically inactive persons [that is $(\hat{T}^u + \hat{T}^n)(I - T)^{-1}$] who lose unemployment and subsistence benefits, respectively.

Next, we turn to the variant of the general model that is specifically designed for estimation of the expenditure effects of in-migrants.

4 Economic effects of the consumption of in-migrants

To estimate impacts of the consumption expenditure of migrants into the north, solutions (28) or (29) are not adequate. First, we are not interested in the effects of other exogenous or lagged endogenous variables. Hence, the r_{ex} vector in equation (26) is set equal to $\boldsymbol{0}$. Second, and more importantly, the consumption effects of endogenous in-migrants are double counted in equation (17). Hence, we have to use equation (18). These two adaptations to our more general model result in the following purpose-specific impact model [compare equations (28) and (29)]:

$$\Delta x = (I - A - Q^w + Q^u + Q^n + Q^m)^{-1}\Delta f_{\text{ex}}\,, \tag{31}$$

$$\Delta e = \hat{L}(I - A - Q^w + Q^u + Q^n + Q^m)^{-1}\Delta f_{\text{ex}}\,, \tag{32}$$

where Q^m corrects for double counting, since

$$Q^m = q^w(c^q)^{\text{T}}\hat{W}\hat{T}^m(I - T)^{-1}\hat{L}\,. \tag{33}$$

Here it should be remembered that equation (9) still holds. This implies that

$$(t^u + t^n + t^r + t^m)^{\text{T}}(I - T)^{-1} = i^{\text{T}}(I - T)(I - T)^{-1} = i^{\text{T}}\,, \tag{34}$$

that is, all (new) jobs are either directly or indirectly filled by unemployed economically inactive persons (with and without benefits) and migrants (see table 3 for their direct shares). Hence $\mathbf{Q}^m$ forms a direct, although sectorally different, proportion of $\mathbf{Q}^w$. The last column of table 4 shows the significance of subtracting the influence of endogenous consumption expenditure of migrants. All employment multipliers for our migration-impact model are slightly lower than the multipliers from our general model.

Besides employment effects and employment multipliers, *income* effects and income multipliers may also be calculated. This is simply done through replacing Δe and $\hat{\mathbf{L}}$ in equation (32) by the change in regional income and the income/production ratios per regional industry, respectively.

Next, the exogenous expenditure of the eleven different categories of migrants are calculated for twenty-eight industries for each family type by multiplying the total consumption per family by the number of families and the corresponding q vectors, which are all derived in section 2. These results are substituted in the income-generation equation [compare equation (32)]. Table 5 summarises the results of this operation. It appears that Dfl.249.9 million of migrants' consumption demand (inclusive of nonpaid government services) causes total regional value added to rise by Dfl.157.6 million. Per guilder of expenditure on northern products, the regional income effect of students and school-leavers and large families with heads with medium education is clearly larger than that of the other categories of migrants.

Table 5. Endogenous income effects (in millions of guilders) due to the expenditure of migrants into the north of the Netherlands in 1979.

Family type[a]	Exog. final demand[b]	Endogenous effects on			Total value added effect	Total as % of exog. effect[e]
		gross wages	social security[c]	incomes and deprec.[d]		
Working head						
1	18.9	4.9	1.4	4.6	10.9	58
2	44.1	12.4	3.8	10.5	26.7	61
3	34.9	11.1	3.5	7.5	22.1	63
4	49.9	15.6	4.9	12.9	33.4	67
5	45.8	13.7	4.2	10.6	28.5	62
Subtotal	193.6	57.7	17.8	46.1	121.6	63
Student head	25.7	8.5	2.7	6.0	17.2	67
Inactive head	30.6	8.9	2.7	7.2	18.8	61
Total	249.9	75.1	23.2	59.3	157.6	63

[a] See table 1 for full description of types of family.
[b] Exogenous final demand on products produced in the north (compare table 1).
[c] Employers' premiums for social security.
[d] Remaining incomes and depreciation.
[e] Total endogenous effect as percentage of exogenous final demand.

The results of the substitution of the same eleven Δf_{ex} vectors into equation (32) are shown in table 6. In 1979 the consumption demand of 6642 migrating families (16500 persons) caused an extra regional employment of 2421 man-years. Obviously, large families with heads with a higher education induce relatively more endogenous employment. The largest part of this employment effect is created in the service industries, which is not too surprising as it concerns the impacts of consumption expenditure. The second largest part is created in the form of government employment, of which only a small part depends on the purchasing power of the migrant. The largest part of this government employment depends on provision of collective services related to population size (compare table 2).

In fact, part of the assumed exogenous inflow of migrant workers is endogenously induced by the consumption demand of the remaining migrants. The endogenous consumption of endogenously caused migration [compare equation (5)] is Dfl.13.5 million, that is, about 5% of total exogenous final demand due to migration. This also implies that roughly about 5% (that is, 260) of the 5061 incoming labour migrants fill jobs created through the expenditure of the remaining migrants.

Table 6. Endogenous employment effects (in man-years) of the expenditure of migrants to the north of the Netherlands in 1979.

Family type[a]	Number of in-migrant families	Endogenous effects on			Total employment effect	Total per 100 exogenous families
		goods sector[b]	service sector	public sector		
Working head						
1	779	21	123	25	169	22
2	1137	52	268	90	409	36
3	724	41	190	115	347	30
4	918	58	287	150	496	54
5	729	52	277	115	444	61
Subtotal	4287	224	1145	496	1865	43
Student head	1466	27	160	81	268	18
Inactive head	889	38	176	74	288	32
Total	6642	289	1481	651	2421	36

[a]See table 1 for full description of types of family.
[b]Primary and secondary sectors, SIC 0–5.

5 Conclusions

As mentioned in the introduction, we have a special interest in the relation between migration and (un)employment. In the foregoing sections, a methodological framework is developed for one of these relations, viz, the production, income, and employment effects of consumption demand of in-migrants. This framework is then applied to the northern Netherlands, a region characterised by relatively high unemployment rates and net in-migration.

The model used is of the demoeconomic type. The economic system is modelled in the input–output tradition. A traditional input–output model with a consumption function is extended with a public sector which accounts for changes in government production arising from changes in the size of the population and with a labour-market model which makes it possible to reckon with sectoral wage differentials and feedbacks with the social security system.

The labour-market submodel explicitly uses information on the filling of vacancies. This process is modelled with a Markov-chain approach applied at the industry level of the input–output model. It reckons with vacancies being filled by workers from regional industries, in-migrants and local unemployed of three types. First, unemployed with unemployment benefits which depend on former labour incomes, second, unemployed with subsistence inactive person benefits and, third, unemployed who were inactive without benefits. The final part of the model ties the changes in labour-market status of different population groups to the corresponding changes in their consumption expenditures.

Our general model is slightly adapted to estimate the impacts of migrants' consumption demand. In 1979, 6642 families entered the northern region of the Netherlands, embodying 16 500 individuals of which 5061 became employed in the region[1]. Their consumption demand caused a rise in final demand of Dfl.250 million. By means of our combined input–output/labour-market model we estimated that this expenditure led to the creation of 2421 man-years of employment.

In table 7 the employment effects of the consumption demand of *all* migrants are compared with the increase in labour supply from *in-migration*. Hence, we compare the indirect employment effects of expenditure of the average mix of in-migrants with the direct labour-supply effects of migrants entering the region. The results indicate that when *two* employed migrants (plus four not employed) enter the north this leads to the creation of *one* additional job in the north. Of these additional jobs, 90% are filled by native job seekers. The remaining 10% are filled by endogenously induced migrants. From table 7 it is obvious that the demand, as well as the supply effects of migration, are heavily concentrated in the service sector and in the public sector.

The foregoing leads to the conclusion that average in-migration increased employment and lowered unemployment in the north in 1979. It should be

---

[1]The figure of 5061 embodies all persons (heads and other family members) who belong to the labour force, minus the unemployed. By means of industry-specific ratios of full-time equivalents to part-time jobs, the 5061 persons correspond to the 4796 man-years of employment shown in table 7 (see also the first note of table 3).

stressed that our positive conclusion with regard to the economic consequences of in-migration is related to the *total migration* to the northern region of the Netherlands in 1979. The effects of course differ strongly for the various types of migrant families with which we have dealt. The 779 employed single people, for instance, create only 169 man-years of employment. Inactive persons and students, on the other hand, have a more favourable effect because they do not fill any jobs at all.

Table 7. Employment effects per sector of in-migration to the north of the Netherlands in 1979.

Sector	Employment effects due to migrants' expenditure (man-years) (1)	Number of migrants who found a job (man-years) (2)	(1) as percentage of (2)
Agriculture	76	142	54
Industry	123	887	14
Construction	90	480	19
Services	1481	3287	45
Government	651		
Total	2421	4796	51

The policy implications of this conclusion are that a policy of stimulating migration to problem regions will in general equalise regional unemployment differences. This will especially be the case when a migration policy is selective. Actual Dutch policy encourages the migration to the north of workers who fill jobs for which no natives are available, hence, for which no preemption occurs. Stimulating the in-migration of unemployed workers or workers who crowd out natives will negatively affect the regional economy because the positive indirect expenditure effect is more than offset by the negative direct effect on unemployment. A possible successful extension of the present policy may be the stimulation of in-migration to the north of inactive persons, such as students, retired people and, as was suggested recently, prisoners.

Acknowledgements. We gratefully acknowledge the help of Ronald Stoffelsma for gathering and compiling the consumption data and for research assistance. Because of space limitations only limited information about the data is given. More details are available from the authors upon request. This research has been supported by a grant from the Regiopool of the University of Groningen.

References
Batey P W J, 1985, "Input–output models for regional demographic–economic analysis: some structural comparisons" *Environment and Planning A* **17** 73–99
CBS, 1980 *Sociale Maandstatistiek* (Bulletin of Social Statistics) Central Bureau of Statistics (CBS, Voorburg)
CBS, 1981 *Nationale Rekeningen 1979* (National Accounts) Central Bureau of Statistics (Staatsuitgeverij, The Hague)

CBS, 1982 *Regionale Input–Output Tabellen 1975* (Regional Input–Output Tables) Central Bureau of Statistics (Staatsuitgeverij, The Hague)

CBS, 1983a, "Arbeidskrachtentelling 1979" (Labour Force Survey) Central Bureau of Statistics (Staatsuitgeverij, The Hague)

CBS, 1983b *Regionale Economische Jaarcijfers 1979* (Annual Regional Economics Figures) Central Bureau of Statistics (Staatsuitgeverij, The Hague)

CBS, 1984, "Budgetonderzoek 1978–1981" (Budget Survey) Central Bureau of Statistics (CBS, Voorburg)

Clark W A V, 1982 *Progress in Planning, Volume 18, Part 1. Recent Research on Migration and Mobility: A Review and Interpretation* (Pergamon Press, Oxford)

CPB, 1981 *REGAM* (Regional Labour Market Model) Central Planning Bureau (CPB, The Hague)

Dahlberg A, Holmlund B, 1978, "The interaction of migration, income, and employment in Sweden" *Demography* **15** 259–266

FNEI, 1983 *De constructie van de Input–Output Tabel Noorden 1975* (The construction of an input–output table for the North) Federation of Northern Economic Institutes (FNEI, Groningen)

Grais B, 1983 *Lay-offs and Short-time Working in Selected OECD Countries* (OECD, Paris)

Greenwood M J, 1975, "Research on internal migration in the United States: a survey" *Journal of Economic Literature* **13** 397–433

Greenwood M J, 1981 *Migration and Economic Growth in the US: National, Regional and Metropolitan Perspectives* (Academic Press, New York)

Muth R F, 1971, "Migration: chicken or egg?" *Southern Economic Journal* **37** 295–306

Oosterhaven J, 1981 *Interregional Input–Output Analysis and Dutch Regional Policy Problems* (Gower, Aldershot, Hants)

Oosterhaven J, 1984, "Dutch regional and multiregional interindustry tables" RM 160, Faculty of Economics, State University of Groningen, Groningen, The Netherlands

Oosterhaven J, Folmer H, 1983, "Review and evaluation of Dutch regional socio-economic policy" in *Dilemmas in Regional policy* Eds A Kuklinski, J G Lambooy (Mouton, The Hague) pp 227–244

Oosterhaven J, Stol K, 1984, "De positie van het Noorden in het stimuleringsbeleid en het ontwikkelingsbeleid" (The position of the North with regard to regional economic policy in The Netherlands) RM 144, Faculty of Economics, State University of Groningen, Groningen, The Netherlands

Richardson H W, 1972 *Input–Output and Regional Economics* (Weidenfeld and Nicolson, London)

Richardson H W, 1978 *Regional and Urban Economics* (Penguin Books, Harmondsworth, Middx)

Rogerson P, MacKinnon R D, 1981, "A geographical model of job search, migration and unemployment" *Papers of the Regional Science Association* **48** 89–102

Salvatore D, 1984, "An econometric model of internal migration and development: extensions and tests" *Regional Science and Urban Economics* **14** 77–88

SCPB, 1981 *Profijt van de Overheid in 1977* (Gain of public policy) Social-Cultural Planning Bureau (Staatsuitgeverij, The Hague)

SCPB, 1983 *Profijt van de Overheid* Social-Cultural Planning Bureau (SCPB, Rijswijk)

Sjaastad L A, 1962, "The costs and returns of human migration" *Journal of Political Economy* **70** 80–93

Steinnes D M, 1978, "Causality and migration: a statistical resolution of the 'chicken or egg' fowl up" *Southern Economic Journal* **45** 218–226

Van Dijk J, Bartels C P A, 1982, "Internal labour migration and its effects on regional labour markets in The Netherlands" paper presented at the 22nd European Congress of the Regional Science Association, RM 109, Faculty of Economics, State University of Groningen, Groningen, The Netherlands

Van Dijk J, Folmer H, 1985, "Entry of unemployed into employment: theory, methodology and Dutch experience" *Regional Studies* **19** 243–256

Van Dijk J, Folmer H, 1986, "The consequences of interregional migration for the regional labour market: theory, methodology and Dutch experience" *Review of Economics and Statistics* (forthcoming)

Van Weeren H, Van Praag B M S, 1984, "The inequality of actual incomes and earning capacities between households in Europe" *European Economic Review* **24** 239–256

APPENDIX

Table A1. Consumption expenditure by five types of migrant families whose head belongs to the labour force, for twenty-eight industries in the north of the Netherlands in 1979 (in ‰ of private total spending).

SIC[a]	Type of migrant family[b]					Total[c]
	1	2	3	4	5	
0	7.6	9.2	10.8	10.9	9.9	9.7
19	0.2	0.1	0.1	0.1	0.1	0.1
20.1–20.2	13.2	18.3	24.3	19.7	15.5	18.2
20.3–21.3	9.3	11.5	16.6	15.0	11.4	12.7
21.4–21.7	2.1	2.5	2.6	2.1	1.8	2.2
22	0.1	0.0	0.1	0.0	0.0	0.0
23–24	1.4	1.5	1.8	1.7	1.4	1.5
25	2.5	1.8	1.9	1.5	2.3	2.0
26	0.0	0.0	0.0	0.0	0.0	0.0
27	6.1	4.5	3.7	3.6	4.0	4.4
12,28	0.0	0.0	0.0	0.0	0.0	0.0
29–31	0.5	0.5	0.5	0.6	0.4	0.5
32	0.7	0.8	0.7	0.7	0.7	0.8
33	0.0	0.0	0.0	0.0	0.0	0.0
34–35	0.1	0.1	0.1	0.1	0.1	0.1
36	0.4	0.4	0.3	0.3	0.3	0.4
37	0.5	0.5	0.4	0.5	0.5	0.5
38–39	0.1	0.0	0.1	0.1	0.1	0.1
40	31.7	34.3	37.6	34.3	32.6	34.1
51–52	14.4	14.9	12.9	15.4	14.5	14.5
6	148.4	138.5	143.8	139.7	128.2	139.7
7	48.1	44.4	35.4	36.6	41.6	41.4
81–82	0.9	1.2	0.9	1.2	1.2	1.1
83–85	131.6	129.9	111.7	118.0	140.8	126.5
93	72.5	76.9	70.6	69.7	57.4	70.2
95–96	58.6	64.8	57.0	60.4	72.2	62.7
9	33.4	29.7	36.2	45.5	48.3	38.0
PGS	19.9	21.6	20.2	19.0	20.4	20.3
Subtotals						
northern industries[d]	604	608	590	597	606	606
value added tax	78.8	77.0	79.6	79.1	76.4	78.1
import from other countries	121.1	116.9	125.1	123.8	115.2	120.2
import from rest of the Netherlands	194.8	199.1	201.3	199.4	198.9	198.7
Total private consumption expenditure[d]	1000	1000	1000	1000	1000	1000
Northern public government services[e]	94.1	176.3	354.3	310.6	235.1	230.2
Grand total[d]	1094	1176	1354	1311	1235	1230

[a]SIC Standard Industrial Classification; PGS paid government services.
[b]1 single person families; 2 families of two persons; 3 three or more persons, head with low level of education; 4 three or more persons, head with medium level of education; 5 three or more persons, head with high level of education.
[c]Weighted average of 1 to 5. The shares of each type of migrant family are used as weights.
[d]Discrepancies in totals caused by a cumulation of weighting and rounding errors.
[e]For which no direct payments are required.

Socioeconomic Impact Models: A Review of Analytical Methods and Policy Implications

F L LEISTRITZ
North Dakota State University, Fargo
R A CHASE
University of Wisconsin, Madison
S H MURDOCK
Texas A and M University, College Station

1 Introduction

Large-scale resource and industrial development projects are having profound effects on many rural areas in the western United States of America. These developments present both opportunities and problems for the areas where they are located. Although resource and industrial development projects offer the benefits of new jobs and provide a stimulus to the local economy, they also may lead to rapid population growth—frequently creating problems that many rural communities are not prepared to manage effectively. Because large projects sometimes have profound effects on small rural communities (for example, doubling or trebling of population in only a few years), policymakers and planners have accorded high priority to estimating the economic, demographic, public service, and fiscal effects (often termed *socioeconomic impacts*) of such large-scale projects in advance of their development. Such socioeconomic impact assessments have come to serve as a basis for federal and state policy decisions concerning the location, scale, and timing of such projects (for example, federal mineral leasing and state plant-permitting decisions) and as a basis for state and local planning to cope with the effects of these developments (Murdock and Leistritz, 1979; Leistritz and Murdock, 1981; Gilmore et al, 1982; Leistritz et al, 1983).

Meaningful assessment of the economic, demographic, public service, and fiscal impacts of large-scale development projects requires that important interactions among these impact categories be taken into account. In addition, each of these aspects of socioeconomic impact assessment may require a large number of very precise calculations. Because the sheer volume of these calculations can become quite burdensome, it has become increasingly attractive to systematise the computational procedures. In response to the need to account more systematically for interrelationships among the various impact categories and to provide for integration of impact-assessment techniques, many analysts have attempted to develop comprehensive models which incorporate a number of impact dimensions and provide for specific linkages among these impact categories (Murdock and Leistritz, 1980).

Other important factors influencing the development of socioeconomic impact-assessment techniques are the needs of decisionmakers. Local decisionmakers, in particular, not only want specific answers; they want timely ones. A characteristic of large-scale projects is the frequency of changes in factors central to the determination of local socioeconomic impacts, such as alterations in construction schedules and changes in workforce requirements (Gilmore et al, 1982). As a result, impact projections must be updated frequently if they are to remain meaningful as guides for impact mitigation and growth-management planning. In recognition of this need, impact-monitoring requirements have been incorporated into the permitting process of several regulatory agencies, and these monitoring systems often include capabilities for impact-assessment updating (Leistritz and Chase, 1982). As a result of the volatility which appears to be inherent in many types of development plans, then, decisionmakers and planners have increasingly demanded impact assessments and impact-assessment methods that provide local area projections for a wide range of socio-economic factors under a variety of possible development scenarios and that do so with only a limited time delay in the preparation of such projections (Leistritz and Murdock, 1981).

In response to these demands, a substantial number of computerised socioeconomic assessment models have been developed. These models all provide a relatively wide range of outputs and do so in a timely and flexible manner. Further, they provide a valuable mechanism for systematically accounting for interactions among the various impact dimensions. Such models thus represent the result of a concerted effort to develop methods that provide integrated analyses of regional systems and of the response of such systems to major exogenous forces. It is unfortunate, therefore, that there have been few attempts to integrate the lessons learned from these efforts at model development into the mainstream of the regional science literature. Few of these models have been described in professional journals, and information concerning the design and capabilities of such systems is available largely in scattered reports of limited circulation which are frequently quite difficult to access. Our aim, then, is to identify, compare, and evaluate a number of these socioeconomic modelling systems and thus to provide at least an initial assessment of the state of the art in this significant area of regional analysis.

The purpose of this paper is to review the structure and historical development of such modelling systems in the USA and to evaluate a number of existing US socioeconomic assessment models in terms of their analytical methodology and utilisation in the policy process. To do this adequately, it is necessary to understand the basic structure and capabilities of such systems and the historical context of their development and to compare and contrast key features of several typical models. Thus, the remainder of the paper is organised into five sections. First, an overview of the general structural features of such models is presented in section 2.

Second, the history of development of socioeconomic assessment models in the USA is briefly described. In the fourth section, criteria for model evaluation are discussed, and in the fifth section, selected models are compared and evaluated on the basis of the criteria discussed earlier. Finally, in a concluding discussion we summarise positive and normative aspects of impact modelling and present recommendations for improving modelling performance.

2 Overview of model structure

Although socioeconomic assessment models differ substantially with respect to their input-data requirements, computational procedures, specific forms of output, and many other aspects, many are quite similar in overall structure and in the general categories of impacts they predict. An overview of the major components typically found in socioeconomic impact assessment systems is provided in figure 1. Such models generally include, at a minimum, an economic impact module, a demographic module, and a component to reconcile projections of labour supply and demand (variously known as economic–demographic interface or labour-market simulation modules). In addition, many socioeconomic impact-modelling systems include a residential allocation module to distribute population changes from the regional or county level to individual towns or other jurisdictions. Some systems also contain modules which project both changes in public service and facility requirements and effects on the costs and revenues of various local jurisdictions (counties, towns, and school districts).

The general types of data-input requirements, estimation methods, and outputs associated with each component of such modelling systems are also shown in figure 1. Examination of this figure reveals that most economic impact modules utilise one of three alternative estimation methods: employment multipliers, income multipliers, or input–output coefficients. Similarly, demographic modules generally utilise some form of cohort-survival method or use employment–population ratios. The techniques utilised in the economic–demographic interface (or labour-market simulation) components of these models are not as readily categorised as those used in the economic and demographic modules. In general, however, the procedures used in these components represent an attempt to estimate: (1) the proportion of new project-related jobs that will be filled by local residents and (2) distinctions among various classes of project-related jobs (for example, construction, operations, secondary) with respect both to demographic profiles of migrating workers and to the potential for local recruitment. (For a more detailed discussion of these characteristics, see Leistritz and Murdock, 1981.) In comparing, contrasting, and evaluating such systems, it is helpful to keep in mind these general characteristics.

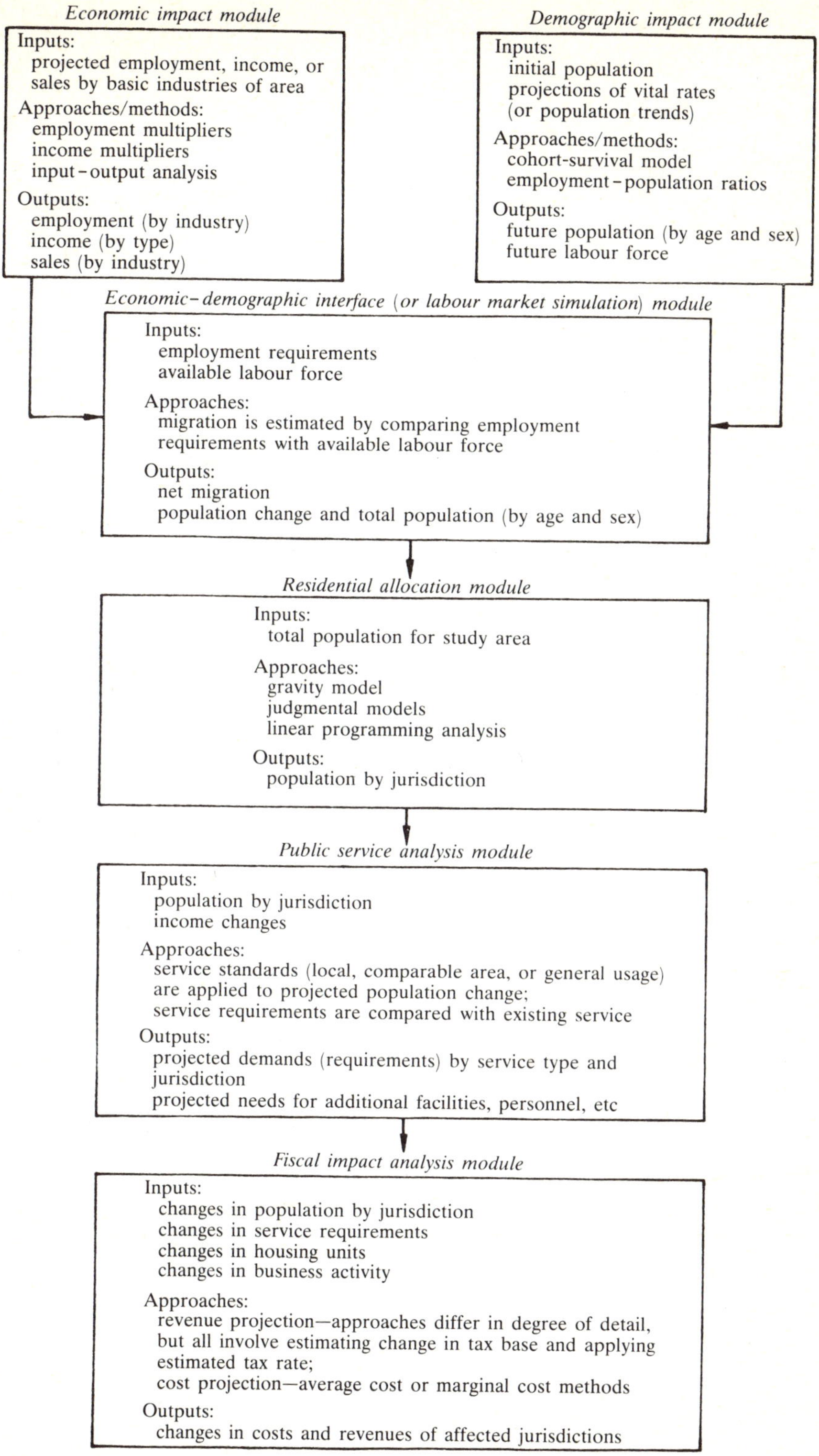

Figure 1. Major components of socioeconomic impact-assessment systems.

3 Historical background of socioeconomic assessment models

The basic techniques for economic and demographic impact assessment
have been developed and refined over a considerable period in the USA.
During the 1960s, however, there was growing recognition of the inter-
dependence of various forces and hence an increasing interest in finding
ways of taking such interdependencies into account. During the same
period, the capability for developing more complex models which would
integrate multiple dimensions was greatly enhanced by the increasing power
and availability of electronic computers. Early work emphasised both
developing more complete detailed models for single dimensions (for
example, economic, demographic) and attempting to integrate various
dimensions (for example, economic activity and population, population and
land use). Early activity in social science modelling was concentrated in
the areas of national econometric models and urban land-use models. By
the end of that decade, however, some attention had been given both to
(1) integration of the economic and demographic areas of study and
(2) application of integrated economic–demographic models in rural areas.

One regional economic–demographic model which was developed
during the late 1960s had a substantial influence on subsequent socioeconomic modelling efforts. The Susquehanna River Basin Model differed
from most earlier models by providing for a specific linkage of the economic
and demographic sectors and by including nonmetropolitan areas whereas
previous models had generally focused only on a single large city (Hamilton
et al, 1969). The model made extensive use of feedback loops to link its
various components, a structure which was inspired at least in part by the
earlier work of Forrester (1961).

The research group at Battelle Laboratories which developed the
Susquehanna Model subsequently constructed similar models for the City
of San Diego (San Diego Comprehensive Planning Organization, 1972)
and for the State of Arizona (Battelle Columbus Laboratories, 1973). The
Susquehanna Model also influenced the structure of a regional forecasting
model developed by the Tennessee Valley Authority (Bohm and Lord,
1972). These models, in turn, influenced subsequent model development
efforts (see figure 2). Notable among these were the series of economic–
demographic models developed by the states of Arizona (ATOM—Arizona
Environmental and Econometric Trade-Off Model) and Utah (UPED—
Utah Process Economic and Demographic Impact Model) (Bigler et al,
1972; Anderson et al, 1974; Reeve and Weaver, 1974; Beckhelm et al,
1975; Anderson and Hannigan, 1977), the MULTIREGION Model
developed at Oak Ridge National Laboratory (Olsen et al, 1977), the North
Platte River Basin Model (Matson and Studer, 1975; Carlson et al, 1976),
and the CPE (Colorado Population–Employment) Model developed at the
University of Colorado (Office of the State Oil Shale Coordinator, 1974).

These models all provided for a linkage between the economic and demographic components through a submodel which simulated the operation of the labour market and provided for in-migration or out-migration from the study area in response to changes in labour-market conditions (that is, if the demand for labour increased more rapidly than the 'natural increase' in labour supply, in-migration would occur). The models differed somewhat in the degree of sectoral disaggregation within the economic module, however. For example, whereas the Susquehanna Model utilised only three employment categories, the ATOM-3 Model included eighty-eight employment sectors. The models also differed in the degree of spatial detail of their outputs, with some providing employment and population projections at the county level (for example, ATOM,

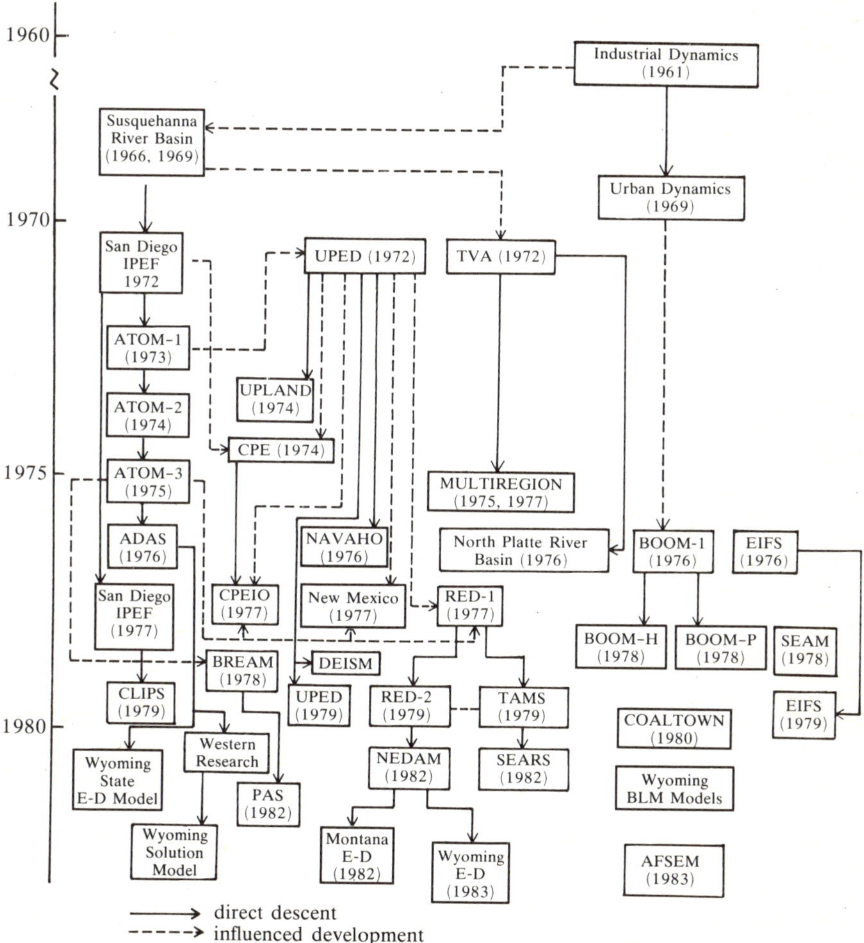

Figure 2. Historical development of socioeconomic impact-assessment models.

UPED, CPE), and others providing projections only at the multicounty
regional level (for example, Susquehanna, MULTIREGION). Last, these
models differed significantly in the time increments associated with their
projections. A few models provided projections annually (for example,
ATOM-3), but several produced estimates only at five-year intervals (for
example, UPED, MULTIREGION).

Socioeconomic projection models developed during the late 1960s and
early 1970s were employed primarily as tools for state and regional
economic planning. As interest in evaluating community-specific impacts
of major projects grew, however, these models were found to have
substantial limitations as impact-assessment tools. The two principal
limitations were failure to include a number of significant impact dimensions,
particularly public service requirements and fiscal effects, and insufficient
spatial and temporal disaggregation of outputs. Thus, in the mid-1970s,
attention turned to developing models which incorporated additional
impact dimensions and provided outputs at county and subcounty levels.
A number of models were developed to meet these needs, including RED-1
and RED-2 [REAP (Regional Environmental Assessment Program)
Economic–Demographic; Hertsgaard et al, 1978; Leistritz et al, 1979];
BREAM (Bureau of Reclamation Economic Assessment Model; Mountain
West Research Inc., 1978); the BOOM models (Ford, 1976; Monts,
1978; Rink and Ford, 1978); SEAM (Social and Economic Assessment
Model; Stenehjem, 1978); WEST (Denver Research Institute, 1979); and
SIMPACT (Huston, 1979).

These 'second-generation' models differ from the earlier economic–
demographic projection models primarily in the number of impact categories
included and in the degree of spatial and temporal disaggregation of their
outputs. Thus, several of these models address public-service requirements
and public-sector cost and revenue effects as well as economic and demographic impacts (for example, RED, WEST, SIMPACT); some provide
projections for individual cities, school districts, or other subcounty areas
as well as for counties and regions (for example, BREAM, RED, WEST);
and most provide annual projections of key impact indicators.

Since about 1979, the emphasis has been on model refinement and update. Only two essentially 'new' models, COALTOWN (Bender et al, 1980)
and AFSEM (Air Force System Evaluation Model; URS-Berger, 1983),
have appeared during this period, but new versions of several earlier
systems have been developed. Examples of this group include UPED 79
(an update of UPED; Weaver et al, 1980), PAS (Planning and Assessment
System, from BREAM; Mountain West Research–Southwest Inc., 1982),
NEDAM (North Dakota Economic–Demographic Assessment Model),
TAMS (Texas Assessment Modeling System; Murdock et al, 1979), and
SEARS (Socio-Economic Analysis of Repository Siting) (from the earlier
RED models; Hamm et al, 1984), and Western Research [from the
ATOM/ADAS (Analysis of Development Alternatives System) line; Western

Research Corporation, 1983]. The early 1980s was also a period in which model adaptation and transfer to other geographic areas became more common. For example, DEISM (Demographic and Economic Impact Simulation Model) represents an adaptation of UPED for use in Nevada, and the Montana and Wyoming economic–demographic (E–D) models involve the use of the basic NEDAM software in conjunction with data-bases develolped for these two states.

4 Model-evaluation criteria

Several recent articles and reports have examined criteria for evaluating socioeconomic impact-assessment models (Murdock and Leistritz, 1980; Winter et al, 1981; ECOS Management Criteria Inc., 1982). Although the perspectives of the authors and the terminology they employ differ some-what, there appears to be general agreement that three sets of factors are central to the evaluation of such models. Model-evaluation criteria should thus include (1) information requirements, (2) use characteristics, and (3) methodological acceptability. Each of these criteria is discussed briefly below.

4.1 *Information requirements*
The information needs of the user are clearly the starting point in selecting a modelling system—what information is needed, for what area, and for what periods of time. Although these needs can be expected to differ somewhat among user groups, several types of information appear to be necessary for the completion of an adequate assessment of socioeconomic impacts under almost any circumstances. Thus, projections generally are needed for a number of economic, demographic, public-service, and fiscal indicators under both baseline (without project) and impact (with project) conditions and for both construction and operational phases of project development.

The economic indicators of greatest interest usually include changes in employment, income, business activity, and industry mix. Demographic information usually includes projections of overall population changes for total impact areas and, increasingly, for particular age, ethnic, and other groups, and for small geographic units, such as municipalities. Public-services data include projections of new service facilities and personnel required to serve in-migrating populations, whereas fiscal information emphasises the costs of such increased services and the public-sector revenues likely to be generated by new populations and associated increases in economic activity. (Social changes, usually measured by the population's perceptions of development, goals for their community, community satisfaction, and likely changes in social structures, are also an important topic of socioeconomic assessments. These effects, however, are not addressed explicitly by any of the computerised models of which we are aware, and hence social changes are not considered further here.)

Realistic assessment of the effects of a major project requires that conditional forecasts for all of these types of indicators be prepared using consistent assumptions. One of the advantages of integrated and computerised models is that they aid analysts in ensuring that consistency in assumptions is maintained through the various steps of the assessment process. Models which address all of the important socioeconomic impact dimensions noted earlier, therefore, are usually most useful.

4.2 *Use characteristics*
Additional factors that must be considered relate to the use characteristics of alternative models. Some important features to be evaluated in this regard are: (1) input-data requirements, (2) model adaptability, (3) flexibility and ease of use, and (4) adequacy of model documentation.

One of the most important use characteristics to be considered is the availability and costs of obtaining the input data required for implementation of a model. Significant differences exist in the input-data requirements and costs associated with the economic and residential allocation components of socioeconomic impact models. It is essential to note, however, that models which reduce data-collection costs by utilising national databases may accentuate problems in projecting local level conditions that depart markedly from national patterns. The trade-off between the need for locally oriented data inputs and the costs of collecting such data must be carefully evaluated.

A distinction also must be made between the overall data requirements for implementing a model and the data which an individual user must supply. Some models have previously developed databases for selected regions, states, and sometimes the entire nation. Utilising such a model may require the user to supply little more than the characteristics (for example, work force, expenditures) of the proposed action (project). At the other extreme, some models require the user to input, at the initiation of each model run, large amounts of data on the characteristics of both the study area and the project.

The adaptability of the model to various site areas is another factor to consider. Two aspects are particularly relevant. The first is the generality of the model structure and logic to different geographic settings. The second is the time and cost required to develop databases and calibrate the model to a new area. Trade-offs may exist between this and other criteria, however, because models which provide more detailed outputs often require a greater level of detail in input data as well. Although an initial evaluation of model adaptability can be made a priori on the basis of model structure and database characteristics, information about previous adaptations of the model is valuable in making a final judgment of its relative adaptability and in estimating the time frame and costs likely to be associated with an adaptation effort. The extent to which the various modelling systems have been used in previous impact-assessment or growth-management planning efforts is another factor to consider. Models which have been utilised extensively in addressing impacts of several types of projects and in a number of geographic areas have to some extent demonstrated the generality of their structure and logic and their feasibility of adaptation to alternative settings.

The flexibility and ease of use of the model also should be evaluated. Impact assessments often involve numerous factors that are difficult to evaluate and predict with precision. Thus, it often becomes important to examine the range of potential impacts under widely varying assumptions for such factors. Models that provide for easy alteration of key parameters and for rapid output of the implications of alternative development scenarios are desirable. Likewise, models that enable users to make such alterations and to select the desired forms of output (for example, variables, geographic areas, years) through a simple dialogue are generally advantageous. ('User friendly' is a popular current phrase describing such model features.)

A final, and very important, consideration is the extent and quality of documentation materials associated with each model. Without some information describing model structure and capabilities, it is not possible even to evaluate the potential of a system and to determine the aptness of the concepts and methods on which it is based. More detailed information would be required to enable a user group to implement the model.

4.3 *Methodological acceptability*

Several aspects of model methodology should enter into evaluations of alternative models. First, the methods used in various model components should be examined in relation to the needs of potential users. For example, if estimating the relative effects of a proposed project or policy on various sectors of the local economy is expected to be a high priority, input–output analysis would appear to be more appropriate than aggregate employment or income multipliers. Similarly, the fact that the effects of development on local schools are typically a major concern suggests that population-projection methods using age cohorts generally will be more useful than those with less detail.

The extent of submodel integration is a second important consideration. In general, the more sophisticated models use multiple rates for various factors during different phases of the projection period (such as changes in labour-force participation rates or fertility rates), utilise factors that most closely differentiate between key dimensions (such as industries or age cohorts), and incorporate procedures that feed back changes (such as alterations of population age distribution or changes in economic structures). For example, with respect to the economic–demographic interface (or labour-market simulation) component, it appears important that a modelling system have the capability of differentiating among various classes of project-related workers (for example, construction, operations, secondary) with regard to such factors as the local versus nonlocal composition of the work force and the demographic profile of in-migrating workers (Wieland et al, 1979; Halstead and Leistritz, 1983).

Finally, an overriding factor in model selection must be an evaluation of the probable accuracy of the system in predicting impact and baseline conditions. Although the accuracy of a model in predicting future conditions can never be known in advance, validation can provide some indication of its potential reliability. It is unfortunate, therefore, that most existing model descriptions contain little or no information on the results of attempts to test their validity. Some initial empirical evaluations of selected models have recently been published, however (Chase et al, 1982; Coon et al, 1983; Murdock et al, 1984), and evidence on the validity of other systems could be derived by comparing samples of model projections with information from published sources. Such analyses constitute an important step in model evaluation.

5 Evaluation of selected models

Several factors were considered in selecting the specific models to be examined. First, attention was focused on models that address multiple impact dimensions and that provide projections at the county or subcounty levels. Second, those models that have been applied extensively in assessing impacts of resource-development projects or which were designed for such applications have been given greatest attention. After models had been identified, we attempted to obtain complete documentation materials for each. In some cases, lack of available documentation materials precluded detailed examination of a model.

The models selected for detailed examination include the following
1 AFSEM (URS-Berger, 1983; Henningson, Durham, Richardson, Inc., 1982),
2 BOOM-1 (Ford, 1976),
3 BREAM/PAS (Mountain West Research Inc., 1978; 1981; Mountain West Research–Southwest Inc., 1982),
4 COALTOWN (Bender et al, 1980),
5 NEDAM (Leistritz et al, 1982),
6 SEAM (Stenehjem, 1978; South and Bragen, 1981),
7 UPED 79 (Weaver et al, 1980).

The comparison of these models is presented in two tables. The informational characteristics of the models are addressed in table 1. The impact categories included in each model and the project phases, geographic units, and time periods for which projections are made are discussed. In table 2, some of the methodological and use characteristics of the models are compared. The methodological features examined include the methods used in each major component and the extent of validation of each model. Use characteristics addressed in table 2 include input-data requirements, extent of previous use, ease of use, and adequacy of documentation. In examining this table, one should note that the extent of validation and the use characteristics of each model have been rated on a scale from A (extensive/exceptional) to C (marginal/difficult). These ratings, of course, reflect the evaluation, interpretation, and opinions of the authors and hence are somewhat subjective. The ratings do, however, provide a general indication of the relative attractiveness of the systems with respect to the attributes indicated. At this point it is also essential to note that the documentation available for the seven systems is quite variable. Whereas the descriptive materials for some systems discuss data sources, methods, user procedures, and outputs in considerable detail, documentation for other models leaves a good deal to be desired. Thus, in some cases available documentation simply did not provide sufficient information to enable a particular model attribute to be evaluated. In these instances, the table contains the designation 'inp' (information not provided) instead of a rating.

Although it is impossible to discuss the information in tables 1 and 2 in detail, even a brief description of the items in these tables indicates how diverse these models are in overall capabilities and characteristics. As is evident from table 1, only four models (AFSEM, BOOM-1, NEDAM, and SEAM) contain as many as five dimensions. All provide projections for each of the three vital project phases, but areal coverage varies widely.

Table 1. Informational characteristics of selected socioeconomic impact-assessment models.

Characteristics	Model[a]						
	AFSEM	BOOM-1	BREAM/PAS	COALTOWN	NEDAM	SEAM	UPED 79
Impact dimensions included							
Economic	•	•	•	•	•	•	•
Demographic	•	•	•	•	•	•	•
E–D interface	•	•	•	•	•	•	•
Residential allocation	•		•		•		
Public service	•	•			•	•	•
Fiscal	•	•[b]		•	•	•[c]	
Project phases analyzed							
Baseline	•	•	•	•	•	•[d]	•
Construction	•	•	•	•	•	•	•
Operation	•	•	•	•	•	•	•
Geographic areas included	region, counties, cities	city only	region, counties, cities	county	region, counties, cities	county	region counties, cities
Total number of areal units	NLS	any given city	up to 50 counties	any given county	53 counties, 350 cities	any given county	NLS
Projection period	NLS (usually 10 years)	NLS	50 years	NLS	25 years	30 years	NLS
Time increments	yearly	yearly	yearly	yearly	yearly	yearly	yearly

[a] NLS no limit specified.
[b] Costs are aggregated.
[c] Revenues are not calculated.
[d] Baseline projections of population only.

Only four models analyse impacts both at county and at city levels. All provide yearly outputs, but several are limited in the total number of units that can be included in a model analysis.

In terms of methodological characteristics (table 2), similar differences can be noted. Four systems use an employment-multiplier approach, two incorporate input–output analysis, and one employs income-multiplier methods. Similarly, four systems use some form of cohort-component demographic-projection techniques, whereas the remainder use more aggregate employment–population multiplier methods. All of the models utilise an economic–demographic interface procedure that involves the matching of available and required employment to determine migration levels. These interface procedures differ substantially, however, in their capability for differentiating among classes of project-related workers with

Table 2. Methodological and use characteristics of selected socioeconomic impact-assessment models.

	Model[a]						
	AFSEM	BOOM-1	BREAM/PAS	COALTOWN	NEDAM	SEAM	UPED 79
Methodological forms by component							
Economic	I-O	E-M	I-M	E-M	I-O	E-M	E-M
Demographic	E-P	E-P	CC-S	E-P	CC-S	CC-S	CC-S
E-D interface	E-M-M	E-P-I	E-M-M	E-P-I	E-M-M	E-M-M	E-M-I
Residential allocation[b]	% share, gravity	na	% share, gravity	na	% share, gravity	na	% share, gravity
Public service[c]	demand facility	demand	na	demand	demand	demand facility	na
Fiscal[d]	per capita	per capita	na	per capita	per capita	per capita (costs only)	na
Extent of empirical validation[e]	B	inp	C	B	A	C	B
Input data requirements[f]	A	A	B	B	C	A	B
Extent of previous use[e]	B	C	A	B	A	B	B
Ease of use[e]	A	A	A	inp	A	A	inp
Adequacy of documentation[e]	B	B	B	C	B	B	C

[a]Abbreviations for models:
economic
I-O input–output
E-M export base–employment multiplier
I-M export base–income multiplier

demographic
CC-S cohort component survival
E-P employment–population ratio

economic–demographic interface
E-M-I employment–migration–one phase
E-P-I employment–population–one phase
E-M-M employment–migration–multiphase procedure

inp information not provided
na not applicable.

[b]% share is the distribution to subareas on bases of employment or population ratio gravity indicates gravity allocation model.

[c]Demand indicates estimates of service demand (for example, school-age population) facility indicates projections of facility requirements are also completed.

[d]Per capita means per-capita costs and revenues.

[e]Rating scale:
A extensive or exceptional
B adequate or moderate
C marginal or difficult.

[f]Cost of database development: A low cost.

respect to both (1) the extent to which local workers will be able to participate in project-related jobs and (2) demographic profiles of workers and dependents. Whereas AFSEM and NEDAM incorporate mechanisms to account for different characteristics for five to seven classes of project-related workers, some other models (for example, BREAM/PAS, COAL-TOWN, UPED) either provide for only one category of project workers or fail even to distinguish between project and baseline workers. The interface procedures of the various models also differ in their capability to reflect potential changes in the labour-force participation rates of the pre-development population in response to project-related job opportunities.

Contrasts among the systems are substantial in the area of empirical validation. Results of extensive validation tests have been reported for one system (NEDAM) and three others have been evaluated on a more limited scale (AFSEM, COALTOWN, UPED). For the remaining models, however, no validation efforts have been reported.

The use characteristics of these models again show considerable differences. NEDAM has the greatest input-data requirements, whereas those of AFSEM, BOOM-1, and SEAM are quite modest. The use history of the systems offers interesting contrasts. BREAM/PAS and NEDAM have been utilised in a wide variety of impact assessments, in a number of states, and under the auspices of several regulatory agencies. Use of the other systems has typically been limited to a single state, agency, and/or type of project. The quality of available documentation limits the evaluation of the ease of use of the models. Although it is clear that most of the systems have been designed to encourage use in an inter-active mode and to allow the user easily to alter a variety of key model parameters through a simple dialogue process, the descriptive materials available for UPED and COALTOWN simply do not discuss these important use characteristics. With respect to model documentation, it must also be noted that, although published descriptions of most systems are adequate to provide a general understanding of basic model structure, capabilities, and user procedures, none is sufficiently detailed to enable a potential user to adapt the model to a new setting without substantial assistance from the model development team.

Overall, the comparisons in tables 1 and 2 suggest that available models differ significantly in the methods employed, information provided, and in use characteristics. Potential users should conduct careful analyses of models that appear appropriate for their particular information needs.

6 Conclusions and implications

The development of integrated socioeconomic assessment models represents an ambitious attempt to understand better and to simulate realistically the processes of economic growth and community change. Given the increasing recognition of the need for informed planning and policymaking at regional and community levels, the development and utilisation of such systems appear likely to increase in the future. The results of the review and evaluation of these models reported here suggest several considerations relative to such utilisation.

First, it is clear that the methodologies employed in such models require continued development. The unknown validity of most of these models requires careful attention. More extensive empirical testing and evaluation should be a high priority for model developers, and prospective users of these systems should increasingly demand such evaluations. In addition, it is obvious that many of the socioeconomic assessment models are in need of greater refinement in order realistically to simulate the processes of growth and change. The economic–demographic interface components of such systems in particular often appear overly simplistic.

It should be recognised of course that data limitations inherent in sparsely populated areas have been a major factor limiting model refinement. The demand for such systems thus often is greatest in the very areas where the data for estimating model relationships are least adequate (for example, because of census data-suppression procedures). Nevertheless, model refinements must be pursued. In some cases additional basic research may be needed to provide the understanding of the dynamics of economic and demographic change essential for realistic modelling (for example, response of labour-force participation rates to increased employment opportunity). In other instances, substantial research already has been completed which could serve as the basis for significant refinements in most existing models (for example, differential characteristics of different types of project-related workers).

A second major need is to consider additional applications of such systems. For example, virtually all of these models were designed for analysis of growth resulting from major development projects. Although community economic decline associated with closure of major industrial and resource extraction facilities has become a widespread concern in recent years, we know of few serious efforts to apply socioeconomic modelling techniques to the problems created by closure. [A major exception is the work of Batey and Madden (1981; 1983). These authors not only point out modelling considerations particularly relevant to the problems of economic decline, such as differences in expenditure patterns for social security payments versus wage income, but also examine more general issues concerning the effects of changing demographic structures on regional economic activity.] Greater attention should be given to determining the applicability of these systems to a wider range of settings and situations.

Third, although the systems discussed here all were developed in the United States of America, some may be applicable for analysis of development impacts in other areas. For instance, the impacts of North Sea oil development on communities in northern Scotland appear similar in many respects to those arising in energy-development regions of the western USA (Sewel, 1983; Murdock and Leistritz, 1979). Models of the type reviewed here, then, might prove useful in facilitating ex ante evaluation of such projects and in guiding impact-management efforts (Leistritz et al, 1983).

Finally, the model comparisons indicate that various systems differ significantly with respect to a number of informational, methodological, and use characteristics. There is no single best socioeconomic assessment model, because the different systems have counterbalancing strengths and weaknesses. It is very important, therefore, for prospective users of such systems to evaluate carefully the alternative models in light of their specific needs. If the selection of such models is done with care, however, this analysis suggests that the integrated socioeconomic assessment models may be useful tools for the analysis of regional systems and thus may provide valuable input to regional planning and policymaking.

Acknowledgements. The authors acknowledge the excellent editorial assistance of Brenda L Ekstrom. Financial support from the North Dakota Agricultural Experiment Station, the Texas Agricultural Experiment Station, and the Center for Energy and Mineral Resources of Texas A and M University is gratefully acknowledged.

References

Anderson E, Chalmers J, Hogan T, Beckhelm T, 1974, "ATOM 2: part 1 of final report" Arizona Office of Economic Planning and Development, Phoenix, AZ

Anderson E, Hannigan B, 1977, "Arizona economic–demographic projection model: a summary report and technical description" Arizona Office of Economic Planning and Development, Phoenix, AZ

Batey P W J, Madden M, 1981, "Demographic–economic forecasting within an activity–commodity framework: some theoretical considerations and empirical results" *Environment and Planning A* **13** 1067–1083

Batey P W J, Madden M, 1983, "The modelling of demographic–economic change within the context of regional decline: analytical procedures and empirical results" *Socio-Economic Planning Sciences* **17** 315–328

Battelle Columbus Laboratories, 1973, "Final report of the Arizona Environmental and Economic Trade-off Model" Arizona Office of Planning and Development, Phoenix, AZ

Beckhelm T L, Chalmers J A, Hannigan W M, 1975, "A description of the ATOM 3 and of the research related to its development" Four Corners Regional Commission, Washington, DC

Bender L D, Temple G S, Parcels L C, 1980, "An introduction to the COAL-TOWN impact assessment model" EPA 600/7-80-146, US Department of Agriculture and US Environmental Protection Agency, Washington, DC

Bigler C, Reeve R, Weaver R, 1972, "Report on the development of the Utah process: a procedure for planning coordination through forecasting and evaluating alternative state futures" Utah State Planning Coordinator, Salt Lake City, UT

Bohm R A, Lord J H, 1972, "Regional economic simulation modeling—the TVA experience" paper presented at the Annual Meeting of the Northeast Regional Science Association, University Park, PA; copy available from the authors at Tennessee Valley Authority, Knoxville, TN

Carlson J F, Doll G F, with Phillips C, Lofgren J, Brock J W, 1976, "The North
    Platte River Basin Economic Simulation Model: a technical report" University
    of Wyoming Water Resources Research Institute, Laramie, WY
Chase R A, Coon R C, Chase C L, Vocke C F, Vuchetich R J, Leistritz F L,
    Hertsgaard T A, Ransom-Nelson W, Murdock S H, Yang P S, Sharma R, 1982,
    "Expansion and adaptation of the North Dakota Economic–Demographic
    Assessment Model (NEDAM) for Montana: technical description" Agricultural
    Economics miscellaneous report number 61, North Dakota Agricultural
    Experiment Station, Fargo, ND
Coon R C, Vocke C F, Chase R A, Ekstrom B L, Ransom-Nelson W, Rathge R W,
    Hertsgaard T A, Leistritz F L, Vuchetich R J, Ranganathan B, 1983,
    "Expansion and adaptation of the North Dakota Economic–Demographic
    Assessment Model (NEDAM) for Wyoming: technical description" Agricultural
    Economics miscellaneous report number 63, North Dakota Agricultural
    Experiment Station, Fargo, ND
Denver Research Institute, 1979, "Socioeconomic impact of Western energy
    resource development" Council on Environmental Quality, Washington, DC
ECOS Management Criteria Inc., 1982, "The validation and improvement of
    socioeconomic forecasting methodologies" US Geological Survey, Washington, DC
Ford A, 1976, "User's guide to the BOOM-1 model" LA-6396-MS, Los Alamos
    Scientific Laboratory, Los Alamos, NM
Forrester J W, 1961 *Industrial Dynamics* (MIT Press, Cambridge, MA)
Gilmore J S, Hammond D, Moore K D, Johnson J F, Coddington D C, 1982,
    "Socioeconomic impacts of power plants" EPRI EA-2228, Electric Power
    Research Institute, Palo Alto, CA
Halstead J M, Leistritz F L, 1983, "Impacts of energy development on secondary
    labor markets: a study of seven Western counties" Agricultural Economics
    report number 178, North Dakota Agricultural Experiment Station, Fargo, ND
Hamilton H R, Goldstone S E, Milliman J W, Pugh A L, Roberts E B, Zellner A,
    1969 *Systems Simulation for Regional Analysis: An Application to River-basin
    Planning* (MIT Press, Cambridge, MA)
Hamm R, Murdock S, Leistritz L, 1984, "A socioeconomic impact model for
    assessing the effects of a high-level nuclear waste repository site" *Impact
    Assessment Bulletin* **3** 6–19
Henningson, Durham, Richardson, Inc., 1982, "A generalized regional socio-
    economic analysis system" US Air Force, Norton AFB, CA
Hertsgaard T, Murdock S, Toman N, Henry M, Ludtke R, 1978, "REAP
    economic–demographic model: technical description" North Dakota Regional
    Environmental Assessment Program, Bismarck, ND
Huston M, 1979, "The United States steel project—a comprehensive approach to
    socioeconomic analysis" in *Boom Towns: Managing Growth* proceedings of
    SME-AIME Annual Meeting, New Orleans; Arthur D Little Inc., Cambridge,
    MA
Leistritz F L, Chase R A, 1982, "Socioeconomic impact monitoring systems: a
    review and recommendations" *Journal of Environmental Management* **15**
    333–349
Leistritz F L, Halstead J M, Chase R A, Murdock S H, 1983, "Socioeconomic
    impact management: programme design and implementation considerations"
    Minerals and the Environment **4** 141–150
Leistritz F L, Murdock S H, 1981 *Socioeconomic Impact of Resource Development:
    Methods for Assessment* (Westview Press, Boulder, CO)

Leistritz F L, Murdock S H, Toman N E, Hertsgaard T A, 1979, "A model for projecting localized economic, demographic, and fiscal impacts of large-scale projects" *Western Journal of Agricultural Economics* **4**(2) 1–16

Leistritz F L, Ransom-Nelson W, Rathge R W, Coon R C, Chase R A, Hertsgaard T A, Murdock S H, Toman N E, Sharma R, Yang P S, 1982, "North Dakota Economic–Demographic Assessment Model (NEDAM): technical description" Agricultural Economics report number 158, North Dakota Agricultural Experiment Station, Fargo, ND

Matson R A, Studer J B, 1975, "Simulating the employment impact of coal development in Wyoming" *Regional Science Perspectives* **5** 43–60

Monts J K, 1978, "BOOMP user's guide" University of Texas Center for Energy Studies, Austin, TX

Mountain West Research Inc., 1978, "Bureau of Reclamation Economic Assessment Model (BREAM) technical description" US Bureau of Reclamation, Denver, CO

Mountain West Research Inc., 1981, "BREAM technical description and user's guide" US Bureau of Reclamation, Denver, CO

Mountain West Research–Southwest Inc., 1982, "Description of the Mountain West planning and assessment system" Mountain West Research, Tempe, AZ

Murdock S H, Leistritz F L, 1979 *Energy Development in the Western United States: Impact on Rural Areas* (Praeger, New York)

Murdock S H, Leistritz F L, 1980, "Selecting socioeconomic assessment models: a discussion of criteria and selected models" *Journal of Environmental Management* **10** 1–12

Murdock S H, Leistritz F L, Hamm R R, Hwang S S, Parpia B, 1984, "An assessment of the accuracy of a regional economic–demographic projection model" *Demography* **21** 383–404

Murdock S, Leistritz L, Jones L, Andrews D, Wilson B, Fannin D, deMontel J, 1979, "The Texas Assessment Modeling System: technical description" department technical report 79-3, Department of Rural Sociology, Texas Agricultural Experiment Station, College Station, TX

Office of the State Oil Shale Coordinator, 1974, "IMPACT—an assessment of the impact of oil shale development—Colorado planning and management region II" State of Colorado, Office of the State Oil Shale Coordinator, Denver, CO

Olsen R J, Westley G W, Herzog H W Jr, Kerley C R, Bjornstad D J, Voyt D P, Bray L G, Grady S T, Nakosteen R A, 1977, "MULTIREGION: a simulation forecasting model of BEA economic area population and employment" ORNL/RUS-25, Oak Ridge National Laboratory, Oak Ridge, TN

Reeve R, Weaver R, 1974, "Report on the development and implementation of the Utah Land Use and Tax Base Model (UPLAND)" Utah State Planning Coordinator, Salt Lake City, UT

Rink R, Ford A, 1978, "A simulation model for boom town housing" LA-7342-MS, Los Alamos Scientific Laboratory, Los Alamos, NM

San Diego Comprehensive Planning Organization, 1972, "Technical user's manual for the interactive population/employment forecasting model" San Diego Comprehensive Planning Organization, San Diego, CA

Sewel J, 1983, "Social consequences of oil development" Scottish Development Department, Edinburgh

South D W, Bragen M J, 1981, "The Social and Economic Assessment Model (SEAM)—a county level energy facility impact assessment model: user's guide" Argonne National Laboratory, Argonne, IL

Stenehjem J, 1978, "'Summary description of SEAM: the Social and Economic Assessment Model" Argonne National Laboratory, Argonne, IL

URS-Berger, 1983, "AFSEM user's guide: Air Force System Evaluation Model, version 1.0" AFRCE-BMS/DEV, Norton Air Force Base, CA

Weaver R, Hachman F C, Wilcox A S, Reeve T R, 1980, "UPED 79: report on revisions of the Utah Process Economic and Demographic Impact Model (UPED)" Bureau of Economic and Business Research, University of Utah, and Utah State Planning Coordinator's Office, Salt Lake City, UT

Western Research Corporation, 1983, "Regional economic model technical document" Western Research Corporation, Laramie, WY

Wieland J S, Leistritz F L, Murdock S H, 1979, "Characteristics and residential patterns of energy-related work forces in the northern Great Plains" *Western Journal of Agricultural Economics* **4**(1) 57–68

Winter R C, Santini D J, South D W, Hotchkiss C M, Bragen M J, 1981, "Selection of economic impact assessment models for use by communities in the Tennessee–Tombigbee corridor: phase 1" ANL/EES-TM-160, Argonne National Laboratory, Argonne, IL

The Socioeconomic Impacts of a Regional Synthetic Fuels Industry: An Integrated Econometric Analysis

B D SOLOMON
Federal Energy Regulatory Commission, Washington

1 Introduction

As the uncertain future of the world oil market continues to plague developed and less developed nations alike, numerous questions about substitute fuel sources remain unanswered. In the United States of America, one energy alternative that has received serious attention in recent years is synthetic liquids from coal. A new multibillion dollar federal agency, the US Synthetic Fuels Corporation, was established by the Congress in 1979 to help finance a synthetic fuels industry. However, since commercial operating experience is still unavailable outside of wartime Nazi Germany and contemporary South Africa, little is known about the likely socioeconomic impacts of commercial-scale synthetic fuels projects in the USA.

Proposals have been advanced by state agencies and private industry to develop a commercial synthetic fuels (coal-liquefaction) industry in Western Kentucky (Kentucky DOE, 1982). A previous static input–output analysis has shown that such a development scenario could dramatically expand employment and real income in a multistate region (Rubin and Solomon, 1983). Since energy from synthetic fuels represents a form of techno-logical change, it is clear that a dynamic econometric modelling method has the greatest potential for accurately portraying development impacts (compare Rose, 1984). Furthermore, the impacts of energy projects will span economic, fiscal, demographic, environmental, and other dimensions, and will distribute unevenly over space and time (Solomon, 1983). This common characterisation of many large-scale development projects under-scores the need for an integrated economic modelling method with a spatial component.

The purpose of this paper is to develop an improved econometric modelling approach for impact-analysis studies, and then to apply the model to the scenario of a three-plant synthetic fuel industry in Western Kentucky. Preceding this, the second section is a description of the energy-development region, and the third section is a review of other relevant studies of regional economic impact-analysis. In the fourth section is presented the Evansville Area Econometric Model, which is more fully integrated than previous regional econometric impact-analysis models. After a description of the socioeconomic and environmental equation structures of the model, the model is then applied to an energy-development scenario. A discussion of the implications of the study for energy policy concludes the paper.

2 The energy-development region

A guiding principle in regional science is that regional studies require the delineation of a *meaningful* region (or system of regions) as a "dynamic organism" (Isard, 1975, page 5). In energy-development studies, the region may be a state or province, coal basin, river basin, utility-company service district, or a metropolitan area. However, other meaningful regions can be defined (Rose et al, 1982). In the present study, where counties are the spatial unit of analysis, focus is placed on an impact-analysis region where the energy-project impacts will be most pronounced, and where data are available and relevant to local governments. As such, six contiguous counties have been chosen as the impact region, which surrounds Evansville, IN—Posey, Spencer, Vanderburgh, and Warrick in Indiana, and Daviess and Henderson in Kentucky (figure 1). The six counties actually host five potential coal-conversion project sites—three for coal-liquefaction projects, and two for coal-fired electric power plants—and contain all but one county in the Evansville and Owensboro Standard Metropolitan Statistical Areas. Although the study utilises pooled cross-sectional time-series data from seven other adjacent counties, the six-county focus provides for a more pragmatic impact-analysis study.

The completion of three (or more) synthetic fuels projects in Western Kentucky would be unprecedented for a small region in the USA. Although numerous synthetic fuels development schemes of comparable scale have been proposed for other regions (National Coal Association, 1981), only a few small plants have thus far been completed. Thus, the

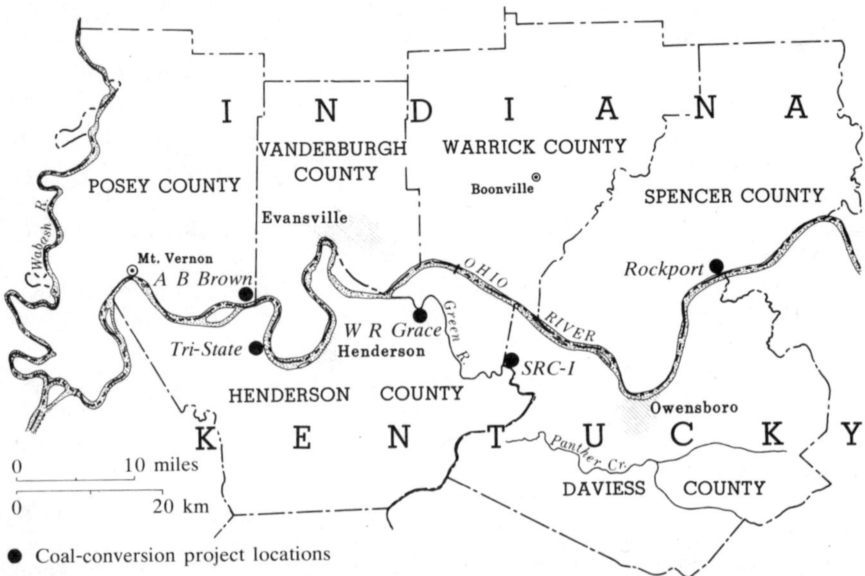

Figure 1. The impact-analysis region.

Western Kentucky development scenario can provide important quantitative information on the development impacts and their distribution for this nascent industry (Schweitzer et al, 1983).

A coal-liquefaction plant is best described as a cross between a crude-oil refinery and a coal-fired electric power plant (Jones and Enoch, 1981). A brief profile of the Western Kentucky projects is presented in table 1. Concentrated commercial-scale development *could* have a boomtown-type effect, since a large but temporary construction work force would be followed by a much smaller operation and maintenance labour force (compare Gilmore, 1976; Schweitzer et al, 1983). Moreover, much of the construction work force would be highly skilled labourers, dominated by job categories such as pipefitters, insulators, and electricians, which are often in scarce supply locally (Finn and Gaston, 1980). Thus, a large but possibly transitory immigration stream could result.

Table 1. Profiles of synthetic fuel projects (costs given for 1984; source: Kentucky DOE, 1982; and author's calculations).

	Project			
	SRC-I (International Coal Refining Co.)[a]		W R Grace and Co.[b]	Tri-State (Texas Eastern Corp.)[b]
	dem	com		
Capital investment[c] ($ billion)	1.77	3.00	3.00	3.00
Construction employment (peak)	3500	7400	6600	10000
Operation and maintenance employment (peak)	725	2200	1500	1300
Peak construction annual payroll ($ million)	90	190	172	260
Equivalent barrels of oil per day	20000	100000	50000	37000

[a] dem demonstration; com commercial projects of International Coal Refining Co.
[b] Commercial projects of Texas Eastern Corporation.
[c] US billion, that is, 10^9.

3 Regional economic impact-analysis studies
3.1 Background
The most appropriate method of regional economic impact-analysis depends of course upon the problem being addressed, and a large variety of approaches are possible (see Isard, 1960; 1975; Richardson, 1978b; Leistritz and Murdock, 1981). The earliest efforts in regional economic impact-analysis modelling were in economic-base analysis and in regionalising national input–output (I–O) models (Leontief, 1953; Isard and Kuenne, 1953). Later applications of regional I–O analysis have come in the areas

of defence spending, the space program, urban policy, and the environment, among *many* other areas (for example, see Leontief et al, 1965; Miernyk et al, 1967; Bergmann, 1969; Richardson, 1972; 1978b; Isard, 1975; Miernyk, 1982; Solomon, 1985).

Although economic-base analysis and regional I–O models are very useful in certain applications, such models also have some major drawbacks. For example, these models cannot be fully dynamic in structure, nor can they have a spatial focus. In the case of large-scale energy-resource development projects, these drawbacks are severely limiting. The impacts of major energy projects do not confine themselves to a single year, but will be distributed unevenly over the plant construction and operation and maintenance phases (Rubin and Solomon, 1983). It is therefore important that the regional modelling structure can trace both direct and indirect and induced effects of energy development over a mid-range time horizon (for example, ten to fifteen years).

The importance of the spatial orientation here arises from the comparatively small land area of counties in the Western Kentucky region, where the energy projects of interest are proposed. This could result in a 'trichotomy' between plant sites, existing population centres, and the likely location of much of the in-migrating construction work force. As a result, development impacts will be distributed unevenly over geographic space, which would be neglected by the aspatial regional I–O model.

In recent years, significant attention has been given to the development of simultaneous equation econometric models as pragmatic approaches to impact analysis in substate regions. Such models have found growing applications in resource-development problems (for example, see Krutilla and Fisher, 1978; Temple, 1978; Brown, 1981; Lakshmanan, 1983). Although a variety of econometric models now exists at the substate regional level (for references, see Duobinis, 1981), none have been specifically developed to estimate the full range of impacts arising from large-scale energy-development projects. This is partly a result of the relative recency of econometric modelling techniques used at this geographic level and partly a result of data problems which often limit the scope of such applications (Richardson, 1978b). Many of the data problems arise from the general paucity of lengthy time-series data at the regional level, and can be overcome via the increasingly popular pooled time-series, cross-sectional approaches (Judge et al, 1980, pages 323–380). Furthermore, regional econometric models have historically been very dependent upon estimates of activity exogenous to the regional system (Knapp et al, 1978). Fortunately, this latter characteristic is a major *advantage* when modelling the impacts of large-scale development projects at the regional level, since the exogenous component of most interest—the level of energy-plant development activity—will often be known precisely.

3.2 *Integrated econometric structures*

Regional econometric analysis has a much shorter history than its I–O counterpart, dating back to the pioneering model developed for the Commonwealth of Massachusetts (Bell, 1967)[1]. Regional econometric modelling has many similarities to regional I–O modelling, since both approaches are direct descendants of models of national economic systems, both are attempts to model the structure of a regional economic system (albeit at varying levels of detail), and both can be estimated at a variety of subnational scales (state, county, river basin, metropolitan area, etc).

Whereas regional I–O models portray regional economic structure deterministically, regional econometric models rely upon stochastic equations as well, generally at a higher level of data aggregation. Econometric models, however, can also be more integrated and more flexibly estimated, since alternative modelling structures and functional forms can easily be tested. This flexibility also applies to the model sectoral coverage and level of detail. For instance, whereas Bell's 1967 model consists of a mere eight stochastic equations, a recent econometric model of Arizona has about three hundred stochastic equations, and a state and three substate levels (Charney and Taylor, 1983).

Bell's Massachusetts model came at a time when there were few national econometric models to provide guidelines, although it was 'driven' by the gross national product (GNP)[2]. Elements of economic-base theory are incorporated into this model, which uses growth in GNP to determine growth in income in export industries, which in turn determines total local income. In addition, this model estimates manufacturing and nonmanufacturing investment, total production, and other variables. However, the model lacks simultaneity between the endogenous variables and does not explain interactions among the local variables.

Substantial improvements were made in the specification and performance of regional econometric models in the 1970s. Among these efforts, the most important is the fourth version of the Philadelphia Metropolitan Area Model (Glickman, 1977). This model consists of a total of 228 equations, including both areal and industrial disaggregation. The model reflects well the diversity of the metropolitan regional economy, by including nineteen industrial sectors and a full range of economic, demographic, and government fiscal variables. The Philadelphia model is area stratified by containing equations for the entire region, the central city, and the suburbs. The government block of the model contains several policy variables, including

---

[1]Actually, regional econometric models were developed earlier, but were based upon very simplistic structures. For an example, see Research Seminar in Quantitative Economics (1965).

[2]Most subsequent regional econometric models have relied upon predictions of national economic variables to drive the regional economy, a structure suggested by Klein (1969). See also Knapp et al (1978).

intergovernmental revenues, defence spending, and tax rates. It is with alternative assumptions for the policy variables in the model that Glickman analyses the impacts of the federal Comprehensive Employment and Training Act program, the 1973 oil embargo by the Organization of Petroleum Exporting Countries, a slowdown in industrial growth, a cut in federal defence spending, and increased decentralisation of employment in the region. Overall, the simulation and forecasting ability of the revised Philadelphia model represented a marked improvement in the field (see also Glickman, 1976).

Ballard and Glickman (1977) developed a multiregional econometric model for the Delaware Valley to show the spatial interaction between a river valley and its component counties and metropolitan areas. Their model is a landmark in spatial impact-analysis studies, since no linkages with the national economy are included and the series of subregions are linked for purposes of impact analysis. After an estimation of differences in the counties and for the entire region in gross product, employment, income, and population, the model is used to simulate the spatial impacts of a hypothetical industrial park to be located in two of the counties.

Although several other regional econometric models for important metropolitan areas have been developed in the past ten years, they have typically been fragmented, incomplete, or lacking in spatial orientation. Regional econometric models of energy-development impacts have had the same problems, and are also reviewed elsewhere (Rubin and Solomon, 1983). On the other hand, a more successful multiregional model of the USA neglects local issues (Lakshmanan, 1983). Nonetheless, policy-relevant models should include numerous policy or control variables in an integrated, comprehensive, and spatial econometric framework. The Evansville Area Econometric Model accomplishes these objectives by pooling county-level data with time-series data, by including policy variables such as the average rate of property tax and state transfer payments to local governments, and by entering the direct effects of the synthetic fuels projects on employment (both local and regional) and property values as exogenous forecasts in the model.

4 The Evansville Area Econometric Model
4.1 *Overview*
The latest version of the Evansville Area Econometric Model consists of 125 equations: fifty stochastic equations and seventy-five accounting equations and identities. The model is divided into five equation blocks: employment, wage rates and personal income, demographic, fiscal, and environmental. Simultaneous and recursive linkages both exist within the model. The size of the sample period upon which most of the equations of the model are derived is thirteen years (1967 to 1979), with the exception of the labour force, unemployment, and environmental variables, for which only six to ten years of data were available. The time-series

data are pooled with cross-sectional data for a larger thirteen-county impact region in most cases, increasing the sample size to 169 observations in such instances. County observations are represented by two to twelve binary variables, and the model is estimated with ordinary least squares regression for reasons given elsewhere (Solomon, 1983; Solomon and Rubin, 1985).

Data sources for the model include both federal and state (Kentucky and Indiana) agency reports. The major federal source is the Bureau of Economic Analysis (BEA) of the US Department of Commerce, which provides data on employment, wages, income, and population. The US

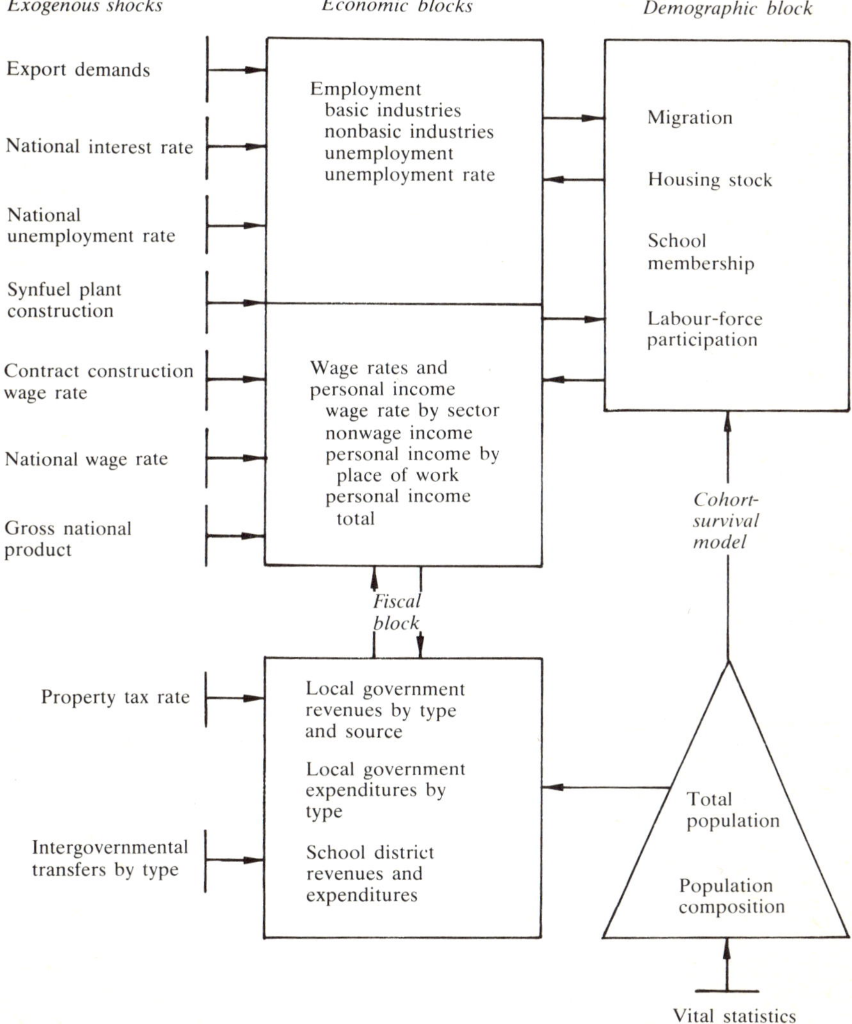

Figure 2. The socioeconomic structure of the Evansville Area Econometric Model.

Department of Commerce's data on the GNP, population, and the housing stock are also utilised. Migration data are estimated by applying a cohort-survival model to BEA population data (see below), and unemployment data are obtained from state employment-security agencies. Last, fiscal and environmental data used in the model are obtained from state departments of revenue, finance, accounts, education, health, environment, and transport.

The present model is a compromise between the highly disaggregated fourth version of the Philadelphia Metropolitan Area Model (Glickman, 1977) and some of the smaller (but incomplete) models that have been developed. The Evansville Area Econometric Model is thus more aggregated in economic detail than some, although it is more integrated and comprehensive than others (particularly in the fiscal block). However, several equations that might appear in many current regional econometric models are left out here, either because of their irrelevancy in the present context, or through the lack of county-level data, or both. These include equations for output and gross regional product, consumer prices, capital stock, and money market conditions. Fortunately, none of these omissions would lead to a misspecified model. The causal flows within the Evansville Area Econometric Model are illustrated in figure 2, and the theoretical bases and estimation results for the stochastic equation structures are described next.

4.2 *The modelling structure*

The employment equations in the model are divided into twelve sectors: agriculture; mining; two sectors for manufacturing (durable and nondurable goods); construction; transport and public utilities; wholesale trade; retail trade; finance, insurance, and real estate; services; state and local government; and the US government. Two regional employment equations are also included.

The general specification for the employment equations in the model integrates a demand-based approach using sectoral wage rates, consumer demand (proxied by population size), national and regional demand (proxied by the GNP), intersectoral economic linkages, and a 'partial adjustment' mechanism. In addition, all of the employment equations best fit a double-log form, thereby accounting for inherent nonlinearities in these relationships.

The use of the sectoral wage rate to estimate employment is based on the work of Dhrymes (1965), who used a constant elasticity of substitution production-function approach to incorporate wage rates into employment equations with a negative coefficient. The use of the wage-rate variable proved statistically significant in ten of the fourteen employment equations.

Local intersectoral economic linkages were found in about a third of the employment equations. Such relationships are based on the assumption that economic activity in key sectors—manufacturing and contract construction—directly stimulates demand for employment in related sectors. For example, the employment equations link mining activity to employment in the contract construction sector; employment in transportation and public utilities and in finance, insurance, and real estate is linked to manufacturing activity; and the regional total employment is also linked to the regional employment in contract construction.

The partial adjustment mechanism in the employment equations is represented by the lagged employment variable, and reflects the fact that most employers are not able to make immediate employment changes in response to changes in demand for their output. This lag in adjusting employment to its optimal level is largely a result of unionisation and contract requirements. Most recent regional econometric models have incorporated this partial adjustment mechanism (for example, see Glickman, 1977; Ballard and Glickman, 1977; Rubin and Erickson, 1980). This specification in the present model proved statistically significant in every local employment equation.

The local unemployment level is modelled stochastically, whereas the unemployment rate is determined by an identity equation. Unemployment is explained on the basis both of local and of national economic conditions, with local conditions being represented by total employment. On the other hand, exogenous factors such as the national unemployment rate and the national interest rate also have a direct influence on local unemployment, and are thus accounted for in the equation.

The equations explaining local real wage rates are estimated for each of the previously mentioned economic sectors, with the exception of construction. The wage rate in construction is utilised as an exogenous control variable in the model to depict the effects of the wages paid to construction workers on synthetic fuels projects.

Each local wage-rate variable is modelled partly as a function of the corresponding national sectoral wage rate. This accounts for the dependence of local wages on national labour-market conditions, because of unionisation and factor mobility (Richardson, 1978a). Local or regional labour-market conditions are captured in these equations through the use of local unemployment or unemployment rate, labour-force participation rate, the average wage rate in the private sector, and wage rates in linked economic sectors. Last, national variables such as GNP, interest rate, and prices are occasionally utilised as further determinants of wage rates.

All of the explanatory variables in the wage-rate equations have positive signs on their respective coefficients, except for the interest rate (Federal Home Loan Bank Board) and labour-force participation rate. Although the other wage-rate, GNP, and price variables provide a positive stimulus to local wage-rate inflation, the previous two variables operate in an opposite fashion. The utilisation of the interest rate and the labour-force variables is based upon an inverse relationship with local wage rates. For example, employers can be expected to increase wages at lower rates when the supply of labour is large. Such an inverse relationship was found in about half of the wage-rate equations.

In addition to the wage equations, stochastic equations are included for nonwage personal income, and the BEA's 'residence adjustment' to transform personal income to a 'place-of-residence' format. The nonwage income equation is explained on the basis of GNP, employment, and unemployment. GNP is included in this equation because a large component of nonwage income is comprised of dividends, profits, and income from unincorporated businesses. This component would vary directly with the overall level of economic activity. Similarly, high levels of unemployment result in high levels of transfer payments (unemployment compensation)—another important component of nonwage income. By way of contrast, high employment levels result in higher levels of wage (and salary) income, so the sign on the total employment coefficient is negative.

Although the demographic block of the model contains only three *stochastic* equations, it is a critical component of the impact-analysis structure. It is here that population composition, net migration, labour-force participation, school membership, housing stock, and residential location patterns are determined. This is accomplished largely through recursively linking the demographic block to a cohort-survival population model (Rogers, 1975).

Migration is modelled as a function both of local and of national economic conditions, as well as of local housing stock. Because of the well-known scarcity of time-series migration data, local net migration data has to be synthesised indirectly. First, the 1960 US Bureau of the Census population counts in standard five-year age–sex cohorts are 'survived' to 1965 for each county in the impact region. These population estimates are compared with the actual BEA population counts for 1965, and the difference is assumed to be net migration for the five-year period. Migration is then allocated on an annual basis, assuming 20% per year of the five-year estimate. Next, the annual migration estimate is allocated to age–sex cohorts, based on national age-group migration rates (Rogers et al, 1978). The result of this process is the creation of the 'best estimate' for the county-level total population composition of 1965. A similar procedure of estimating natural increase and migration for the population of the impact region is completed through 1980. However, another 'migration allocation' to age groups is needed only in 1975, since Bureau of the Census population-composition data are available for 1970 and 1980. Although problems with the use of the net migration variable have been discussed in the literature (Clark, 1982), no alternative in this case is available and the benefits appear to outweigh the costs. The relationship between local and national labour-market conditions is captured via the use of both the national unemployment rate and the level of local unemployment. Although the national unemployment rate should have a direct influence on net migration, the local unemployment variable should have an inverse effect. Since people often move in response to job opportunities, employment in contract construction is also utilised in this equation. The use of the construction variable follows the successful empirical findings of Ledent (1978), who employed a similar specification in his econometric model of the Tucson, AZ metropolitan area. Employment in state and local government is used as a proxy for the quality of public-sector services, also influencing migration. Last, the housing-stock variable is also included since it has a direct effect on the settlement (and departure) pattern of migrants.

Housing stock is modelled on the basis of consumer demand (proxied by population size and personal income by place-of-work, that is, wage and salary income), and the level of housing investment (proxied by nonwage income)[3]. All three explanatory variables were expected to have positive signs on their respective coefficients in this equation, which proved to be the case.

The final stochastic equation of this block depicts school-district member-ship (enrollment) as a logarithmic function of population. The cohort-survival component of the demographic block is contained in nineteen identity equations.

Fiscal equations in the model are included both for municipal and for county governments (aggregated to the county level) and for school districts. Relatively few regional econometric models include fiscal blocks and even fewer have estimated fiscal equations based on the public finance literature (Rubin and Erickson, 1980). This situation is partly because of the lack of data or because of its poor quality at the level of local government—particularly common are inconsistencies in data recording over time and space. In the present model, these problems are compounded by the need to collect fiscal data from two different states. Although the use of the cross-sectional, time-series pooling technique allows some of these problems to be overcome and makes it possible to address endogenously a substantial number of public-sector fiscal components, the number of fiscal equations is still fewer than would be optimal. Nevertheless, the number of stochastic equations estimated in the fiscal block is greater than in most comparable econometric models.

Local government general own-source revenue from nonproperty-tax sources is derived from user charges and several miscellaneous sources of income from the business and residential sectors of the local economy. The general revenue equation is thus structured on the basis of employment in the private sector and the size of the housing stock.

---

[3]Housing-stock data were no easier to come by than migration data, and also had to be synthesised. Actual housing-stock data available from the decennial census were taken as starting observations, and intervening year observations were inter-polated based on housing construction permit data available in the US Department of Commerce's *Construction* Reports, series C-40. A one-year lag between the issue of construction permits and the completion of construction was assumed.

The equation for municipal and county government property-tax receipts is based on the components of property-tax collections. These include the assessed value of the rateable property, the average millage rate, and the size of the housing stock.

The assessed value of property is portrayed as a function of the local population level and employment in the agricultural sector. The agricultural variable can be considered as a proxy for the degree of urbanisation in a county, with greater concentrations of agricultural employment leading to lower property values.

Municipal and county expenditure for general government activities is modelled as a function of population and total employment. This endogenous variable includes housing and urban renewal, highways and roads, financial administration, general control, health, and public welfare. As such, population represents the demand for services in this expenditure category, and total employment acts as a proxy for the general economic and social condition of a county. A negative sign on the coefficient of this last variable can be interpreted as indicating that the demand for many services (such as welfare or urban renewal) is inversely related to the economic prosperity of the geographic area.

Municipal and county government general expenditure is defined as all municipal and county expenditure other than that for highways and roads, general government, and school districts. This variable then includes hospitals, police and fire protection, sewerage and sanitation, utilities, and general debt. It is modelled on the basis of total employment, unemployment, personal income by place-of-work, and the ratio of the wage rate in state and local government to the wage rate in the private sector. The first two explanatory variables are used as general measures of the demand for government services and thus have positive signs. Since many of the general expenditures in this 'other' category are for a variety of social welfare programmes, personal income by place-of-work (that is, wage and salary income) is used as an indicator of local economic prosperity. Ceteris paribus, the greater the economic prosperity of a county, the lower will be the need for government expenditure in social welfare categories such as hospitals. Thus, an inverse relationship between general expenditure and personal income results. The use of the wage-rate ratio rests on the concept that wages are generally the largest component of government expenditure, and that the public sector must compete with the private sector for many qualified employees. A higher ratio of general public-sector wages to private-sector wages implies relatively lower funding levels for other direct general expenditure, other things being equal. Consequently, an inverse relationship is also expected between the wage-rate variable and other government general expenditure; such a relationship was found in this equation.

School-district property-tax receipts are related to the local average millage rate, school-district transfer payments, and the logged assessed value of property. Transfer payments constitute a major portion of school-district revenues, and relieve some of the burden on the property tax for educational funding. Thus, a negative coefficient for transfer payments is obtained in the estimation process. Conversely, property-tax receipts are directly dependent on the average millage rate and the assessed value of property.

The equation for school-district expenditure includes three explanatory variables—school-district membership, total personal income, and the wage rate in state and local government. Membership depicts the demand for educational services, total personal income represents the ability to pay, and the wage-rate variable is a proxy for teachers' salaries. The inclusion of this wage variable in such relationships has been substantiated by the work of Ehrenberg (1973).

Additional fiscal equations are included which sum the dependent variables described above to yield local government total general expenditure and revenue (includes municipal, county, and school-district figures), and school-district total revenue.

The environmental block of the model covers local ambient air quality, utility-services demands, and traffic levels. The air-quality variables are total suspended particulates, sulphur dioxides, and nitrogen oxides. These variables are explained on the basis of proxies such as employment in manufacturing, employment in transportation and public utilities, passenger car registrations, and regional manufacturing output (for nitrogen oxides only). Water use and wastewater treatment levels per capita are related to per-capita income and total employment; average daily highway traffic is modelled on the basis of total employment, and car registrations per capita are related to population and per-capita income. Last, population density and solid-waste generation are modelled as identity equations, the second of which is explained as a constant multiple of the population level.

In general, the Evansville Area Econometric Model fits the historical data closely, especially considering the poor quality of the county-level data. Thirty-one of the fifty stochastic equations have adjusted R^2 values above 0.9, with the lowest R^2 being 0.52 (wage rate in wholesale trade). In addition, twenty-three of the stochastic equations are estimated with generalised least squares, because of temporal autocorrelation in the disturbance term (Cochrane and Orcutt, 1949). When the model system was solved with the Gauss–Seidel simulation algorithm, the error statistics were generally low as well. For more detailed estimation and simulation results, see Solomon (1983) or Solomon and Rubin (1985).

4.3 *Application*

The Evansville Area Econometric Model is used to forecast county-by-county impacts of synthetic fuels development, yearly to 1995 (although in the interest of brevity only impacts every five years will be shown). This time frame allows the model to capture the full project-construction periods, and part of the operational phases as well. The exogenous variables are projected in the usual manner; for example, whereas national interest rates and unemployment are assumed eventually to stabilise at acceptable levels, national sectoral wage rates and the GNP grow (in real terms) at moderate rates in the model. The direct effects of the synthetic fuels plants are entered into the model by utilising unit coefficients in the following equations: local and regional contract-construction employment, total regional employment, nondurable manufacturing local employment, and the assessed value of property. The direct effects reverberate to all other parts of the model during the simulations.

Three development scenarios are considered. The first is the baseline scenario, in which it is assumed *no* synthetic fuels projects will be completed, although other coal projects are developed. The results of this analysis show moderate growth in most of the important variables. In the other two scenarios it is assumed that one and three projects will be completed, respectively. The results of the three-project case will be summarised here.

The synthetic fuels project impacts are most pronounced in the counties where they are sited—Daviess and Henderson (tables 2 and 3). 'Impact' is defined here as the change in the energy-development forecast over that of the base case. Employment and real income are greatly stimulated in this analysis, primarily because of the contract-construction labour required by the project in the mid-1980s, and later by more modest manufacturing employment needs. Modest growth occurs in the wholesale trade and

Table 2. Definitions of variables.

Variable[a]	Definition
EMCON	Employment in contract construction (thousands)
EMMT	Employment in manufacturing—durable *and* nondurable goods (thousands)
EMWHL	Employment in wholesale trade (thousands)
UNR	Unemployment rate (%)
PITPC	Personal income total per capita ($ thousands)
GNRVD	Local government general revenues—includes schools and inter-governmental transfer payments ($ millions)
GNEXD	Local government general expenditures—includes schools ($ millions)
HOUS	Housing stock (thousands)
MIG	Net migration (thousands)
POP	Total population (thousands)
TSP	Total level of suspended particulates (mean in μg m^{-3})
SOX	Level of sulphur dioxides (mean in μg m^{-3})
WATER	Municipal water use (million gallons per day)
WWATER	Level of municipal wastewater treatment (million gallons per day)
SWG	Solid-waste generation rate (thousand tons per year)

[a] All monetary variables are in constant (1972) dollars.

transportation and utility sectors as well. Real per-capita income rises most noticeably in Henderson County, where most of the construction impacts would be concentrated. The local unemployment rate drops throughout the projection period, very dramatically in Henderson County in the mid-1980s.

The economic growth in the region also stimulates demographic and fiscal expansion. Again, the impacts are the largest and most critical in Henderson County, where migration and population, the housing stock, property values, and local government finances all expand at fast rates. Government expenditure requirements expand faster than revenues in most cases, which is partly a result of the average property-tax rate being held constant during the initial forecast periods. This was done so that county tax rates, as well as transfer payments to local governments and school districts, could be manipulated as policy variables. However, these policy variables had to be expanded greatly in most cases to balance local government finances, which does not bode well for the fiscal impacts of synthetic fuels projects that could actually occur. The coal-liquefaction plants would not contribute to property-tax levies until the operational phases in the late 1980s and beyond, whereas local government expenditure requirements would rise dramatically when the construction periods begin in the mid-1980s.

The environmental impacts forecast by the model are a response to the economic expansion as well. Ambient levels of total suspended particulates rise well *above* federal standards in the two Kentucky counties, with the

Table 3. Net impacts of three synthetic fuels plants on Daviess County and Henderson County, KY.

Variable[a]	Daviess County			Henderson County		
	1985	1990	1995	1985	1990	1995
EMCON	4.589	5.331	0	16.773	0	0
EMMT	− 0.030	0.556	1.702	− 0.088	3.814	3.517
EMWHL	0.096	0.545	1.202	0.211	1.207	2.469
UNR	− 0.716	− 0.761	− 0.321	− 3.628	− 1.342	− 1.112
PITPC	0.230	0.275	0.209	1.698	0.713	0.859
GNRVD	4.841	12.695	12.817	9.571	16.584	16.659
GNEXD	8.397	15.017	22.410	29.840	12.457	16.736
HOUS	0.657	2.085	3.128	1.397	4.182	5.816
MIG	0.968	1.418	0.713	3.353	0.828	1.201
POP	2.040	7.741	11.632	14.028	14.495	20.989
TSP	0.57	2.98	6.45	3.33	20.04	22.59
SOX	− 0.38	− 1.91	− 3.84	− 2.01	− 11.29	− 12.07
WATER	0.615	1.563	2.190	1.908	2.639	4.239
WWATER	− 0.523	− 0.904	0.077	0.664	1.966	3.125
SWG	1.489	5.651	8.491	3.290	10.581	15.322

[a]See table 2.

impacts in Henderson again most severe. However, sulphur dioxides are less serious in the region, and were found actually to *decrease* because of the shift in industrial structure. Nevertheless, the remaining environmental variables grow in most cases, particularly average daily traffic, municipal water use, and solid-waste generation. Some of these environmental impacts may exceed the 'carrying capacity' of the region, and will have to be traded off with the positive economic effects in the eventual energy development scenario that can be realised (see also Fishkind et al, 1978). This could be accomplished through stricter pollution-control standards for the energy plants, greater industrial funding for local infrastructure, or a restriction on the *scale* of permitted synthetic fuels development.

The impacts of synthetic fuels projects are very *small* in the Indiana counties by comparison, and some of the impacts in two of the counties are shown here (table 4). Vanderburgh County, for example, would see a minor stimulus in retail trade, but otherwise most of the impacts on southern Indiana are negligible. Thus, although the impacts on Indiana should not be ignored totally, the policy emphasis should be placed on Kentucky.

Table 4. Net impacts of three synthetic fuels plants on Vanderburgh County and Warrick County, IN.

Variable[a]	Vanderburgh County			Warrick County		
	1985	1990	1995	1985	1990	1995
EMCON	0	0	0	0	0	0
EMMT	0	− 0.004	− 0.006	0	0	0
EMWHL	0	0.001	0.004	0	0	0
UNR	0	− 0.008	− 0.007	0	− 0.006	− 0.005
PITPC	0	0.005	0.007	0	0.002	0.003
GNRVD	0	0.014	0.024	0	− 0.004	− 0.005
GNEXD	0	0.500	1.644	0	0.027	0.032
HOUS	0	− 0.001	0.004	0	− 0.001	− 0.001
MIG	0	0.002	0.004	0	0	0
POP	0	0.006	− 0.022	0	0	0.001
TSP	0	0.01	0.02	0	0	0.01
SOX	0	− 0.01	− 0.02	0	− 0.01	0
WATER	0	0.021	0.036	0	0.003	0.004
WWATER	0	− 0.121	− 0.179	0	0.001	0.002
SWG	0	0.004	0.016	0	0	0

[a]See table 2.

5 Implications for energy policy

The recent 'new federalism' that has slowed the federal synthetic fuels program should be seen as an opportunity for rethinking directions in energy policy. Indeed, before the creation of the US Synthetic Fuels Corporation, many analysts had proposed (almost blindly) major federal subsidies for the creation of a domestic synthetic fuels industry. In one such proposal, federal subsidies for synthetic fuels production were advanced as a crucial means to reduce foreign oil imports and payments, which could *reduce* upward pressure on other energy prices (Ezzati, 1978, page 208). The latter conjecture now seems very doubtful, since it is more likely that higher priced synthetic fuels would increase the demand for and thus the price of competing fuels, including foreign oil. More pertinent, Ezzati does acknowledge that environmental factors need to be accounted for, but does not indicate their likely relationship to an overall energy policy. It is precisely this 'blindspot' that the completion of this study will help to remove.

In recent years, a synthetic fuels promotion policy has been criticised on grounds of distortions induced in regional coal markets (Attanasi and Green, 1981), and the lack of a sequential research and development strategy (Weitzman et al, 1981). Clearly, the ultimate desirability of synthetic fuels should depend on the total social costs: market, environmental, and national security costs, preferably at all spatial scales. This suggests an energy-policy decision process which iterates concerns from

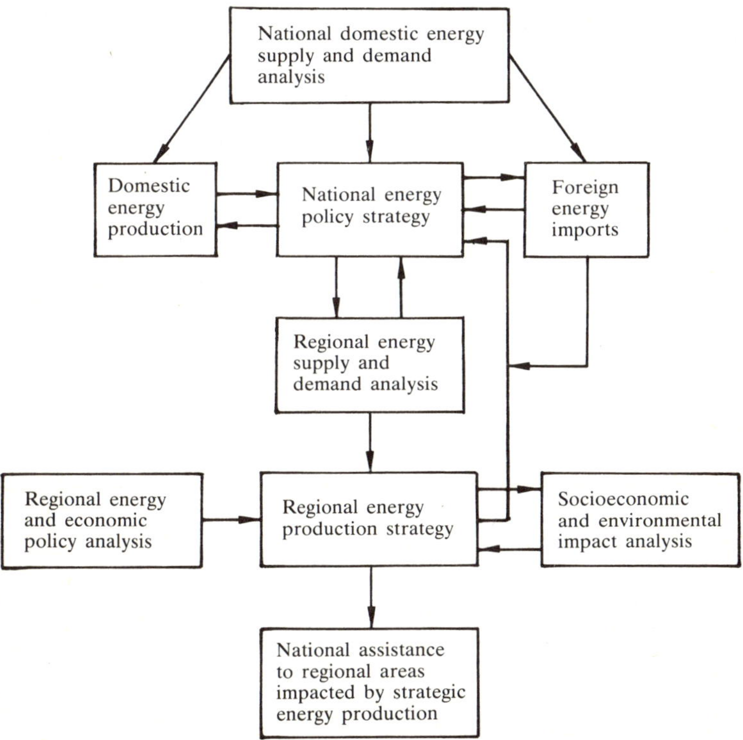

Figure 3. An iterative decision process for national–regional energy policy.

the national level down to the regional level, and back up to the national level again (figure 3).

A socioeconomic and environmental impact-analysis of synthetic fuels development could be used to influence regional production decisions, which ultimately affect national energy policy. In the case of Western Kentucky, the results of the Evansville Area Econometric Model could thus also help to *guide* policy decisions of federal energy agencies. The output of the regional econometric model alone does *not* indicate if the projects *should* be completed, although *if* the projects are pursued, national financial assistance to the negatively impacted local governments in the region might be justified. Such assistance could be used for pollution control, and to meet shortfalls in local government general expenditures. Alternatively, since the US Synthetic Fuels Corporation has considered subsidising individual projects at up to $3 billion, it is reasonable to ask that the *industrial developers* allocate a small fraction of their revenues to strict environmental protection and local area impact mitigation. Although other federal programs for assistance with mitigation of energy-development impact currently exist, these programs are quite modest in scope, and it would be more appropriate to link an assistance program of synthetic fuels development to regional funding for development impact mitigation. Hopefully, the Evansville Area Econometric Model can help to focus these important issues.

Acknowledgement. The partial financial support of the National Science Foundation (grant number SES 81-07355) is gratefully acknowledged. The views expressed herein do not necessarily reflect those of the Federal Energy Regulatory Commission or the National Science Foundation.

References
Attanasi E D, Green E K, 1981, "Some regional costs of a synthetic fuel industry: the case of Illinois" *The Annals of Regional Science* **15** 43–52
Ballard K P, Glickman N J, 1977, "A multiregional econometric forecasting system: a model of the Delaware Valley" *Journal of Regional Science* **17** 161–177
Bell F W, 1967, "An econometric forecasting model of a region" *Journal of Regional Science* **7** 109–127
Bergmann B R, 1969, "The urban economy and the urban crisis" *American Economic Review* **59** 639–645
Brown R J, 1981, "Simulating the impact of an irrigation project on a small regional economy" *Growth and Change* **12** 23–30
Charney A H, Taylor C A, 1983, "Consistent region–subregion econometric models: a comparison of multiarea methods" *International Regional Science Review* **8** 59–74
Clark G L, 1982, "Dynamics of interstate labor migration" *Annals of the Association of American Geographers* **72** 297–313
Cochrane D, Orcutt G H, 1949, "Application of least squares regressions to relationships containing autocorrelated error terms" *Journal of the American Statistical Association* **44** 32–61

Dhrymes P J, 1965, "Some extensions and tests for the CES class of production functions" *The Review of Economics and Statistics* **47** 357–366

Duobinis S F, 1981, "An econometric model of the Chicago Standard Metropolitan Statistical Area" *Journal of Regional Science* **21** 293–319

Ehrenberg R G, 1973, "The demand for state and local government employees" *American Economic Review* **26** 36–48

Ezzati A, 1978, "Impact of government subsidies on market penetration of synthetic fuels" *Energy Policy* **6** 196–208

Finn M, Gaston R, 1980, "Construction labor assessment for Solvent-Refined-Coal project I at phase zero" Oak Ridge Associated Universities, Oak Ridge, TN

Fishkind H H, Milliman J W, Ellson R W, 1978, "A pragmatic econometric approach to assessing economic impacts of growth or decline in urban areas" *Land Economics* **54** 442–460

Gilmore J S, 1976, "Boom towns may hinder energy resource development" *Science* **191** 535–540

Glickman N J, 1976, "A note on simultaneous equation estimation techniques applications with a regional econometric model" *Regional Science and Urban Economics* **6** 275–287

Glickman N J, 1977 *Econometric Analysis of Regional Systems: Explorations in Model Building and Policy Analysis* (Academic Press, New York)

Isard W, 1960 *Methods of Regional Analysis: An Introduction to Regional Science* (MIT Press, Cambridge, MA)

Isard W, 1975 *Introduction to Regional Science* (Prentice-Hall, Englewood Cliffs, NJ)

Isard W, Kuenne R E, 1953, "The impact of steel upon the greater New York–Philadelphia industrial region" *The Review of Economics and Statistics* **35** 289–301

Jones J, Enoch H, 1981, "The Kentucky synfuel industry: a basis for assessment and planning" Kentucky Department of Energy, Lexington, KY

Judge G G, Griffiths W E, Hill C R, Lee T C, 1980 *The Theory and Practice of Econometrics* (John Wiley, New York)

Kentucky DOE, 1982, "Coal conversion projects summary" Kentucky Department of Energy, Lexington, KY

Klein L R, 1969, "The specification of regional econometric models" *Papers and Proceedings of the Regional Science Association* **23** 105–115

Knapp J L, Fields T W, Jerome R T, 1978, "A survey of state and regional econometric models" Tayloe Murphy Institute, The University of Virginia, Charlottesville, VA

Krutilla J W, Fisher A C, with Rice R E, 1978 *Economic and Fiscal Impacts of Coal Development: Northern Great Plains* (The Johns Hopkins University Press, Baltimore, MD)

Lakshmanan T R, 1983, "A multiregional model of the economy, environment, and energy demand in the United States" *Economic Geography* **59** 296–320

Ledent J, 1978, "Regional multiplier analysis: a demometric approach" *Environment and Planning A* **10** 537–560

Leistritz F L, Murdock S H, 1981 *Socioeconomic Impact of Resource Development: Methods for Assessment* (Westview Press, Boulder, CO)

Leontief W W, 1953, "Interregional theory" in *Studies in the Structure of the American Economy: Theoretical and Empirical Explorations in Input–Output Analysis* Eds W W Leontief, H B Chenery, P G Clark, J S Duesenberry, A R Ferguson, A P Grosse, R N Grosse, M Holzman, W Isard, H Kistin (International Arts and Sciences Press, White Plains, NY) pp 93–115

Leontief W W, Morgan A, Polenske K R, Simpson D, Tower E, 1965, "The economic impact–industrial and regional–of an arms cut" *The Review of Economics and Statistics* **47** 217–241

Miernyk W H, 1982 *Regional Analysis and Regional Policy* (Oelgeschlager, Gunn and Hain, Cambridge, MA)

Miernyk W H, Bonner E R, Chapman J H Jr, Shellhammer K L, 1967 *Impact of the Space Program on a Local Economy—An Input–Output Analysis* (West Virginia University Foundation, Morgantown, WV)

National Coal Association, 1981, "Coal synfuel facility survey" National Coal Association, Washington, DC

Research Seminar in Quantitative Economics, 1965 *Econometric Model of Michigan* (University of Michigan Press, Ann Arbor, MI)

Richardson H W, 1972 *Input–Output and Regional Economics* (John Wiley, New York)

Richardson H W, 1978a *Regional Economics* (University of Illinois Press, Urbana, IL)

Richardson H W, 1978b, "The state of regional economics: a survey article" *International Regional Science Review* **3** 1–48

Rogers A, 1975 *Introduction to Multiregional Mathematical Demography* (John Wiley, New York)

Rogers A, Raquillet R, Castro L J, 1978, "Model migration schedules and their applications" *Environment and Planning A* **10** 475–502

Rose A Z, 1984, "Technological change and input–output analysis: an appraisal" *Socio-Economic Planning Sciences* **18** 305–318

Rose A Z, Nakayama B, Stevens B K, 1982, "Modern energy region development and income distribution: an input–output analysis" *Journal of Environmental Economics and Management* **9** 149–164

Rubin B M, Erickson R A, 1980, "Specification and performance improvements in regional econometric forecasting models: a model of the Milwaukee metropolitan area" *Journal of Regional Science* **20** 11–35

Rubin B M, Solomon B D, 1983, "Economic and fiscal impact analysis of energy development projects: coal liquefaction in the Illinois basin" *Socio-Economic Planning Sciences* **17** 11–20

Schweitzer M, Carnes S A, Soderstrom E J, Braid R B, 1983, "Synthetic fuel development: potential socioeconomic impacts of single and multiple projects" *Energy Policy* **11** 333–345

Solomon B D, 1983 *Environmental Linkages in Regional Econometric Impact Analysis Models* PhD dissertation, Department of Geography, Indiana University, Bloomington, IN

Solomon B D, 1985, "Regional econometric models for environmental impact assessment" *Progress in Human Geography* **9** 379–399

Solomon B D, Rubin B M, 1985, "Environmental linkages in regional econometric models: an analysis of coal development in Western Kentucky" *Land Economics* **61** 43–57

Temple G S, 1978 *A Dynamic Economic System Community Impact Model Applied to Coal Development in the Northern Great Plains* PhD dissertation, Department of Applied Economics, Montana State University, Bozeman, MT

Weitzman M L, with Newey W, Rabin M, 1981, "Sequential R & D strategy for synfuels" *The Bell Journal of Economics* **12** 573–590

State and Local Fiscal Analysis with an Econometric Model of Texas

T R PLAUT
University of Texas, Austin

1 Introduction

Since 1973, increasing oil and gas prices and economic prosperity have allowed Texas state and local governments to keep taxes relatively low, while increasing spending to meet the needs of a growing population. In 1981, nonseverance state and local taxes accounted for 8.2% of Texas personal income and 11.0% of personal income nationwide (US Bureau of the Census, 1982a). Texas has no individual or corporate income tax (although it does have a corporate franchise tax), and the last major increase in state tax rates (up to 1984) was in 1972, when the sales tax was increased from 3% to 4% and local governments were given the option to add 1%. (In July 1984, however, a $4.6 billion tax increase to fund increased education and highway spending passed the Texas legislature.)

Over the decade 1973–1983, Texas avoided the need to increase taxes mainly because of the increasing value of oil and gas production and the resulting flow of revenues from the severance tax and rents and royalties from state oil land. In 1981, 21.6% of total state government revenues were from severance taxes and rents and royalties, which is almost five times the national figure of 4.4% (US Bureau of the Census, 1982b).

In contrast to the past decade, the ability of Texas state and local governments to increase revenues to meet growing expenditure needs, with the current system of revenue and expenditure, looks less promising. State oil and gas production is declining, and even increasing petroleum prices can do little to slow this trend. Declining production, coupled with only a moderate rate of increase in oil and gas prices (especially oil), indicates that the value of state oil and gas production will increase relatively slowly and that revenues will need to be increased or the rate of increase in expenditures reduced to keep the state and local revenue–expenditure system in balance.

The addition of a detailed state and local government expenditure and revenue submodel to the Texas Economic–Demographic Forecasting Model (TEDFM) allows for long-term structural analysis of governmental finances in the state. The submodel forecasts five types of state and local expenditures and fifteen types of revenues, including several significant nontax revenues. Forecasts are generated to the year 2000 and state and local fiscal pressure is gauged by observing the ratio of expenditures to revenues and comparing it with historical norms.

The organisation of the rest of this paper is as follows: section 2 is an overview of the overall structure of TEDFM, and section 3 is a more detailed description of the expenditure–revenue submodel. Forecast assumptions underlying the baseline forecast are discussed in section 4 and in section 5 are presented the results of the baseline (most likely) expenditure–revenue forecast. Given the sensitivity of the expenditure– revenue submodel to alternative assumptions about oil and gas prices and production and because of the uncertainty of the future path of these variables, it is useful to run the model with alternative forecast assumptions. The results of low price, low production, and high price, high production alternative forecasts are thus presented in section 6. Finally, section 7 is a summary of the major results of the paper, in which some suggestions are made for future analysis.

2 Overall structure of TEDFM

The Texas Economic–Demographic Forecasting Model is a large-scale forecasting and policy-analysis model for the state. The model summarises in equations the historical relations between economic growth and population growth in Texas. This system of equations, along with forecasts of US growth, is then used to forecast the future path of economic and population growth in the state.

TEDFM is made up of 135 stochastic equations and 190 deterministic equations and identities. The model contains 325 endogenous variables and 125 exogenous variables. The equations are estimated on annual time-series data, which span the period 1958 to 1981.

The main idea behind TEDFM is that the relative attractiveness of Texas to business and to people determines its long-term growth. The relative attractiveness of Texas to business, as measured by the growth in markets and the costs of doing business in Texas in comparison with market growth and costs in the whole of the United States of America, determines business investment in Texas. Business investment is then summed over time to give the Texas capital stock—that is, the stock of plant and equipment available to produce output.

The relative attractiveness of Texas to people, as measured by wages, the availability of jobs, and environmental conditions in Texas compared with the whole of the USA, determines population migration into Texas. Population migration is then combined with the numbers of births and deaths to give the state population.

Texas population is the major determinant of the labour force—the number of people willing and able to work. The growth in Texas capital stock and labour force are then combined to determine the long-term growth in Texas output.

2.1 *Submodels and industrial–demographic detail*

TEDFM is made up of four interacting submodels (see figure 1). The demographic submodel determines population migration, births, deaths, and population for six broad age groups and for thirty-two age and sex groups. The manufacturing submodel determines manufacturing investment, capital stock, worker hours, and output (gross product) for fifteen industries. The production submodel and labour-market submodel determine output, employment, and wages for nine major economic sectors, three mining industries, and two government industries, as well as determining personal income by source. For more information on the structure of the submodels in TEDFM see Plaut (1981; 1982b; 1985a; 1985b).

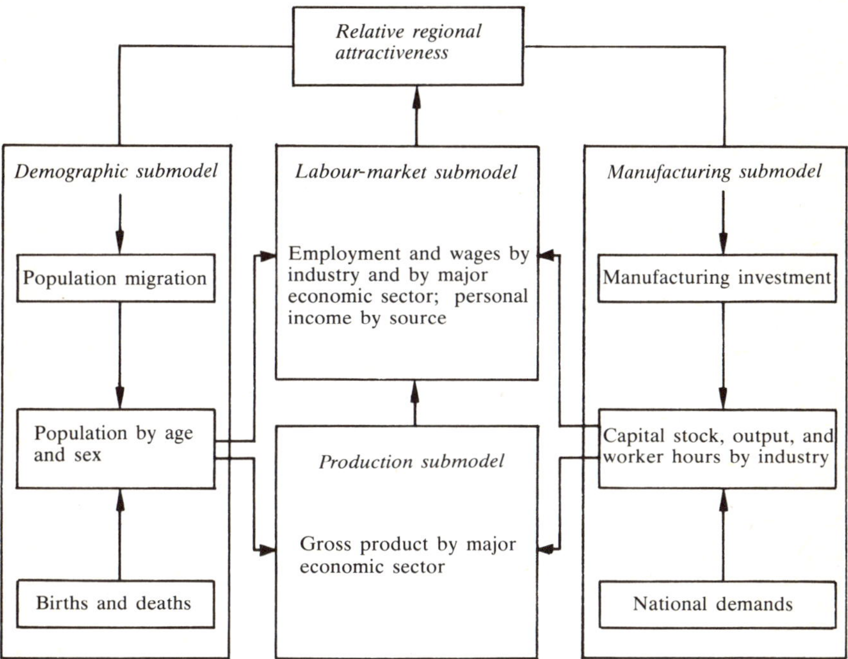

Figure 1. Overall structure of the Texas Economic–Demographic Forecasting Model.

2.2 *Model verification*

Throughout its development, TEDFM has been subjected to continuous tests of forecasting accuracy, stability, and 'reasonableness'. The evaluation of model accuracy and stability is performed at two levels. First, as each equation is estimated, it is analysed in terms of its consistency with economic theory, its overall explanatory power, the reasonableness and significance of estimates of individual coefficients, and the accuracy of its specification. Second, the operation of the entire equation system as an integrated unit is tested through a dynamic in-sample simulation of the model over the sample period.

Model accuracy in predicting aggregate Texas economic and demographic variables is quite high. The root mean squared percentage errors in in-sample predictions of four summary variables—gross product, personal income, nonagricultural employment, and population—range from 1.0% to 1.7%. Generally, prediction errors increase with increased variable disaggregation, but this is to be expected since more disaggregate variables are smaller, and more volatile over time.

Judging the 'reasonableness' of model forecasts is much more subjective than the in-sample analysis of model accuracy and stability. As each set of model forecasts is produced, it is analysed in terms of its consistency with historical trends and general expectations of future economic and population growth. If a model forecast is deemed to be 'unreasonable', the process generating the forecast—the relevant equations and data—is reevaluated.

2.3 *Model updates and forecast results*
Once a year, the entire structure of TEDFM is reexamined and all of the stochastic equations in the model are reestimated with an additional year of data. Forecast results from the model were first made available to users in 1982 (Plaut, 1982a) and the forecasts have been updated and published annually since then (see Plaut, 1983; Plaut et al, 1984). A wide variety of users use the forecast results from TEDFM including government agencies, people running small businesses, strategic planners in large corporations, banks and savings and loans institutions, utilities, and real-estate developers.

3 Expenditure–revenue submodel
The expenditure–revenue detail used in the submodel is outlined in table 1. Three types of state expenditures (education, other, and state grants to local governments) and two types of local expenditures (education and other) are determined in the simultaneous block of TEDFM. Total state and local expenditures then drive state and local government output and employment. In general, state and local government expenditures are determined by the demand for government services as measured by population, school-age population, and personal income (see table 2).

At the state level, noneducation expenditures are by far the most important component in spending. The estimated equation for state noneducation expenditures is:

$$EOS = -1436.58^{***} + 0.25^{***}POP + 0.39^{**}RFS, \qquad (1)$$
$$ (-5.22) \qquad\quad (6.52) \qquad\quad (2.30)$$

$$\overline{R}^2 = 0.98, \qquad DW = 1.38,$$

(t-statistics are shown in parentheses, significance levels are ***1%, **5%, and *10%, DW is the Durbin–Watson statistic),
where
EOS is state noneducation expenditures (in 1972 dollars),
POP is the total state population,
RFS is state federal funding (in 1972 dollars).

Noneducation expenditures are also the most important component of spending at the local government level, but until recently, education spending has been more important. The estimated equation for local education spending is

$$EEL = -1135.77^{***} + 0.67^{***}POP517 + 1.22^{***}RSL,$$
$$(-2.81) \qquad\quad (4.11) \qquad\qquad (16.33)$$
$$\tag{2}$$

$$\overline{R}^2 = 0.99, \qquad DW = 2.22,$$

where
EEL   is local education expenditures (in 1972 dollars),
POP517 is the state population of 5 to 17 years old,
RSL   is local government grants from the state (in 1972 dollars).

State and local government revenues are determined by a block of equations that takes forecasts of state income, population, oil and gas production, oil and gas prices, and other driving variables as exogenous.

Table 1. State and local government expenditure and revenue detail in the Texas Economic–Demographic Forecasting Model.

Expenditures
State education
State other
State grants to local governments (mostly for education)
Local education
Local other

Revenues
State general sales tax
State selective sales tax (motor vehicle, motor fuels, cigarette, alcoholic beverages, etc)
State severance taxes (oil and gas production)
State license taxes (corporate franchise tax, motor vehicle registrations, insurance tax, utility taxes)
State other taxes (property taxes, inheritance taxes)
State current charges (mostly education)
State rents and royalties
State interest and other miscellaneous revenues
State federal funding
Local property taxes
Local sales taxes
Local other taxes
Local charges and miscellaneous revenues
Local government grants from the state
Local federal funding

Revenues in each category are determined by direct or indirect measures of the revenue base (see table 2), and each equation is estimated over the period when the most recent tax rate has been in effect (for example, the state general sales tax equation is estimated over the period 1973–1981).

In total, nine types of state government revenues are determined—these include five types of taxes (general sales, selective sales, severance, license, and other) and four nontax revenues (current charges, rents and royalties, interest and miscellaneous revenues, and federal funding). Six types of local government revenues are determined, including three types of taxes (property, sales, and other) and three nontax items (local charges and miscellaneous revenues, local government grants from the state government, and local federal funding). Note that a significant source of local government revenues—state grants to local government—is also a state expenditure item. This fact illustrates the strong linkage of state and local governments in Texas.

Table 2. State and local government expenditure and revenue determinants.

Variable	Determinants
State government expenditures	
Education	School-age population, personal income
Other	Population, state federal funding
Grants to local governments	Population
Local government expenditures	
Education	School-age population, state grants to local government
Other	Population
State government revenues	
General sales taxes	Retail sales, manufacturing investment
Selective sales taxes	Personal income, US motor vehicle consumption, US gasoline consumption
Severance taxes	Oil production, natural gas production, oil prices, natural gas prices
License taxes	Personal income
Other taxes	Personal income
Current charges	Personal income
Rents and royalties	Oil production, natural gas production, oil prices, natural gas prices
Interest and other miscellaneous revenue	Commercial bank rate, personal income
Federal funding	Exogenous
Local government revenues	
Property taxes	Personal income
Sales taxes	Retail sales
Other taxes	Personal income
Charges and miscellaneous revenues	Personal income
Grants from state government	Population
Federal funding	Exogenous

The most important source of state government revenues is federal funding, accounting for 23% of total revenues in 1981. The three next most important revenue sources are general sales taxes, selective sales taxes, and the severance tax, which together accounted for 53% of total state revenues in 1981. The estimated equations for those three taxes are

$$\ln \text{RGSS} = \underset{(-10.81)}{-3.62^{***}} + \underset{(16.77)}{0.92^{***}} \ln \text{RS} + \underset{(3.40)}{0.14^{***}} \ln \text{IM}, \tag{3}$$

$$\overline{R}^2 = 0.99, \qquad \text{DW} = 2.60;$$

$$\text{RSSS} = \underset{(-0.10)}{-21.68} + \underset{(10.90)}{0.01^{***}} \text{PI} + \underset{(3.80)}{5.12^{***}} \text{MV} + \underset{(1.73)}{4.31^{*}} \text{GAS}, \tag{4}$$

$$\overline{R}^2 = 0.99, \qquad \text{DW} = 2.74;$$

$$\text{RSEVS} = \underset{(0.40)}{6.78} + \underset{(6.62)}{0.05^{***}} \text{VOIL} + \underset{(4.24)}{0.06^{***}} \text{VNGAS}, \tag{5}$$

$$\overline{R}^2 = 0.99, \qquad \text{DW} = 1.00;$$

where
RGSS   is state general sales tax receipts,
RSSS   is state selective sales tax receipts,
RSEVS   is state severance tax receipts (all revenues are determined in
         current dollars).
The independent variables in these equations are as follows:
RS   Texas retail sales ($),
IM   Texas manufacturing investment ($),
PI   Texas personal income ($),
MV   US motor vehicle consumption ($),
GAS   US gasoline consumption (gallons),
VOIL   Value of Texas oil production ($),
VNGAS   Value of Texas natural gas production ($).

The most important component of local government revenues is property taxes, which accounted for 34% of total revenues in 1981. The estimated equation for this revenue source is

$$\ln \text{RPROPL} = \underset{(-22.76)}{-1.95^{***}} + \underset{(109.14)}{0.87^{***}} \ln \text{PI}, \tag{6}$$

$$\overline{R}^2 = 0.99, \qquad \text{DW} = 0.88,$$

where
RPROPL   is local property tax receipts,
PI   is state personal income ($).

4 Forecast assumptions

The major forecast assumptions underlying the state and local government revenue–expenditure analysis are outlined in table 3. Forecasts of major economic and demographic driving variables such as population, school-age population, personal income, and retail sales are given by TEDFM. Forecasts of oil and gas prices are taken from Data Resources, Inc. (1983), and projections of oil and gas production reflect the average decline rate for state production from 1972 to 1981. Projections of state and local federal funding are based on the assumption that no increase in real funding will occur, so the rate of increase in funding follows the projected rate of increase in the US state and local expenditure price deflator.

Basically, the forecast assumptions reflect the expectation of relatively high, but slowing, state economic and population growth and moderate, but increasing, inflation. Oil and gas production is expected to continue to decline at a moderate rate, while prices increase slowly in the first ten years and moderately thereafter. Natural gas prices increase more rapidly than oil prices over the first ten years of the forecast period because of the continuing process of deregulation under current legislation. Federal funding is expected to remain relatively restricted over the forecast period because of continuing pressures on the federal government to economise.

Table 3. Forecast assumptions underlying the state and local government expenditure and revenue forecasts.

Variable	Average annual growth rate (%)		
	1970–1980	1980–1990	1990–2000
Population	2.5	2.3	1.4
School-age population	0.5	1.0	1.4
Personal income	13.1	10.4	9.8
Retail sales	13.2	10.3	9.7
Oil production	− 2.4	− 3.5	− 3.5
Natural gas production	− 1.5	− 1.9	− 2.1
Oil prices (US wellhead)	21.1	6.7	10.4
Natural gas prices (US wellhead)	25.1	11.5	11.3
State federal funding	12.1	7.0	6.7
Local federal funding	24.7	7.7	6.7

5 Baseline expenditure–revenue forecasts

Figure 2 illustrates the fact that since 1973 the Texas state government has enjoyed a relatively healthy fiscal situation with revenues well in excess of expenditures. The forecast results indicate, however, that the fiscal condition of the state began to deteriorate in 1982 and that by 1986 the ratio of revenues to expenditures drops below 1. The revenue–expenditure ratio drops rapidly over the first ten years of the forecast period, reaching 0.94 by 1990, and drops slowly thereafter to reach a low point of 0.91 in 2000.

The major factors contributing to increasing fiscal pressures on the state government, especially over the decade 1984–1994, are the increasing demand for government services caused by continuing economic and population growth and the inability to extract the revenues necessary to fund such services from a revenue system heavily dependent on declining oil and gas production. With current projections, the rates of increase in oil and gas prices are not sufficient to offset declines in production, and oil- and gas-related revenues become a declining source of state government revenues. For example, the share of total state revenues coming from severance tax peaks at 16.0% in 1981 and is projected to fall steadily to 9.8% in 2000. The other major oil- and gas-related revenue source—rents and royalties—peaks at 6.2% of total state government revenues in 1982 and falls to 5.7% in 2000.

It should be emphasised that the forecast of increasing state fiscal pressures is not a result of the rate of increase in state spending out-stripping the general growth of the economy. State spending (including state grants to local governments) remains a relatively constant percentage of Texas personal income over the forecast period. In 1982, this percentage peaks at 8.0% (the same as its 1973 peak), and it gradually declines to 7.8% by 2000.

The state revenue and expenditure forecasts thus indicate that during the mid-1980s the state government will be facing significant fiscal pressures and that revenues or expenditures will need to be adjusted to keep the state finances in balance. In fact, until the mid-1990s the state will continue to face significant fiscal pressures.

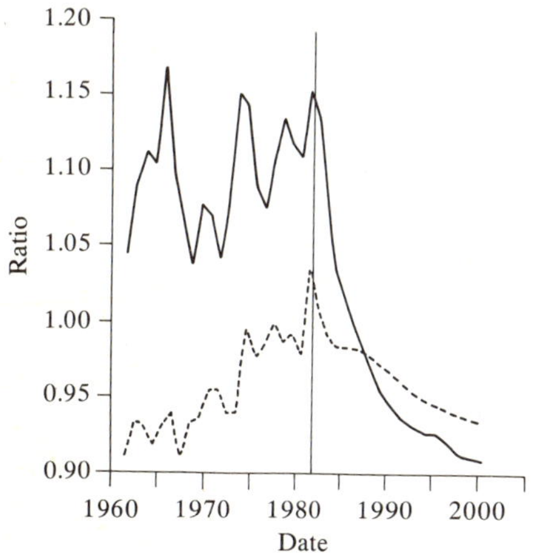

Figure 2. Ratio of Texas state (solid line) and local (dotted line) government revenues to expenditures, 1961–2000.

Like the state government, local governments in Texas will also face increasing fiscal pressures over the next twenty-five years. Figure 2 shows that the ratio of local government revenues over expenditures dropped to a low of 0.94 in 1973, but the addition of the local sales tax option and strong economic growth allowed this ratio to increase to 1.04 by 1981 (this ratio tends to remain below 1 because local governments obtain some revenues from locally owned utilities, a factor which is not included in the existing revenue data).

Over the forecast period, the local revenue–expenditure ratio falls steadily to 0.97 in 1990 and drops slowly thereafter to reach 0.93 in 2000. In general, local government revenues are not as closely linked to oil and gas production as state revenues, so the position of local governments is not as immediately precarious as that of the state government. Still, over the long term some adjustments in revenues or expenditures will be necessary to keep local government finances in balance.

It should be noted that the above assessment of the relatively better fiscal position of local governments in Texas is based on the assumption that the state government will continue to fund a major portion of local government activities. In 1981, the state government provided 27.8% of local government revenues (funds that are almost entirely directed at education) and this ratio is projected to rise gradually to reach 31.9% by 2000. If the state government is forced to cut local government funding to restore its revenue–expenditure balance, the present assessment of the Texas local government fiscal outlook could change dramatically.

6 Alternative forecasts

Today, the future path of world oil prices is extremely uncertain. Some observers argue that the era of rising real oil prices is over and that in the future the rate of increase in oil prices may not even keep pace with the general inflation rate. Others, however, argue that the current fall in oil prices is a result of worldwide economic stagnation and that, once the world economy begins growing, real oil prices will begin to rise (see Jacoby and Paddock, 1981; US Department of Energy, 1982).

Because of the strong link between world oil prices and Texas economic and population growth and state and local government finances, it is useful to analyse the effects of these widely divergent oil forecasts on the revenue and expenditure forecasts. TEDFM is used to examine the effects of two alternative oil and gas price and production possibilities: (1) a low price, low production alternative that assumes extremely slow worldwide economic growth, a continuation of the oil glut, a further fall in oil prices until 1985, and a relatively low rate of increase in prices afterwards; and (2) a high price, high production alternative that assumes rapid world recovery from economic recession and a long-term increase in oil prices well above the overall inflation rate.

The specific alternative oil and gas price and production assumptions are outlined in table 4. In the low price, low production alternative, the US wellhead price of oil is expected to increase 6.6% annually from $21.59 per barrel in 1980 to $77.17 per barrel in 2000. In the high price, high production alternative, oil prices are expected to increase 3 percentage points per year faster than in the low price, low production alternative, and the oil price reaches $142.41 per barrel by 2000.

By 2000, the high price, high production oil price is 85% above the low alternative price. In both alternatives, natural gas prices are expected to increase faster than oil prices, but the gap between the high and low rates of increase remains at about 3 percentage points.

Because changes in oil and gas prices have a significant effect on petroleum exploration efforts and these efforts should eventually increase reserves and oil and gas production, it seems reasonable to associate the two price alternatives with different projections of oil and gas production. Two quite divergent forecasts of Texas oil and gas production are available—a fairly optimistic set of projections from the Texas Energy and Natural Resources Advisory Council (TENRAC, 1980) and three much gloomier projections from industry sources (Texas Research League, 1982).

The TENRAC oil and gas production projections appear to be based on the belief that increasing oil prices will slow the rate of decline in Texas production. Total oil and gas production is projected to decline 1.1% a year from 977 million barrels in 1980 to 734 million barrels in 2000.

The industry oil and gas projections, on the other hand, are based on a fairly low expected rate of increase in world oil prices. The average of the three projections indicates that Texas oil and gas production will decline 5.3% a year to 326 million barrels in 2000.

Because of the apparent assumptions about oil prices behind the two disparate sets of oil and gas projections, the industry projection is

Table 4. Forecast assumptions underlying the alternative state and local government expenditure and revenue forecasts.

Variable	Average annual growth rate, 1980–2000 (%)	
	low price, low production	high price, high production
Population	1.6	2.0
School-age population	0.9	1.3
Personal income	9.5	10.6
Retail sales	9.5	10.5
Oil production	−5.3	−1.4
Natural gas production	−3.7	−1.1
Oil prices (US wellhead)	6.6	9.9
Natural gas prices (US wellhead)	9.9	12.6

associated with the low price, low production alternative, whereas the
TENRAC projection is associated with the high price, high production
alternative.

6.1 *Forecast results*
As might be expected, the low price, low production forecast results in an
even gloomier outlook for the Texas state and local government finances
than the baseline forecast, whereas the high price, high production forecast
generates much more optimistic results.

Because the Texas economy is heavily oriented toward energy production
rather than energy consumption, the low price, low production forecast
results in somewhat lower projections of state economic and population
growth than in the baseline scenario, and the resulting lower demands for
government services give lower forecasts of state and local government
expenditure growth. This reduction in expenditures, however, is more
than counterbalanced by lower revenues from oil- and gas-related sources.
Consequently, the ratio of state government revenues to expenditures is
projected to fall to 0.85 by 2000 as compared with an expected decline to
0.91 in the baseline forecast (see table 5).

Local governments are also adversely affected by low oil and gas prices
and production, but not nearly as much as the state government. In the
low price, low production alternative, the local government revenue/
expenditure ratio is projected to fall to 0.91 by 2000 as compared with
0.93 in the baseline scenario.

With the high price, high production alternative, the long-term outlook
for Texas state and local government finances looks much better. In this
case, the state government revenue/expenditure ratio is projected never to
drop below 1 over the forecast period and the local government ratio
declines only slightly to 0.96 by 2000 (see table 5). Given these results, it
appears that with high oil and gas prices and production, only small
adjustments in the state and local government revenue and expenditure
system will be necesary to keep finances in balance over the next twenty
years.

Table 5. Alternative ratios of state and local government revenue to expenditure,
1980–2000.

Alternative	1980	1990	2000
State government			
Low	1.11	0.90	0.85
Baseline	1.11	0.94	0.91
High	1.11	1.00	1.00
Local government			
Low	0.98	0.95	0.91
Baseline	0.98	0.97	0.93
High	0.98	0.98	0.96

The major reason that the high price, high production forecasts of Texas state and local finances turn out to be so much more favourable than the low price, low production projections is, of course, because of the much higher forecasts of state oil- and gas-related revenues. In the low price, low production alternative the proportion of total state revenues from oil and gas severance taxes and rents and royalties from state oil lands falls from 21.6% in 1981 to 9.3% in 2000; in the high price, high production alternative this ratio is projected to remain at about its 1981 level throughout the forecast period.

7 Summary and future analysis

Texas state and local governments are heavily reliant on oil- and gas-related revenues; state oil and gas production is declining; and only a moderate rate of increase in oil and gas prices is expected in future years. Given these facts, baseline forecasts of Texas state and local expenditures and revenues indicate that a major adjustment in revenues and/or expenditures will be necessary fairly soon to keep the state fiscal situation in balance, and, over the longer term, an adjustment in local government expenditures and revenues will also be necessary. Alternative forecasts with low and high oil and gas price and production assumptions generate more pessimistic and more optimistic results, but the baseline scenario is probably the most likely.

The revenue and expenditure forecasts presented in this paper offer an initial understanding of the fiscal outlook for Texas state and local governments. Given the importance of this subject, however, there are at least two ways in which the analysis can be expanded and deepened.

First, the expenditure equations should perhaps be broken into capital expenditures and spending for current operations. Breaking capital spending out separately may be important since such expenditures are aimed at meeting long-term needs and, with the slowing economic and population growth of the state, the rate of this spending may also slow.

Second, the expenditure–revenue submodel may be used to analyse what kinds of spending should be reduced or what kinds of revenues should be increased to meet the state's growing revenue gap most effectively. The entire model can also be used (with some modifications) to study the effect of such measures on overall state economic and population growth.

References

Data Resources Inc., 1983 *Drilling Service Forecast Summary* Data Resources Inc., Lexington, MA

Jacoby H D, Paddock J L, 1981, "World oil prices and economic growth in the 1980s" WP MIT-EL 81-060 Massachusetts Institute of Technology, Cambridge, MA

Plaut T R, 1981, "An econometric model for forecasting regional population growth" *International Regional Science Review* **6** 53–70

Plaut T R, 1982a, "A supply-side model of the Texas economy: detailed forecasts to the year 2000" *Texas Business Review* **56** 49–55

Plaut T R, 1982b, "Personal income determination in the Texas economic–demographic forecasting model" BP-82-9, Bureau of Business Research, University of Texas, Austin, TX

Plaut T R, 1983 *Texas Economic and Population Growth: The Next Quarter Century* Bureau of Business Research, University of Texas, Austin, TX

Plaut T R, 1985a, "Economic–demographic interactions in an econometric model of Texas" in *Population Change and the Economy: Theory and Models* Ed. A Isserman (Kluwer-Nijhoff, Hingham, MA) forthcoming

Plaut T R, 1985b, "A survey-side model of Texas manufacturing growth" *Journal of Regional Science* (forthcoming)

Plaut T R, Tully S M, Henaff P J, 1984 *Texas Economic Outlook: Long-term Forecasts* Bureau of Business Research, University of Texas, Austin, TX

TENRAC, 1980 *Texas Energy Outlook: 1980–2000* Texas Energy and Natural Resources Advisory Council, Austin, TX

Texas Research League, 1982 *Public Revenues from Oil and Natural Gas in Texas: What Lies Ahead?* Texas Research League, Austin, TX

US Bureau of the Census, 1982a *Governmental Finances in 1980–81* 6F81 number 5 (US Government Printing Office, Washington, DC)

US Bureau of the Census, 1982b *State Government Finances in 1981* 6F81 number 3 (US Government Printing Office, Washington, DC)

US Department of Energy, 1982 *Outlook for World Oil Prices* DOE/EIA-0336, Energy Information Administration, Washington, DC

Applications of a Biregional Input–Output Model in Regional Policy Analysis

S CASINI BENVENUTI, A CAVALIERI
Regional Institute for Economic Planning of Tuscany, Florence

1 Introduction

In 1980, a scientific cooperation between the Regional Development Group at the International Institute for Applied Systems Analysis (IIASA) and the Regional Institute for Economic Planning of Tuscany (IRPET) was established to apply system-analytic methods to regional planning in a small open market economy such as that of the Tuscany region.

The main aim of the integrated model implemented within the project is to provide consistent forecasts and economic impact assessments in the Tuscany region derived by a priori scenarios as far as regional and national policy choices, as well as international exogenous variables, are concerned. The project was completed in Autumn 1983; the main results were presented at the IIASA–IRPET conference on Model Systems for Regional Planning held in Pistoia in September of that year.

More recently, the SMART (System of Models for the Analysis of the Tuscany Region) model has been used to analyse regional economic structure, as well as in several impact exercises (public health expenditure, public building projects, modifications of exchange rates, tourist expenditure, changes in fiscal policy, evaluation of import substitution) and in some forecasting applications (estimation of the regional needs of electric energy until 1992).

All these applications have been carried out by the Regional Planning Department, which is highly interested in the results of the project.

The modular design (Lakshmanan, 1982) of the SMART model has permitted applications from the beginning, although the different modules were not at the same level of completeness.

At present, only a provisional version of the model has been implemented; so far the medium-term module for private investment and the adjustment algorithm for interregional trade coefficients are not operational.

All the exercises and applications presented in this paper have been carried out according to this simplified version of the SMART model, briefly described in the next section.

2 The present analytical structure of the SMART model

The SMART model developed at IRPET is composed of seven interlinked submodels (figure 1); the central 'core' of the model is the biregional input–output module closed with respect to interregional trade and private consumption. The base year is 1978; for that year an intersectoral table of Tuscany built from direct survey is available (Grassini, 1983), as well as the national input–output table for Italy.

Because most exercises have used this module, it is useful to present very briefly the analytical structure, in the present version, of the submodel TIM:

$$x + m + w = \mathbf{A}x + c + g + j + e + d , \tag{1}$$

$$m - e = \mathbf{B}(\mathbf{A}x + c + g + j + d) , \tag{2}$$

$$w = \hat{\mathbf{M}}(\mathbf{I} - \mathbf{B})(\mathbf{A}x + c + g + j) , \tag{3}$$

$$c = \mathbf{H}x + k , \tag{4}$$

where

A   is a technical coefficients matrix,

B   is the interregional trade coefficients matrix,

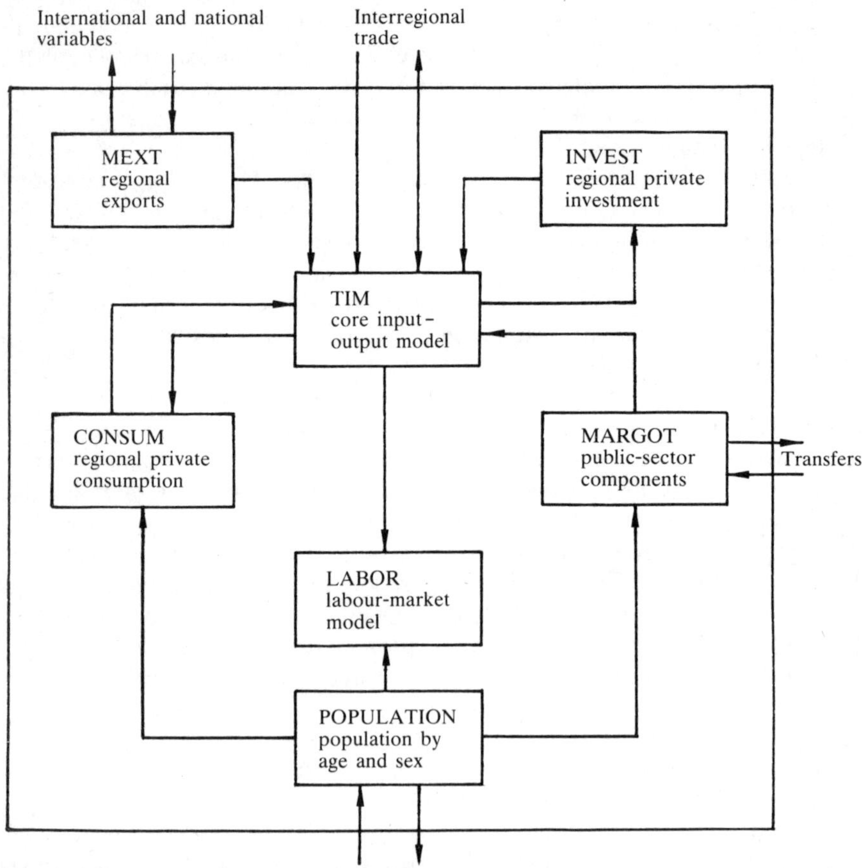

Figure 1. Structure of the regional part of the model system in the Tuscany study.

$\hat{\mathbf{M}}$ is a diagonal matrix of foreign import coefficients,
H   is a matrix of endogenous private consumption,
I   is an identity matrix,
x   is the gross output vector,
m   is the interregional imports vector,
w   is the foreign imports vector,
c   is the private consumption vector,
g   is the public consumption vector,
j   is a vector of private fixed investment plus inventory changes,
d   is a vector of foreign exports,
e   is a vector of interregional exports,
k   is a vector of the exogenous fixed part of private consumption.

All the above variables have a dimension of eighty-eight (forty-four branches × two regions). The **A** matrix has been computed from the Tuscany and Italy input–output tables for 1978; it has the following usual structure:

$$\mathbf{A} = \left(\begin{array}{c|c} \mathbf{A}_T & \mathbf{0} \\ \hline \mathbf{0} & \mathbf{A}_R \end{array} \right) , \tag{5}$$

where $\mathbf{A}_T$ and $\mathbf{A}_R$ are the matrices of total technical coefficients of the two regions, namely, Tuscany (T) and the rest of Italy (R). The interregional trade [equation (2)] is computed by premultiplying matrix **B** by intermediate and final demand. The **B** matrix is composed of four submatrices:

$$\mathbf{B} = \left(\begin{array}{c|c} \hat{\mathbf{B}}_{TR} & -\hat{\mathbf{B}}_{RT} \\ \hline -\hat{\mathbf{B}}_{TR} & \hat{\mathbf{B}}_{RT} \end{array} \right) , \tag{6}$$

where $\hat{\mathbf{B}}_{TR}$ is a diagonal matrix of import coefficients of the two regions; vice versa for $\hat{\mathbf{B}}_{RT}$. The coefficients of the blocks of the main diagonal allow the computation of regional imports, whereas regional exports are given by the other two blocks. The products of **B** and total demand are set equal to the flows of imports minus the flows of exports $(\boldsymbol{m} - \boldsymbol{e})$.

The estimate of the **B** coefficients is based on the survey carried out during the construction of the Tuscany input–output table. Whereas in equation system (1)–(4) only a single **B** matrix is presented, it has been possible to estimate and to use three different **B** matrices: the first for intermediate demand, the second for consumption and investment, and the third for foreign exports. This last matrix is aimed at evaluating the relevant intermediary role of the two regions in foreign trade (Tuscany exports goods produced in the rest of Italy, and vice versa).

Foreign imports [equation (3)] are computed by postmultiplying the **M** matrix by final demand (minus foreign exports) previously allocated in the two regions by the $(\mathbf{I} - \mathbf{B})$ matrix.

Also in this case different matrices for the components of total demand have been estimated. Matrix $\hat{\mathbf{M}}$ has the following structure:

$$\hat{\mathbf{M}} = \left(\begin{array}{c|c} \mathbf{M}_T & \mathbf{0} \\ \hline \mathbf{0} & \mathbf{M}_R \end{array} \right) , \tag{7}$$

where $\mathbf{M}_T$ and $\mathbf{M}_R$ are full matrices calibrated on the basis of the input–output tables of Tuscany and the rest of Italy for 1978. According to the inner structure of the $\mathbf{B}$ and $\hat{\mathbf{M}}$ matrices the equations (1)–(4) ought to be modified because they do not correctly represent the algebraic solution algorithm, even if their compact form has to be preferred in this brief presentation of the analytical structure of the TIM module. The consumption function is defined in equation (4). Private consumption is split into two parts: endogenous and exogenous.

The $\mathbf{H}$ matrix of endogenous consumption has the single element h_{ij} which represents the amount of consumption of good i given by a production unit of sector j (Miyazawa, 1976).

The estimates of the endogenous private consumption vector by input–output branches are obtained according to the following four steps:
Step 1 An estimate is made of a disposable income matrix by sectors and income earners, taking the fiscal system into account;
Step 2 Total consumption is linked to disposable income via an aggregate Kaldorian function;
Step 3 The consumption by commodity sector is derived from the total consumption via a linear econometric estimate of the share coefficients;
Step 4 The consumption vector by commodity sector is converted into a consumption vector by input–output sectoral branches via a bridge matrix.

The exogenous part of private consumption ($\mathbf{k}$) is defined as the part which is not affected by the level of production in the region, that is, tourist consumption and expenditure induced by transfer payments.

Equation system (1)–(4) can be expressed in reduced form:

$$\mathbf{x} = [\mathbf{I}-(\mathbf{I} - \hat{\mathbf{M}})(\mathbf{I} - \mathbf{B})(\mathbf{A} + \mathbf{H})]^{-1}[(\mathbf{I} - \hat{\mathbf{M}})(\mathbf{I} - \mathbf{B})(\mathbf{k} + \mathbf{g} + \mathbf{j}) + (\mathbf{I} - \mathbf{B})\mathbf{d}] . \tag{8}$$

By defining

$$(\mathbf{I} - \hat{\mathbf{M}})(\mathbf{I} - \mathbf{B})(\mathbf{A} + \mathbf{H}) = \mathbf{R} , \tag{9}$$

$$(\mathbf{I} - \hat{\mathbf{M}})(\mathbf{I} - \mathbf{B}) = \mathbf{G} , \tag{10}$$

$$(\mathbf{k} + \mathbf{g} + \mathbf{j}) = \mathbf{f} , \tag{11}$$

we obtain

$$\mathbf{x} = (\mathbf{I} - \mathbf{R})^{-1}[\mathbf{G}\mathbf{f} + (\mathbf{I} - \mathbf{B})\mathbf{d}] , \tag{12}$$

which will be used in the following sections.

The other submodels around the TIM core are used either to produce input vectors, or to estimate certain parameters and coefficients, as is

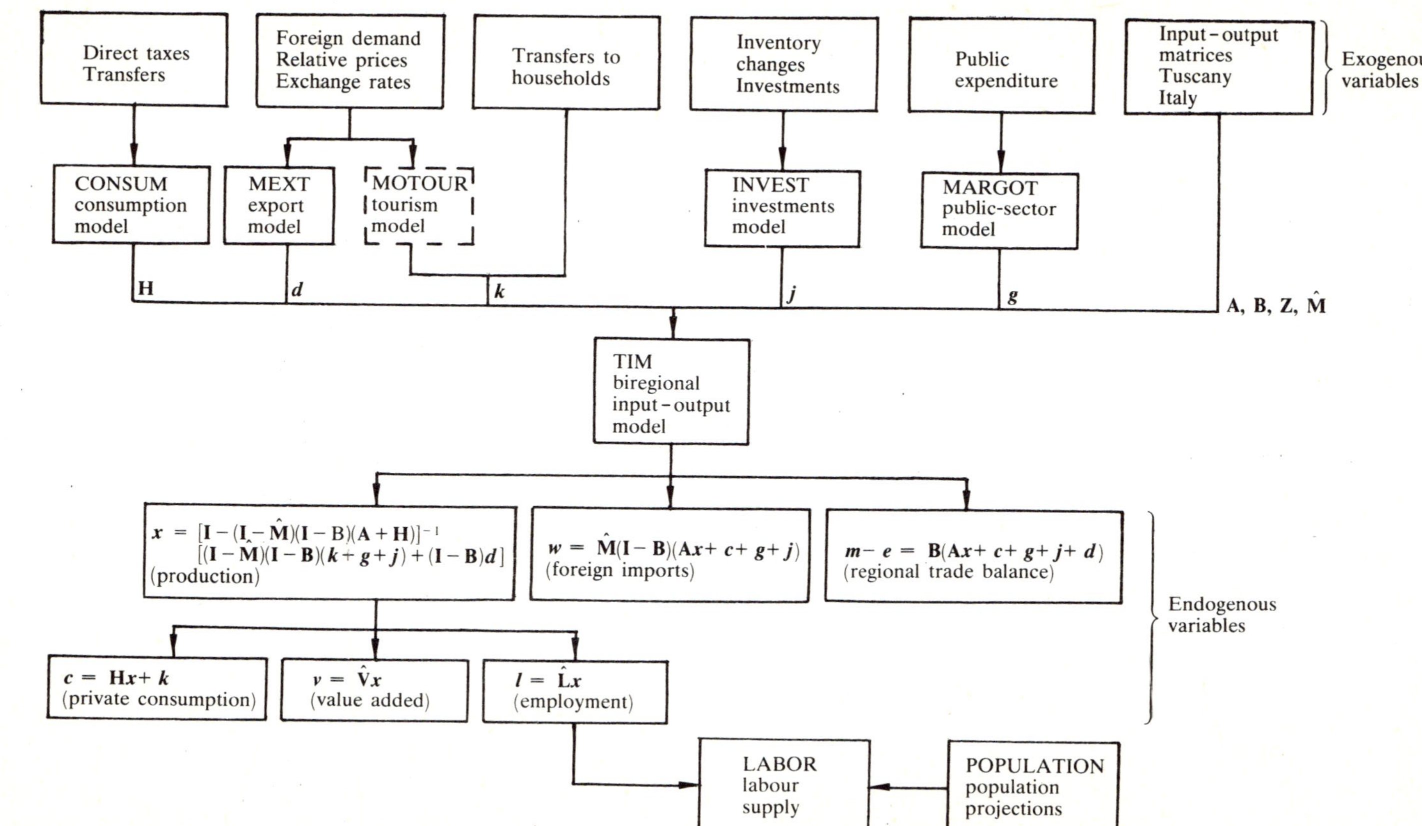

Figure 2. Exogenous and endogenous variables in the SMART model.

shown in figure 2. Several comments can be made about these submodels:
1 the export model (MEXT) has as output the foreign exports vector as a
function of foreign demand, relative prices, and exchange rates (Cavalieri,
Casini et al, 1983; Cavalieri, Martellato et al, 1983). The tourism model,
of which estimation is in progress, has a similar structure;
2 the public-sector model (MARGOT) splits total public expenditure into
seven social functions, each one with a specific input shares structure
(Petretto et al, 1983);
3 the interregional trade coefficients can be modified according to the
level of production and capacity in the two regions (Martellato, 1983),
and/or updated via an appropriate updating computer program operating
on the biregional input–output tables;
4 private investment is exogenous in the present version and the INVEST
module is used to convert investment by origin sector into sectors
producing capital goods. Work on the estimation of capital coefficients
(Johansson and Persson, 1983) is in progress;
5 the labour model (LABOR) produces forecasts of labour supply (Meini
and Rampichini, 1983) and labour productivity trends aimed at updating
the labour coefficients.

If the endogenous variables are expressed as a function of the exogenous
ones, the whole model system, in the present version, can be expressed by
the following relationships;

$$x, \, l, \, w, \, e = \mathrm{f}(\underline{z}, \, y, \, p, \, \underline{s}, \, \underline{t}, \, j, \, \underline{g}) \, , \tag{13}$$

where the new notation denotes:
l an employment vector,
z a direct taxation vector,
y a foreign-demand vector,
p a relative prices vector,
s an exchange rates vector,
t a transfer payments vector,
(the underlined variables can be considered, to some extent, to be the
instrumental ones).

In the following sections two different empirical applications of the
SMART model are analysed, using the TIM module structure presented in
this section. The applications demonstrate the analysis of regional structure
and regional impact analysis.

3 Applications in the analysis of regional structure

Multiregional input–output modelling is often used to describe the economic
structure of a regional and/or national economy through a detailed
analysis of the parameters and the coefficients computed in the model.

Several types of structural analysis may be carried out in a biregional
input–output context; in this section the focus is on the study of aggregate
regional multipliers.

In some analyses, in addition to direct and indirect effects, induced effects are also computed by endogenising private consumption. In the SMART model, the so-called Keynesian–Leontievian multipliers of the components of final demand have been computed separately for the endogenous variables included in the model (production, value added, employment, import, interregional trade).

Whereas the sectoral value-added multipliers are reported in the appendix, in this section the global multipliers are analysed from two different points of view and computed on the basis of the final demand structure in 1983: the division into direct, indirect, and induced effects and the division into internal, spillover, and feedback effects (table 1).

Before evaluating the division into the different effects, we can make some remarks on the total values. First, the public consumption multiplier is, as expected, the highest, and the low value of the export multiplier can be explained by the fact that most inputs of exported products in Tuscany are imported from abroad (leather, wool, chemicals). In the rest of Italy the multipliers are generally lower than in Tuscany (as can be seen in the appendix). This is because of the presence of higher multipliers in the industrial sectors and lower ones in the service sector. In fact, the only higher multiplier in the rest of Italy is in public consumption.

Table 1. Division of the Keynesian–Leontievian multipliers into direct, indirect, and induced effects and into internal, spillover, and feedback effects.

	Foreign export	Private consumption	Investment	Public consumption	Total
Tuscany					
direct	0.43	0.53	0.47	0.73	0.54
indirect	0.36	0.28	0.31	0.22	0.29
induced	0.44	0.47	0.42	0.65	0.49
total	1.23	1.28	1.20	1.60	1.33
Rest of Italy					
direct	0.43	0.52	0.45	0.75	0.54
indirect	0.33	0.27	0.31	0.19	0.28
induced	0.38	0.39	0.36	0.76	0.47
total	1.14	1.18	1.13	1.70	1.29
Tuscany					
internal	0.814	0.765	0.701	1.211	0.873
spillover	0.405	0.501	0.490	0.379	0.444
feedback	0.011	0.011	0.012	0.009	0.010
total	1.230	1.277	1.203	1.599	1.327
Rest of Italy					
internal	1.112	1.139	1.088	1.656	1.249
spillover	0.027	0.032	0.035	0.029	0.031
feedback	0.004	0.013	0.009	0.012	0.009
total	1.143	1.184	1.132	1.697	1.289

As far as the specification of induced effects is concerned, it can be noted that the differences between the multipliers in Tuscany and the rest of Italy are mainly a result of these effects, whereas the direct and indirect effects are fairly similar. Because of the approach followed in the endogenising of private consumption, these results imply that in Tuscany both the propensity for consumption and the income distribution are more oriented towards consumption.

The division of the multipliers into internal, spillover, and feedback effects shows the minor role of feedback and the strong spillover effect in Tuscany, with special regard to exogenous consumption, where tourist expenditure is preeminent. In the investment component, the high spillover effect, in addition to the low value of the total multiplier, determines the low level of the internal effect.

The total spillover effect in Tuscany is about one third of the total multiplier; it is a matter of discussion whether regional policy has to be oriented towards a reduction of this high degree of openness or not. In general, the strength of the internal linkages *versus* the breadth of the external ones is taken as a relevant goal of economic planning; some doubts arise when the level to be taken into consideration is the regional one within a national context. In this case the local goals can be different, or opposite, to the national ones with reference to the degree of openness of the regional economy.

4 Applications in impact analysis

Impact analysis is aimed at evaluating the economic effects on sectoral productions and employments of public decisions and/or exogenous scenarios. Special attention is devoted to some instrumental variables connected both with the public final demand components at regional and national level and with national economic policies, such as fiscal tools, sectoral transfers, exchange rates, and so on.

Three different cases are presented here as examples of several applications of the SMART model to problems of public expenditure, import substitution, export, and tourism impact, and some recent developments on applications such as energy, pollution, environment, and so on.

When public consumption is taken into account, in many cases it is necessary to consider the possibility of the treatment of those disaggregated public branches with their own specific input-shares structure. This detailed information is, in fact, often provided by the Regional Planning Department.

In analytical terms, it is necessary in the first run of the model to modify column k of the $\mathbf{A}$ and $\mathbf{H}$ matrices, that is, equation (12) must be changed in the following way:

$$x = (\mathbf{I} - \mathbf{R})^{-1}(\mathbf{I} + \mathbf{R}^*)\mathbf{G}f, \tag{14}$$

where

$$\mathbf{R^*} = (\mathbf{I} - \mathbf{M})(\mathbf{I} - \mathbf{B})(\mathbf{A^*} + \mathbf{H^*}) \ .$$

In the matrices $\mathbf{A^*}$ and $\mathbf{H^*}$, column k is replaced by a new one, derived from the new disaggregated information. This possibility of modifying the column related to the public sector has been included in the software package and has been employed in several impact exercises executed by the Planning Department. As part of this work, an assessment has been made of the economic impact of regional public expenditure during the period 1978-1983. The results, relative to the year 1983, are presented in table 2, which reports the aggregate values for the Tuscany region, distinguished by seven social functions, current and investment expenditures, and the effects in terms of value added.

The multiplier effects are similar to those already analysed for general public consumption and investments, and the differences are marked within the seven social functions, especially for public investments. This application is only an example of several impact exercises on public projects, executed by the Regional Planning Department in order to obtain funds from FIO (Fund for Investment and Employment) at national and European levels.

This procedure can also be used in other kinds of analysis when the components to be evaluated are a specific and more disaggregated part of

Table 2. Impact analysis of regional budget expenditure by public service, Tuscany, 1983 (thousands of millions of lire).

	Current expenditure	Investment	Value added		
			Tuscany	rest of Italy	total
Expenditure					
Public administration	96.2		134.0	33.0	167.0
Sanitation, water	2.5		2.9	0.9	3.8
Culture, sport, recreation	8.8		8.8	3.3	12.1
Social assistance	32.6		36.8	10.9	47.7
Economic activity	142.2		185.2	51.4	236.6
Education	62.5		72.4	25.7	98.1
Health care	1435.2		1592.0	608.0	2200.0
Total	1780.0		2032.1	733.2	2765.3
Investment					
Public administration		1.1	0.7	0.6	1.3
Sanitation, water		2.7	2.7	1.1	3.8
Culture, sport, recreation		0.0	0.0	0.0	0.0
Social assistance		0.9	0.7	0.4	1.1
Economic activity		182.9	152.5	74.2	226.7
Education		4.9	4.6	2.0	6.6
Health care		12.7	4.8	5.6	10.4
Total		205.2	166.0	83.9	249.9

the sectoral classification (forty-four branches) of the input–output tables; that is, cotton products within the textile industry and so on.

The second application is related to the effects of a reduction in some sectors which are strongly dependent on foreign imports. These reductions should meet an increase of the same amount in foreign exports or in tourist expenditure, in order to evaluate the different effects on the regional and national trade balance, as well as on the value added at regional level (table 3).

It has been assumed that the reduction in foreign imports in Tuscany is balanced by an increase in internal production with no influence on the interregional trade coefficients. In other words, the aim of this exercise is to evaluate whether it is better to augment the degree of foreign openness of the regional economy or to enforce the internal interrelationship.

In fact, one of the major issues in regional economic planning in Tuscany is the role to be given to tourism, that is, whether it is better to promote this sector or to invest regional funds in other directions, such as the promotion of export flows or the substitution of imports. IRPET was requested to analyse the different impacts of these three components, in order to evaluate some alternatives. The attention given to these components is justified by the fact that tourist consumption in Tuscany is about 15% of total consumption and the export flows are more than 30% of the regional domestic product.

The results must be interpreted in the light of the following points:
(a) export growth and the import cutbacks, even if of the same amount, cannot be properly generalised—whereas in the export case the model is linear, for the import cutbacks the model is not linear;
(b) it has been assumed unrealistically that all the substituted import is internally produced.

Nevertheless, some interesting remarks can be made. First, it seems that the import policies are more effective than the export ones, in terms of both value added and trade balance; second, the specialised sector of

Table 3. Reduction in foreign imports versus increase of the same amount (thousands of billions of lire) in tourist consumption and foreign exports: impact effects on the national trade balance and value added.

	National trade balance	Value added		
		Tuscany	rest of Italy	total
Tourist consumption	698	857	456	1313
Total exports	605	825	405	1230
Exports of mechanical goods	538	821	503	1324
Exports of textiles	601	796	440	1236
Total imports	748	1043	270	1313
Imports of petrochemicals	843	1078	291	1369
Imports of food products	829	1309	274	1583

the Tuscan export (textiles) gives the lowest internal multipliers and a low net contribution to the trade balance—about 40% is lost because of its import dependence; last, tourist consumption has the highest internal effects among the foreign-demand components, even if table 1 shows that this is mainly a result of the induced effects.

A number of applications of the SMART model to energy, pollution, and the environment are currently in progress.

In particular an input–output matrix of energy flows at regional level has been constructed and has been used to evaluate the needs of different energy sources as a result of alternative scenarios of industrial structure. We are also working on an extension of the SMART model aimed at including the pollution process by adding a new row and column to the **A** matrices for Tuscany and the rest of Italy. The methodology we have followed is similar to the computation of the equations of the environmental balance (Costa, 1982) estimated at regional level on the basis of the pioneering work of Leontief (1970).

Finally, also under study is the feasibility of adapting the current version of the SMART model, mainly driven by the demand side, to a new version where relevant changes in the supply side can be analysed, to study the impact effects of the restructuring of industrial sectors (Martellato, 1984).

5 Final remarks
The applications of the SMART model, in its present simplified version, have proved the validity of this tool in many structural and impact analyses initiated by the Regional Planning Department. In this analytical work, interesting results have been achieved relating to the differentiated effects of the final demand components.

The economy of Tuscany is mainly driven by foreign exports, highly specialised in light industry, and tourism. Because of the low internal backward linkages, the spillover effect is very relevant both for exports and for tourist consumption. It has been proved that an industrial policy aimed at substituting some import flows is more effective, both at regional and at national levels, than increasing foreign exports and tourism by the same amount. In addition, the sectoral specialisation of regional exports determines a relatively low multiplier of this final demand component. These two considerations have helped regional policy in identifying some guidelines for a sectoral restructuring policy.

Last but not least, the use of the model has pointed out the role of endogenous consumption in input–output modelling. Whereas attention is often focused on the productive and trade system, that is, technological and interregional flows, the weight of the linkages between the value added and the consumption activity is so relevant, from both the quantitative and qualitative viewpoints, that the final results in terms of direct, indirect, and induced effects are highly influenced by the endogenisation of consumption.

More attention to this part of input–output multiregional modelling ought to be paid by the builders and the users of this kind of analytical tool.

Finally, we offer some comments on the future prospects of the work on the SMART model. When the investment module is fully implemented within the whole system, more comprehensive considerations from the supply side will be included in the analysis. In addition to the capital constraints derived by estimation of the capacity-change process, a more detailed study of the labour market is also planned from the point of view of both demand and supply.

All these new applications will be based on an updated version of the SMART model. In fact, whereas the structure of the model is mainly calibrated on the input–output accounting of the base year (1978), through an updating program of the input–output tables (at present the version for 1983 is available), it is possible to apply relatively recent matrices of technical, interregional, and consumption coefficients.

This solution is able to meet the needs of impact analysis, but is not an appropriate one for the estimation of a development path of the coefficients in the long term, as would be required in forecasting applications. For this kind of use experience has shown the weakness of such a model, because of the lack of the price effect, relevant in the income distribution, and of the technological changes in the production process.

Whereas it is possible, to some extent, to get around the absence of prices, as far as income distribution and linked endogenous consumption are concerned, by making the consumption exogenous, it is more difficult to avoid the problem of changes of the technological coefficients in the long term.

In fact, the interregional input–output models have to be used in a time span which does not exceed five years from the most recently updated calibration.

Longer term applications need strong assumptions about the stability of the structural coefficients or about some scenarios both of the exogenous variables and of the internal parameters of the model.

References

Cavalieri A, Casini S, Viviani A, 1983, "MEXT: regional export model" in *Model Systems for Regional Planning* IRPET, Florence, Italy, and IIASA, Laxenburg, Austria; pp 375–402

Cavalieri A, Martellato D, Snickars F, 1983, "A model system for policy impact analysis in the Tuscany region" *Papers of the Regional Science Association* **52** 105–124

Costa P, 1982, "Inquinamento e disinquinamento in Italia: un'analisi input–output" *Ricerche Economiche* **4** 355–375

Grassini M, 1983, "MIT: Tuscany input–output tables" in *Model Systems for Regional Planning* IRPET, Florence, Italy, and IIASA, Laxenburg, Austria; pp 235–266

Johansson B, Persson H, 1983, "INVEST: capacity change and capital formation model" in *Model Systems for Regional Planning* IRPET, Florence, Italy, and IIASA, Laxenburg, Austria; pp 403–428

Lakshmanan T R, 1982, "Integrated multiregional economic modeling for the USA" in *Multiregional Economic Modeling: Practice and Prospect* Eds B Issaev, P Nijkamp, P Rietveld, F Snickars (North-Holland, Amsterdam) pp 171–188

Leontief W, 1970, "Environmental repercussions on the economic structure: an input–output approach" in *Review of Economics and Statistics* **52** 262–271

Martellato D, 1983, "TIM—system core: the biregional model" in *Model Systems for Regional Planning* IRPET, Florence, Italy, and IIASA, Laxenburg, Austria; pp 267–284

Martellato D, 1984, "Restructuring the industrial sector: the case for a new input–output model" paper presented at the 5th Italian Conference of Regional Science, Bari, November; copy available from Department of Economic Science, University of Venice, Venice

Meini M, Rampichini C, 1983, "Labor supply model" in *Model Systems for Regional Planning* IRPET, Florence, Italy, and IIASA, Laxenburg, Austria; pp 429–452

Miyazawa K, 1976 *Input–Output Analysis and the Structure of Income Distribution* (Springer, New York)

Petretto S, Maltinti G, Vignetti C, 1983, "MARGOT: government and fiscal policy model" in *Model Systems for Regional Planning* IRPET, Florence, Italy, and IIASA, Laxenburg, Austria; pp 285–330

APPENDIX

Table A1. Value-added multipliers of the four components of final demand.

	Private consumption	
	Tuscany	rest of Italy
1 Agricultural, forestry, and fishery	1.709	1.601
2 Coal mining	0.144	0.000
3 Coke	0.421	0.407
4 Crude petroleum, natural gas, oil refining	0.573	0.509
5 Electric, gas, and water services	0.795	0.678
6 Nuclear fuel	1.155	1.113
7 Iron and nonferrous metal mining	0.985	1.025
8 Stone and clay products	0.454	0.885
9 Chemical and pharmaceutical products	0.964	0.933
10 Metal products	0.856	0.859
11 Farm and industrial machinery	0.546	0.896
12 Office machines, scientific instruments	0.770	0.383
13 Electric lighting and wiring equipment	1.022	0.894
14 Motorcars, lorries, and equipment	0.602	0.632
15 Other transportation equipment	0.890	0.916
16 Fresh and corned meat	0.945	0.893
17 Milk and related products	1.206	1.179
18 Other food	1.202	1.077
19 Alcoholic and nonalcoholic drinks	1.210	1.130
20 Tobacco products	0.886	0.892
21 Textile products and apparel	1.327	1.348
22 Leather, leather products, footwear	1.041	0.964
23 Lumber and wood products, furniture	1.305	1.141
24 Paper products, printing, and publishing	1.225	1.159
25 Rubber and plastic products	1.128	1.032
26 Miscellaneous plastic products	0.723	0.702
27 New construction and public works	1.411	1.366
28 Scrap, used goods, repair services	1.394	1.378
29 Trade	1.459	1.453
30 Hotels and lodging places	1.468	1.344
31 Land transportation	1.365	1.470
32 Sea and air transportation	1.249	1.248
33 Warehousing and related services	1.441	1.525
34 Communications	1.446	1.446
35 Finance and insurance	1.518	1.595
36 Business services	1.509	1.573
37 Real estate and rental	1.620	1.537
38 Market research and educational services	1.528	1.609
39 Marketing of sanitary services	1.463	1.560
40 Marketing of amusement and cultural services	1.507	1.590
41 Nonmarketing: miscellaneous services	1.642	1.713
42 Nonmarketing: research and educational services	1.563	1.669
43 Nonmarketing: sanitary services	1.652	1.716
44 Nonmarketing: household services	1.586	1.686

Table A1 (continued).

Public consumption		Investment		Foreign exports	
Tuscany	rest of Italy	Tuscany	rest of Italy	Tuscany	rest of Italy
1.898	1.762	0.475	0.308	1.956	1.760
1.006	1.005	1.006	1.005	1.006	1.005
0.421	0.407	0.421	0.407	0.421	0.407
0.582	0.516	0.582	0.516	0.635	0.515
0.795	0.682	0.795	0.682	0.807	0.682
1.155	1.113	1.155	1.113	1.155	1.113
0.985	1.025	0.985	1.025	0.985	1.027
1.362	1.336	1.185	1.149	1.391	1.333
1.060	1.039	1.060	1.039	1.089	1.037
1.219	1.106	0.939	0.836	1.328	1.101
1.208	1.179	0.901	0.868	1.279	1.176
1.315	1.210	0.326	0.405	1.425	1.205
1.245	1.208	1.004	0.924	1.304	1.207
1.158	1.152	0.823	0.807	1.236	1.150
1.157	1.126	0.958	0.922	1.254	1.103
1.071	1.008	1.071	1.008	1.161	1.007
1.410	1.374	1.410	1.374	1.455	1.374
1.263	1.142	1.263	1.142	1.337	1.138
1.333	1.261	1.333	1.261	1.342	1.257
1.022	1.026	1.022	1.026	1.022	1.026
1.425	1.450	1.425	1.450	1.373	1.456
1.103	1.006	1.103	1.006	1.112	1.001
1.342	1.184	1.303	1.149	1.402	1.168
1.321	1.233	1.321	1.233	1.397	1.227
1.245	1.104	1.187	1.045	1.452	1.098
0.817	0.808	0.350	0.326	0.890	0.808
1.411	1.366	1.411	1.366	1.411	1.366
1.404	1.393	1.404	0.000	1.405	1.393
1.459	1.453	1.459	1.453	1.459	1.453
1.468	1.344	1.468	1.344	1.470	1.344
1.365	1.470	1.365	1.470	1.364	1.472
1.249	1.248	1.249	1.248	1.095	1.249
1.441	1.525	1.441	1.525	1.441	1.526
1.446	1.446	1.446	1.446	1.446	1.446
1.518	1.595	1.518	1.595	1.511	1.595
1.509	1.573	1.509	1.573	1.488	1.575
1.620	1.537	1.620	1.537	1.620	1.537
1.528	1.609	1.528	1.609	1.528	1.609
1.463	1.560	1.463	1.560	1.463	1.560
1.507	1.590	1.507	1.590	1.498	1.590
1.642	1.713	1.642	1.713	1.642	1.713
1.563	1.669	1.563	1.669	1.563	1.669
1.652	1.716	1.652	1.716	1.652	1.716
1.586	1.686	1.586	1.686	1.586	1.686

Previous volumes in the series

Volume 1

Volume 2

Contents of previous volumes

Volume 9

Volume 10

Volume 11

Volume 12